THE RELIGION AND THEOLOGY OF PAUL

THE KERR LECTURES

DELIVERED IN THE UNITED FREE CHURCH
COLLEGE, GLASGOW, DURING SESSION 1914-15

BY

W. MORGAN, D.D.

PROFESSOR OF SYSTEMATIC THEOLOGY AND APOLOGETICS
IN QUEEN'S THEOLOGICAL COLLEGE, KINGSTON, CANADA

EDINBURGH : T. & T. CLARK, 38 GEORGE STREET
1917

Printed by
MORRISON & GIBB LIMITED,

FOR

T. & T. CLARK, EDINBURGH.

LONDON: SIMPKIN, MARSHALL, HAMILTON, KENT, AND CO. LIMITED.
NEW YORK: CHARLES SCRIBNER'S SONS.

TO

MY LIFE-LONG FRIEND

W. L. DAVIDSON, LL.D.

PROFESSOR OF LOGIC IN THE UNIVERSITY OF ABERDEEN

TO WHOM I OWE MORE THAN I CAN EXPRESS

THIS BOOK IS DEDICATED

THE KERR LECTURESHIP.

THE "KERR LECTURESHIP" was founded by the TRUSTEES of the late Miss JOAN KERR of Sanquhar, under her Deed of Settlement, and formally adopted by the United Presbyterian Synod in May 1886. In the following year, May 1887, the provisions and conditions of the Lectureship, as finally adjusted, were adopted by the Synod, and embodied in a Memorandum, printed in the Appendix to the Synod Minutes, p. 489.

On the union of the United Presbyterian Church with the Free Church of Scotland in October 1900, the necessary changes were made in the designation of the object of the Lectureship and the persons eligible for appointment to it, so as to suit the altered circumstances. And at the General Assembly of 1901 it was agreed that the Lectureship should in future be connected with the Glasgow College of the United Free Church. From the Memorandum, as thus amended, the following excerpts are here given :—

II. The amount to be invested shall be £3000.

III. The object of the Lectureship is the promotion of the Study of Scientific Theology in the United Free Church of Scotland.

The Lectures shall be upon some such subjects as the following, viz. :—

A. Historic Theology—
> (1) Biblical Theology, (2) History of Doctrine, (3) Patristics, with special reference to the significance and authority of the first three centuries.

B. Systematic Theology—
> (1) Christian Doctrine—(a) Philosophy of Religion, (b) Comparative Theology, (c) Anthropology, (d) Christology, (e) Soteriology, (f) Eschatology.
> (2) Christian Ethics—(a) Doctrine of Sin, (b) Individual and Social Ethics, (c) The Sacraments, (d) The Place of Art in Religious Life and Worship.

Further, the Committee of Selection shall, from time to time, as they think fit, appoint as the subject of the Lectures any important Phases of Modern Religious Thought or Scientific Theories in their bearing upon Evangelical Theology. The Committee may also appoint a subject connected with the practical work of the Ministry as subject of Lecture, but in no case shall this be admissible more than once in every five appointments.

IV. The appointments to this Lectureship shall be made in the first instance from among the Licentiates or Ministers of the United Free Church of Scotland, of whom no one shall be eligible who, when the appointment falls to be made, shall have been licensed for more than twenty-five years, and who is not a graduate of a British University, preferential regard being had to those who have for some time been connected with a Continental University.

V. Appointments to this Lectureship not subject to the conditions in Section IV. may also from time to time, at the discretion of the Committee, be made from among eminent members of the Ministry of any of the Nonconformist Churches of Great Britain and Ireland, America, and the Colonies, or of the Protestant Evangelical Churches of the Continent.

VI. The Lecturer shall hold the appointment for three years.

VII. The number of Lectures to be delivered shall be left to the discretion of the Lecturer, except thus far, that in no case shall there be more than twelve or less than eight.

VIII. The Lectures shall be published at the Lecturer's own expense within one year after their delivery.

IX. The Lectures shall be delivered to the students of the Glasgow College of the United Free Church of Scotland.

XII. The Public shall be admitted to the Lectures.

PREFACE

——◆——

DURING the last fifteen or twenty years, much has been done to elucidate the Pauline theology, and the chief outcome of the most recent work has undoubtedly been the discovery that Hellenistic religion and religious philosophy were vital factors in its formation. It is not too much to say that a flood of light has been thrown on much that was formerly obscure. A new epoch has been created in the study of the Apostle, with the inevitable result that the older expositions have to a considerable extent become antiquated. While many recent books have dealt with particular aspects of his religion and thought from the standpoint of the newer knowledge, there is not one, so far as the writer knows (with the exception of the sketch in the second edition of Holtzmann's *Lehrbuch der neutestamentlichen Theologie*), that has attempted a full and systematic presentation. To supply this lack is the aim of the present volume. It will give a systematic account of the Apostle's religion and theology in the light of modern research. While primarily intended for students, the endeavour has been made to render it intelligible and interesting also to the non-professional reader.

The Epistles on which the exposition is based are Romans, First and Second Corinthians, Galatians,

Philippians, Colossians, and First and Second Thessalonians. The Epistle to the Ephesians has not been used as an independent source.

My warmest acknowledgments are due to my friend and colleague, Professor E. F. Scott, D.D., not only for revising the proofs, but for constant stimulus and endless suggestion.

W. MORGAN.

KINGSTON, CANADA,
25th December 1916.

CONTENTS

PART I.

THE REDEEMER AND HIS REDEMPTION.

PART II.

THE LIFE IN SALVATION.

PART I.

THE REDEEMER AND HIS REDEMPTION.

CHAPTER I.

PAUL'S WORLD-VIEW.

JESUS CHRIST, Redeemer and Lord, the redemption He has accomplished or will accomplish, the life in salvation which is the fruit of His redemptive activity—on these three great realities Paul's religion hangs, and they form the subject-matter of his theology.

In the innermost shrine of the Apostle's soul stands the figure of the crucified and exalted Jesus. To Jesus he looks as the slave to his master, as the ransomed to his ransomer, as the worshipper to his God; and he cherishes the idea of a union with Him the most intimate that can be conceived. "I have been crucified with Christ," he can say, "yet I live; and yet no longer I, but Christ liveth in me: and the life which I now live in the flesh I live in faith, the faith which is in the Son of God, who loved me and gave Himself for me." If Paul is dominated by the thought of Christ, he is hardly less so by the thought of the Christ-redemption. The Cross is ever before his eyes. It is the great divine fact for which the ages have been waiting, for which they have been preparing. Fallen are the hostile powers that from the beginning have enslaved and desolated the life of man: the demons, the Law with its curse, sin seated in the flesh—Christ has triumphed over them in His death. The long and bitter reign of these powers lies behind, and it is a new world on which the sun looks down, a world under

3

the reign of grace and of the Spirit and of the enthroned Christ. That the forces of evil are still active, that the consummation has still to come, the Apostle knows; but with serene confidence he anticipates the near day when Christ will return to perfect His work; and he is sure that in the intervening period the believer is safe in Christ's keeping. In this invincible belief in the great redemption accomplished on Calvary and soon to be completed, the note of assurance, boldness, victory, so characteristic of his piety, has its ground. "Who is he who shall condemn? It is Christ that died. For I am persuaded that neither death, nor life, nor angels, nor principalities, nor things present, nor things to come, nor powers, nor height, nor depth, nor any other creature, shall be able to separate us from the love of God, which is in Christ Jesus our Lord." Finally, Paul's religion has at the heart of it the consciousness that it is a life in salvation. Through his faith in Christ he has become a partaker in the great redemption. He is a new man and lives under a new dispensation. Emancipated from the Law, he knows himself justified and a child of God; emancipated from the sinful flesh, he is conscious of supernatural powers stirring within him, the spring of all his victorious achievement. By the grace of God, by the indwelling of the Spirit, by the power of Christ, he is what he is. And his citizenship is in heaven; from whence also he waits for a Saviour, who shall fashion anew the body of his humiliation that it may be conformed to the body of His glory.

It is with the same great realities underlying his piety that Paul is everywhere occupied in his theological activity. In all the evolutions of his thought he has no other purpose than so to expound, commend and defend these realities as that men shall be led to embrace his own faith. He will establish the claim of Jesus to be the one Lord and Saviour, exhibit His moral glory, His divine dignity, His saving power. He will demonstrate the necessity for the great redemption, demonstrate also its sufficiency, by relating it to man's practical situation in the world, nay, to the constitution of the world itself. He will show what salvation means, the conditions that attach to it, the obligations it imposes, and trace it to its ground in Christ's finished work and continued activity. Throughout, his motive is a practical one. Of speculation, elaboration or system for their own sakes we find nothing. His thoughts are developed to meet the need of the occasion, and they are pursued only so far as edification requires. Substantially his theology and his gospel are one and the same.

In attempting to reproduce Paul's gospel we shall follow the order of subjects we have indicated—the Redeemer, His work of redemption, the new life in salvation. Strictly speaking, eschatology falls under Christ's redemptive work, but since it represents the consummation of the whole world-drama we have reserved it till towards the end. The last chapter will be devoted to a discussion of the momentous question of the relation of the teaching of Paul to that of the Master.

But before proceeding to these cardinal themes a preliminary task must first be undertaken. Paul's gospel is set in the framework of a general world-view, which bears upon it the stamp of the age and cannot without some exercise of the historical imagination be reproduced. From this world-view the categories in which it is stated are derived. In expositions designed for edification it is inevitable that the original framework, foreign as it has to a large extent become, should be for the most part discounted, and that the Apostle's essential ideas should receive a more modern setting. With such procedure no fault can be found ; and that it is possible is a proof that these ideas are at bottom of permanent validity. When, however, our aim is to understand Paul's gospel in its

historical objectivity, the method is one which cannot be
followed.   A knowledge of its precise presuppositions and
categories becomes then a matter of first-class importance.
To obtain such knowledge is the task that lies immediately
before us.

How does the world mirror itself in the Apostle's
mind?   What powers does he see active in it?   To what
goal is it tending?   What was the situation that demanded
so tremendous an interposition as the descent of the Son
of God to earth and His submission to a shameful death?
Such are the questions that must occupy us in this opening
chapter.

Paul's outlook is at bottom that of Jewish Apocalyptic.
While conceptions from other sources have, as we shall
see, to be taken into account, they are superimposed on an
apocalyptic groundwork.   This type of religious thought
is of such fundamental importance, and we shall have so
often to refer to it, that it is necessary at the outset to give
some account, however brief, of its main ideas.

Jewish Apocalyptic had its roots in the hope held up
before Israel by her great prophets, particularly in times
of national declension and disaster, of a glorious day in the
future, "the day of the Lord," when her oppressors should
be overthrown, and she, purified by the fires of affliction,
should be exalted to a position of unparalleled splendour
and power.   Through her fidelity to God and her supremacy among the nations God's rule on earth would be
visibly realised, and nature itself would be made fairer and
more generous to grace the new era.   Isaiah, Micah,
Jeremiah, the prophet of the Restoration, Zechariah, all
point forward to the great consummation and depict it
in the most glowing colours.   This national hope proved
itself vital enough to survive the most disillusioning experiences ; but somewhere in the dark days of Persian or
Greek ascendancy it was subjected to radical modification

and fitted into a world-view widely different from that of the prophets.

The new development of Hebrew religion is characterised in the first place by a thoroughgoing pessimism. In the eyes of apocalyptic writers the existing world or age is radically and incurably evil, incapable by any conceivable reformation of being transformed into a kingdom of God. It is not only that human beings are in the mass hopelessly corrupt, that the reins of power are in the hands of wicked men and that the righteous are a despised and downtrodden remnant. A portentous development of the belief in evil spirits gives to apocalyptic pessimism a still darker hue. The world is the haunt of throngs of such spirits, who, under Satan their head, form a demonic hierarchy. With unwearied activity they prosecute their hellish work, thwarting the will of the Almighty, hounding on the heathen persecutors of His people, inciting men to idolatry and scourging them with disease. To these sinister powers God, by an inscrutable decree, has surrendered the government of the world. Though there is no question of setting up a prince of evil co-ordinate with God, the world is regarded as Satan's rather than God's. Satan is its real master.[1] Over against this demonic hierarchy we find a hierarchy of ministering angels, who form the court of the Almighty and whose business it is to carry into effect His decrees. This belief in angel mediators indicates a trait in Apocalyptic closely akin to its pessimism—a profound sense, namely, of the gulf separating God from creation, and a shrinking from bringing Him into direct contact with it. God is thought of as transcendent, remote from His creatures and transacting with them only through intermediaries.

But dark as apocalyptic pessimism is, it does not, like that of Buddhism, strike at existence itself. Faith in God

[1] Martyrdom of Isa. iii. 4.

and in God's promise to Israel is held fast. Only this faith, finding nothing in the present to which it can attach itself, takes refuge in the future and becomes eschatological. In this we have another cardinal feature of apocalyptic religion. The existing world is surrendered to destruction, and interest transferred to a new and glorious world which God will reveal when the first has been swept away. With passionate eagerness the great catastrophe that shall precede the coming of the Kingdom is anticipated, and the horizon scanned for signs of its approach. For that the end is near, that men are living in the last days, is never for a moment in doubt. Among the looked-for signs are increasing wickedness, devastating invasions, the appearance of the mysterious figure of Antichrist, shakings of the earth and dreadful portents in the heavens. Knowing that his time is short, Satan will muster his forces for a last onset.

These two features of Apocalyptic, its pessimism and its transference of religious interest from the present to the future, are summed up in the doctrine of the two ages or worlds, the present ($\dot{o}$ $ai\grave{\omega}\nu$ $o\hat{v}\tau o\varsigma$, $\dot{o}$ $\kappa\acute{o}\sigma\mu o\varsigma$ $o\hat{v}\tau o\varsigma$: both terms are used, the reference being at once temporal and local), and that which is to come ($\dot{o}$ $ai\grave{\omega}\nu$ $\dot{o}$ $\mu\acute{e}\lambda\lambda\omega\nu$). God, says the writer of 4th Esdras, has not created one age, but two. The first is evil, troubled, transient, laden with a curse; the second full of glory and immortality (4 Esd. 4[11. 27] 7[12. 50. 113], Bar. 44[9] 83[8]). Within this scheme all apocalyptic thought moves. Present and future, the actual and the ideal, are set over against each other in dualistic opposition.

We have said that the advent of the new world of Apocalyptic must be preceded by the destruction of the old. In this final catastrophe the opening scene will be one of judgment. The Almighty will hold a great assize. For the prophets too the " day of the Lord" was a day of judgment ; but while in their conception only the living oppressors of Israel are judged, in Apocalyptic the stage has become world-wide. Jews as well as heathen, and what is of still greater significance, the dead as well as the living, will appear at the bar. This belief in a general resurrection and universal judgment forms a landmark in the history of Hebrew religion. We recognise in it the victory of individualism over the old corporate conception of life. It is no longer the nation but the individual that is the religious unit ; the worth of the individual comes to recognition and he is set solitary before God.

The fate of men decided, their sentence is forthwith carried into effect. The doom of the wicked is variously described, now as destruction and again as eternal torment in hell-fire. In their ruin the devil and his angels are involved, and even the material creation. For the righteous, on the other hand, there is reserved a blessed and deathless life in the presence of God. This new existence has its scene not in Palestine, but in a heavenly world created before the natural and kept in reserve until the appointed hour (4 Esd. 8^{52}, Bar. 51^8). The old demon-ridden age, with its sin and its misery, has run its evil course ; the blessed and immortal age, the reign of God, begins.

We have described this drama of judgment and salvation without introducing the figure of the Messiah, so familiar to us from the New Testament. And indeed the part which he plays in it can scarcely be called essential. In some apocalyptic writings—Daniel and the Assumption of Moses, for example—he does not appear at all, and in others the references to him are of the scantiest. Only in the Book of Enoch and the Psalms of Solomon is he a really prominent figure.[1] When he appears on the scene, it is no longer as the prince of David's house and ideal theocratic king of prophetic expectation. The

[1] E. F. Scott, *The Kingdom and the Messiah*, p. 41.

Messiah has become a heavenly being, created before the sun and stars and kept by God in concealment until the fateful hour. And the rôle assigned to him corresponds with his superhuman character. When he descends with the clouds of heaven, it is to act as the representative and agent of the Almighty. Sitting as judge he pronounces sentence on kings and nations. In his name the righteous are saved, and at his hands wicked men and the demonic hosts meet their doom.

This apocalyptic conception of things first comes clearly into view in the Book of Daniel, written in the crisis of the Maccabæan struggle (165 B.C.). Its rise may to some extent be explained by the calamitous situation of the Jewish people under Persian and Greek rule. A fulfilment of the prophetic promise through the means which the prophets had in view—inner reform, political revolution, a victorious leader—no longer seemed within the range of possibility. A feeling was abroad, reflected in many of the Psalms, that God had forgotten His people and forsaken the earth. In despair of the present world, faith betook itself to the idea of a future and transcendent world. Such an explanation is, however, only partial. The pessimism and dualism of the apocalyptic outlook, its demonology and angelology, its conception of a death-struggle between the kingdom of God and the kingdom of Satan, its conception of a resurrection of the dead and a final judgment, can be accounted for only on the hypothesis of influence from the side of Persian religion.

Apocalyptic was never the faith of more than a circle. Popular messianic expectation, though not unaffected by it, continued to run in more earthly and political lines, attaching itself directly to Old Testament prophecy. But if it never gathered to itself the faith of the mass, its religious vitality is attested by the fact that it was the deepest and most earnest spirits that were attracted to it. When the last of the great prophetic figures appeared in the person of John the Baptist, it was as a preacher of the apocalyptic judgment and Kingdom. And the same grand consummation was before the eyes of Jesus. To prepare men for the coming of the Kingdom was the task to which He knew Himself called. At least in the last days of His life, when the tragic issue of His earthly ministry had become clear to Him, He proclaimed Himself as the Messiah who should come with the clouds of heaven, and taught His disciples to expect His reappearance. It was as an apocalyptic movement that Christianity entered the world. The faith of the disciples, stunned by the shock of the crucifixion, reawakened in redoubled force with the proof afforded by the resurrection appearances that the Master they loved had indeed risen from the dead. The primitive Christian gospel was a proclamation of the crucified Jesus as exalted to the messianic throne, and of His speedy descent to judge the world and bring in the Kingdom.

This primitive outlook is also the outlook of Paul. While introducing elements the ultimate effect of which was to transform it, he never for a moment thinks of breaking with it. With both feet he stands on primitive apocalyptic ground. That this is so will become increasingly clear as we proceed in our study of his thought. Our immediate task is to show that in Apocalyptic his preaching of redemption has, in part at least, its background and setting.

At the basis of all the Apostle's thinking and constituting its ground-plan there lies the apocalyptic doctrine of the two ages or worlds with its pessimistic and dualistic implications. Standing in the old and evil age, Paul looks with eager longing towards the new. For the first is as full of misery as the second is of glory ; and it was to deliver us out of the first and give us a heritage in the

second that the Son of God surrendered Himself to death
(Gal. 1⁴, 1 Cor. 7³¹, Col. 1¹²).   The misery of the evil age
consists first and foremost in the fact that man's lot in it
is one of hopeless bondage to sin.   Sin is not only his
guilt but his inevitable fate ; for he has i.herited a nature
that is radically corrupt and cannot lift a finger to save
himself.   Apocalyptic writers admit at least a few ex-
ceptions to the general sinfulness, but the Apostle will
hear of none.   " There is no distinction, for all have sinned,
and fall short of the glory of God " (Rom. 3²³ 5¹⁹ 7¹⁴).
In the Law, which is the religious institution of the evil
age, men have indeed an ostensible means of salvation ;
but situated as they are, powerless to obey its commands,
its only effect is to plunge them still deeper into the abyss
of sin and to oppress them with the new terror of its
curse (Gal. 3¹⁰, Rom. 4¹⁵ 7⁷ᶠᶠ·).   Of the grace of God the
evil age has no experience, unless indeed as a promise to
be fulfilled in the future ; it knows and can know God
only as a God of commandment and recompense (Gal.
3¹⁸⁻²⁷).   Equally foreign to it is the activity of the life-
giving Spirit (1 Cor. 2⁶ᶠᶠ· 4²⁰, 2 Cor. 10⁴).   Only after the
Christ-redemption has introduced the better day does the
reign of grace and of the Spirit open.

As the result of sin's dominion, man in the evil age
is subjected to another sore evil, that, namely, of death.
Mortality is the law of the existing world, as immortality
of the world to come (Rom. 5¹²ᶠᶠ·).

In describing the existing world as evil it is of course
the lot of man that Paul has mainly in view.   At the
same time he thinks of the material creation as also
involved in the curse.   On it too lies the bondage of
corruption : it " groaneth and travaileth in pain together
until now " (Rom. 8²⁰ᶠᶠ·).

In Paul as in Jewish Apocalyptic the pessimism of
the outlook is deepened by a belief in the all-pervading

activity of evil spirits. Everywhere the shadow of these malignant powers falls across his pages. The angels and principalities of Rom. 8³⁸, the thrones, dominions, principalities and powers of Col. 1¹⁶, the elemental and astral spirits (στοιχεῖα) of Gal. 4⁹ and Col. 2⁸, are different classes of demonic beings. To these the evil age is in large measure in subjection (1 Cor. 2⁶). Satan their head is described as its god (2 Cor. 4⁴). His power is not absolute—Paul sees in history the unfolding of a Divine purpose which Satan himself must unwillingly subserve—but it is extensive enough to make the world his rather than God's. Very real and very horrible for the Apostle are the machinations of the demonic legions. They entice men to evil and blind their eyes (1 Cor. 7⁵, 2 Cor. 4³, Eph. 6¹²). They are the real objects of heathen worship; and when men participate in heathen meals, and observe the calendar, they put themselves under their power (1 Cor. 10¹⁹, Gal. 4⁹). They accuse believers before God, and endeavour to separate them from His love (2 Cor. 2¹⁰, Rom. 8³⁵). Their malice and cunning lie behind all mischief in the Church. The false apostles are Satan's ministers; and it is Satan who hinders Paul from coming to the Thessalonians and inflicts on him the thorn in the flesh. In one passage the crucifixion itself is traced to "the rulers of this age," by whom is clearly meant not Pilate and the chief priests, but the angel-powers who used these human agents as their instrument. Ignorant of the real rank of their victim, they unwittingly carried into effect the Divine plan for their own undoing (1 Cor. 2⁶). The demons in the Apostle's pages are no mere symbolic figures, but personal powers of evil. With them Christ has to wrestle, and His redemption signifies in one aspect of it a deliverance of men from their baleful tyranny.

Compared with the part assigned to angels of darkness

that assigned to angels of light is but inconspicuous. Following Jewish traditions, Paul speaks of the latter as having mediated the Law to Moses and as accompanying Christ at His second coming; but his conception of Christ as the one mediator stands in the way of his attributing to them more than a scenic rôle.

Being such as we have seen, the evil age or world can have but one end—destruction. And the end is close at hand. Paul expects to see it in his lifetime (1 Thess. 4^{15}). As a thief in the night the day of the Lord will come. Christ will descend from heaven with His angels, and the human race be gathered before Him for judgment and sentence (Rom. 14^{10}). We read also of a final struggle between Christ and the demonic powers, ending in their irretrievable ruin (1 Cor. 15^{24}). Saved from the day of wrath, the righteous will ascend with their Lord into the new world of glory and immortality.

In all this Paul departs but little from the traditional Jewish scheme. One interpolation of far-reaching importance has, however, to be noted. Anterior to the messianic redemption of the last days of which alone Apocalyptic knows, the Apostle introduces another redemption, which, indeed, is the decisive one. In fashion as a man, the Son of God is born into the existing evil world, and through His death destroys or mortally wounds the malignant powers that hold it in bondage. The introduction into the apocalyptic drama of this new act to some extent dislocates it. The sharpness of the transition from the old age to the new is blurred. With the death or, more strictly, with the resurrection of Christ the new age has in some sense already begun. Believers are even now living under the reign of grace; and the Holy Spirit, the great messianic gift, is exercising its renewing activity. In some sense the Kingdom is already present. Instead of the single turning-point of Apocalyptic, the day of judgment, we have two. It would be untrue to say that in Paul the second is overshadowed by the first; but this was the final outcome. More and more religious interest was transferred from the redemption of the last day to that already achieved on the Cross.

That the apocalyptic conception of things has small title to be called philosophic will at once be evident. It belongs to the domain not of reasoned thought, but of mythology. Angels and demons, even the Messiah, are mythological figures; a war of heaven with hell, a world-catastrophe and a sudden appearance of the Kingdom of God are events in a mythological drama.

One may wonder that a gospel expressed in terms of such a world-view found acceptance outside Judaism, in circles more or less leavened by Greek thought. But as a matter of fact Hellenistic paganism had much closer affinities with Apocalyptic than might at first sight appear. In both we find the same deep-seated pessimism with respect to the existing order, and the same belief in the malignant and all-pervading activity of evil spirits. Common to both was the belief in redemption, and the idea that redemption, in one aspect of it at least, consisted in deliverance from the tyranny which the evil spirits exercised. And as we can see from the 4th Eclogue of Virgil, there was current in certain pagan circles something analogous to the messianic hope. Indeed, it is by no means easy to decide how much of Paul's demonology is derived from Jewish, and how much from pagan sources. When he speaks of the heathen as being in bondage to the στοιχεῖα or astral spirits, and represents Christ as triumphing over principalities and powers on the Cross, it is in all probability the latter rather than the former that supply the background of his thought (Gal. 4[3, 9], Col. 2[15]).

Although Apocalyptic constitutes the ground-plan of

Paul's general scheme, it is far from providing him with all or even with the most characteristic categories of his thought. His developed doctrine of the evil age, of man and his sin, the world and its bondage, the Redeemer and redemption, carry us outside the circle of apocalyptic ideas. We cannot in the present chapter introduce all his leading conceptions, but there remain two, which occupy a position so fundamental, and are so closely associated with those already noted, that they may claim to be considered at this point. They are the conceptions of the flesh and the Spirit. In these two conceptions the apocalyptic dualism of the old age and the new, the demonic and the Divine, receives a speculative expression and grounding. From the domain of mythology we are led into that of philosophy or quasi-philosophy.

What does the Apostle understand by "the flesh," when he uses the term not in a popular way, as he frequently does, but with a definite dogmatic connotation? In agreement with Hellenistic psychology, he distinguishes in man's being two elements, soul and body, the inner and the outer man. Flesh is the material living substance of the human body. He can use the terms flesh and body indifferently; and if the first is of far more frequent occurrence than the second, it is because the body's fleshly constitution is what gives it its character (Rom. 7^{24}). A body composed not of flesh but of heavenly substance would have properties entirely different (1 Cor. $15^{42ff.}$). With respect to the fleshly body, we have to note the way in which Paul thinks of its connection with the soul or self. With the antique world in general he conceives the two as separate and relatively independent entities. The body is the soul's garment, and like a garment it can be stripped off (2 Cor. $5^{2ff.}$). It is the earthly tabernacle which the soul inhabits; and Paul can entertain the idea that in an ecstatic experience he had temporarily left it behind (2 Cor. 1²³). Further, the fleshly body is conceived as endowed with a life and activity of its own. It is the seat of impulses that are distinguishable from those of the soul united with it and, indeed, at variance with them (Rom. 7²³). When the Apostle speaks of " the mind of the flesh," of " its affections and lusts," his words are not to be taken as a merely figurative description of the pro- pensities of the natural man. Flesh and soul, if bound up together, retain their separate life and motions, and act reciprocally on one another. The modern idea of the unity of the personality must be dismissed from our mind.

And now we come to the main point. The motions of the flesh possess moral quality, and that quality is evil. Fornication, idolatry, sorcery, enmities, jealousies, heresies, drunkenness, revellings and such-like—these are the works to which they provoke (Gal. 5¹⁹ff·). It is not a case of a thing in itself morally indifferent being perverted to evil, but of a thing inherently evil. " The mind of the flesh is enmity against God; for it is not subject to the law of God, neither indeed can be " (Rom. 8⁷). While the body is capable of redemption in the sense of being changed into a spiritual body, the flesh is irredeemable. It can have no place in the Kingdom of God; and the task of the believer is not to transmute its passions and lusts, or even to regulate them, but to mortify and crucify them (1 Cor. 15⁵⁰, Col. 3⁵). In the flesh Paul in fact finds the spring and principle of sin. Sins of every description, whether bearing a sensuous character or not, are traced back to it (Gal. 5¹⁹ff·). It is everywhere set over-against the Spirit, which is the principle of righteousness, as its moral opposite. " The flesh lusteth against the Spirit and the Spirit against the flesh; for these are contrary one to the other " (Gal. 5¹⁷). Sometimes, it is true, Paul speaks of sin as a personal power that entered the world, took up its abode in man

2

and subjected him to its sway; but such personification cannot be regarded as more than figurative (Rom. $5^{12.\ 21}$ $6^{16.\ 23}$ 7^{17}). From a multitude of passages it is abundantly clear that for Paul sin means just the motions or lusts of the flesh. As will appear later, these lusts do not become sinful in the full sense of the word, until confronted by the " Thou shalt not " of the Law.

Against the interpretation of Paul's teaching here adopted various objections have been urged, but none possessing any real force. The Apostle, it is urged, can speak of glorifying God in the body, of cleansing oneself from all defilement of the flesh ; he can speak of the body as a temple of the Holy Ghost and of its sanctification (1 Thess. 4^4, 1 Cor. $6^{19.\ 20}$). But what he means by these assertions is not that the flesh has been altered in its moral character, but only that through the indwelling of the Spirit its sinful lusts have been reduced to impotence.

Such then is the fleshly body. How does Paul think of the soul ? It is the inner as opposed to the outer man, the ego or self as distinguished from the body it inhabits and the bodily lusts that exert an evil power over it (2 Cor. 4^{16}, Rom. 7^{18-23}). More explicitly, it is the mind ($\nu o\hat{v}\varsigma$), the heart, the spirit (Rom. 7^{23}, 1 Cor. 2^{11}, 2 Cor. 7^1). When he describes it as the spirit, the Apostle is simply using popular language and has no intention of suggesting a primordial connection with the divine Spirit. From these designations as well as from the functions ascribed to it, it is clear that Paul thinks of the soul after the Greek fashion as constituted by reason and conscience. It has God's unwritten law imprinted on it, and it is capable of rising through observation of the visible creation to a knowledge of the Creator's eternal power and Godhead (Rom. 2^{15} 1^{20}). What is more, it has its affinities, not with the flesh—against the domination of which it rebels, though impotently—but with the divine law. Transcribing his pre-conversion experience Paul can say, " I delight in the law of God after the inward man " (Rom. 7[15ff.]). But whatever its native leanings, through its connection with the flesh the soul is bound to evil by a chain it can never of itself break, and in cases of flagrant abandonment its spark of light is turned into utter darkness (Rom. 1[19], Eph. 4[18]). No initiative is conceded to it, and in the drama of redemption it plays not the slightest part. In the natural man the tyranny of the flesh is the all-determining fact. The natural man is carnal ($\sigma\alpha\rho\kappa\iota\kappa\acute{o}\varsigma$), or as the Apostle, borrowing a term from Hellenistic religion, again describes him, psychic ($\psi\upsilon\chi\iota\kappa\acute{o}\varsigma$) (Rom. 7[14], 1 Cor. 2[14]). His bondage is absolute. " The Law is spiritual," Paul declares, " but I am carnal, sold under sin; the good which I would I do not; but the evil which I would not, that I do." Only by a divine act of redemption can the soul be delivered; and it is the proper subject of the redeeming process, the field in which the saving activities exercise their power. The flesh is not redeemed but destroyed. Paul has nothing of the Stoic faith in the ability of the mind to control the passions of the body. He leaves no place for the freedom of the will, a property which Jewish writers, even while teaching a radical and innate impulse to evil, were careful to safeguard. The highest the natural man can reach is that cry from the depths, " Wretched man that I am! who shall deliver me from this body of death ? "

It is thus that Paul accounts in a philosophical way for the chief misery that afflicts mankind in the evil age. And the second great misery, which is mortality, is traced to the same source. Like sin, death is the result of man's fleshly constitution. Flesh is in its essential nature corruptible, our body is a body of death, and therefore must we all die (1 Cor. 15[50]).

It has already been observed that in Paul's view the material world no less than man is in subjection to an evil bondage. In what this bondage consists we are not left in doubt. It is in the fact of corruptibleness or transience (Rom. 8²¹). Over nature as over human life death reigns. While the Apostle can speak of nature's bondage as imposed by a divine decree, it is clear that he finds its proximate source in the fact of materiality. " The things that are seen are temporal."

At this point the question inevitably presents itself, whether it is not materiality that is for Paul the ultimate source of sin as well as of transience, and whether therefore we must not attribute to him the Platonic and Hellenistic doctrine that matter is inherently evil. Certainly the logic of his thought points in this direction. His description of the fleshly body as of the earth, earthy, and of earthly goods as carnal, supposes a connection between flesh and the substance of the material world (1 Cor. 15⁴⁷⁻⁴⁹, Rom. 15²⁷). And when he declares that the resurrection body is composed not of earthly but of heavenly substance, he must be regarded as passing a damnatory judgment on the former. At the same time it cannot be too strongly affirmed that Paul himself has no idea of developing his thought to the point of a cosmic dualism. The truth is that in cosmological speculation he has not the slightest interest. His interest is exclusively practical, to demonstrate the need for redemption and to render the process of redemption intelligible. The doctrine of the sinful flesh and of the transience of all material things is developed so far, and only so far, as it serves these ends. Why the flesh should be the seat and principle of sin is a problem he never raises. Nowhere does he assert or imply that it is because of its materiality. Nowhere does he speak of the material world as being not only in bondage but evil. The doctrine that in matter lies the principle of evil is not to be found in Paul, however much the trend of his thought may seem to be toward it. On the contrary, he teaches that "all things were created by Christ and for Christ," that "the earth is the Lord's" and that "nothing is unclean of itself" (Col. 1^{16}, 1 Cor. 10^{26}, Rom. 14^4).

As the flesh is the dominating power of the old order, so is the Spirit of the new order inaugurated by the Christ-redemption. Everywhere the two powers are set over against each other in antithetical relation. "The flesh lusts against the Spirit and the Spirit against the flesh; for these are contrary the one to the other." The first is the principle of sin and death, the second of righteousness and immortality (Rom. 8^2). To the one there attach the predicates of weakness and dishonour, to the other those of power and glory. The one belongs to earth, the other is from heaven (1 Cor. $15^{41ff.}$).

In speaking of the Spirit as the power of the new age we have to keep in view what was said as to the dislocation of the apocalyptic scheme by the introduction of a redemption anterior to that of the last days. Though in strictness the new age does not begin till after the Judgment, in some sense it opens with the Christ-redemption, to run for the intermediate period concurrently with the old.

The conception of the Spirit when Paul took it up had already a long history behind it, but it is not necessary to go farther back than the Old Testament prophets. For the prophets the Spirit of Jahveh meant first and foremost the divine power that in moments of rapture and inspiration descended upon them to overmaster and make them its instruments. This power was conceived, not in primitive fashion as a daimon or spirit-being, still less as a mere personal influence such as one man can exert on another, but in a naively materialistic way. Proceeding from God as if it were His breath—*ruach*, the Hebrew word for the Spirit, means literally breath—and bearing within it something of His life and energy, it can enter into a man

bodily.   It is doubtful if the so-called hypostatising of the
Spirit amounted to much more, even in the later Judaism,
than this idea of it as material and therefore as separable
from its source.   Certainly it was never thought of as a
personal being in the sense in which the angels were
persons.

While the prophetic ecstasy was regarded as the Spirit's
most characteristic, it was far from being its only work.
Extraordinary endowments of various kinds—prowess in
war, skill in judging and even in handicraft—was traced to
its activity.   On the coming Messiah it would rest as a
spirit of wisdom and understanding, of counsel and might,
of knowledge and the fear of the Lord (Isa. 11^2).   From
this and other passages it is clear that ethical workings
were attributed to it and that it was described as holy, not
merely as belonging to God but also as antagonistic to sin.
In view of New Testament developments, it is of particular
importance to notice the close connection into which the
Spirit was brought with the messianic age.   The messianic
age will be signalised by an outpouring of the Spirit, not
merely on a few favoured individuals, but on all flesh
(Ezek. 36^{27}, Joel 2^{28}).   And by the Spirit the messianic King
will be equipped for His high task (Isa. 4^2).

This Old Testament conception of the Spirit and its
activities maintained itself down to primitive Christian days
practically unaltered.   In the outburst of ecstatic phenomena within its ranks the primitive community recognised
the fulfilment of the old prophecies, and in the Spirit's
descent upon Jesus at His baptism, His equipment for the
messianic task (Acts 2$^{15ff.}$).   Comparing the early Christian
conception with that of the Old Testament, the only
observable difference is that in the former the working of
the Spirit is more exclusively identified with phenomena of
an ecstatic character.

Turning to the doctrine of Paul we find that it has its

basis in that of the primitive community. For him too the Spirit is the great messianic gift, its activity the sign that the new age has dawned (Gal. $3^{2ff.}$ 4^{26}, 2 Cor. $3^{6ff.}$). And since the full consummation still lies in the future, he can speak of this gift as the earnest of better things to come (2 Cor. 1^{22}). With the primitive community also he recognises the Spirit's working in the ecstatic gifts and miraculous powers with which believers were endowed. " For to one is given through the Spirit the word of wisdom, to another faith, and to another gifts of healing in the one Spirit, and to another working of miracles, and to another divers kinds of tongues " (1 Cor. 12^8).

But if the Apostle reproduces the primitive doctrine in its main features, he at the same time develops it in a way that gives to it an entirely new character. This development proceeds along three lines.

(1) In the first place, the ethical side of the Spirit's activity, which in the primitive view had been in the background, is brought distinctly and decisively to the front. The chief evidences and fruits of that activity are no longer sought in ecstatic gifts or miraculous powers, but in the everyday virtues—love, joy, peace, longsuffering, kindness, meekness, temperance (Gal. 5^{22}). This ethicising of the Spirit is one of the Apostle's greatest religious and dogmatic achievements. It puts upon Christianity in a decisive way the stamp of an ethical religion.

(2) Along with this ethicising of the Spirit and as its result there goes another development hardly less important. From being a power whose working in the believer is only intermittent and occasional, it becomes his abiding possession, and the spring of all in his life that has religious value. Every believer as such is endowed with the Spirit: he lives by the Spirit and it is his supreme duty to obey its promptings, to walk by it (Rom. 8^9, Gal. 5^{25}). The Spirit is the supernatural power

behind his every motion towards truth and goodness, the supernatural source of his liberty, his knowledge of divine things, his assurance of sonship and of the divine love (2 Cor. 3^{17}, 1 Cor. 2^{10}, Gal. 4^6, Rom. 4^5). It occupies in the redeemed soul the place which the flesh occupies in the unredeemed, being the principle of the higher life as the flesh is of the lower. We may describe it as God immanent in the soul, if we remember that it is never in its working confused with or merged in the soul's native powers.

(3) The third direction in which Paul develops the primitive Christian doctrine is in practically, and in at least one passage explicitly, identifying the Spirit with the exalted and indwelling Christ. We start from the passage, Rom. 8$^{9-11}$: " But ye are not in the flesh, but in the Spirit, if so be that the Spirit of God dwelleth in you. But if any man hath not the Spirit of Christ, he is none of His. And if Christ is in you, the body is dead because of sin, but the Spirit is life because of righteousness. But if the Spirit of Him that raised up Jesus from the dead dwelleth in you, He that raised up Christ Jesus from the dead shall quicken also your mortal bodies through His Spirit that dwelleth in you." The first thing to be noted in this passage is that the Spirit is described now as the Spirit of God and again as the Spirit of Christ. As also in other passages, the two terms are used interchangeably (Gal. 4^6). Still further, the indwelling of the Spirit and the indwelling of Christ are plainly presented as equivalent facts. Between the one and the other no distinction is drawn. With the above passage to support us we can scarcely hesitate to press the letter of the much-discussed passage, 2 Cor. 3^{17} : " Now the Lord is the Spirit (ὁ δὲ κύριος τὸ πνεῦμα ἐστιν): and where the Spirit of the Lord is, there is liberty." This statement means more than that Christ possesses the liberating power asserted in the preceding verse in virtue of the fact that the Spirit constitutes

His essential being. Indeed, one can say that the idea of Christ's power as derivative, dependent on His possession of the Spirit, is foreign to the Apostle's thought. What he asserts is that the Spirit, since it is subject to no external norm, carries with it liberty, and that Christ can liberate those who turn to Him because He is Himself the Spirit. In the verse following the assertion of identity is repeated. Turning from the thought of liberation to that of inward transformation, Paul declares that beholding, not like the Israelites with veiled, but with unveiled face, the glory of the Lord reflected from the face of Christ—a higher glory than that which shone from the face of Moses—the believer is changed into the same image, even as from the Lord, the Spirit (καθάπερ ἀπὸ κυρίου πνεύματος).

How the Apostle was led up to this identification of the Spirit with the risen Christ is not difficult to understand. It was the logical outcome of his Christ-mysticism. As we shall see later, his Christ-mysticism is the outstanding feature of his piety. The life he lives is a life of fellowship with the Christ who dwells in the depths of his soul ; and everything he is he traces to this august presence. There is no single function ascribed to the Spirit which is not taken over by the indwelling Christ. The believer's righteousness, justification, sanctification, liberty, knowledge, love, joy, peace are ascribed now to the one and again to the other (2 Cor. 5²¹, Rom. 14¹⁷, Gal. 2¹⁷, 1 Cor. 6¹¹, 1 Cor. 1², Rom. 15¹⁶, Gal. 2⁴ 5¹⁸, 2 Cor. 13³, 1 Cor. 2¹⁰, 1 Cor. 16²⁴, Col. 1⁸, Phil. 3¹, Rom. 14¹⁷, Phil. 4⁹, Rom. 14¹⁷). Now it is the indwelling Christ that is the principle and power of the new life, and again it is the Spirit (Gal. 2²⁰, 5¹⁶⁻²²). Here it is the first that quickens the mortal body, and there it is the second (2 Cor. 4¹⁴, Rom. 8¹¹). In one passage we read that the possession of the Spirit is the earnest of the future inheritance ; and in another, that Christ in the believer is the hope of glory (2 Cor. 1²²,

Col. I²⁷). Even a function of the Spirit so distinctive as
that of ministering ecstatic gifts is taken over by Christ
(2 Cor. 12¹).

This list of parallels might easily be extended. The
truth is that the idea of the indwelling Christ is so developed
as to render the Spirit as a separate agent superfluous.
By a process of which he was himself probably unconscious,
the Apostle withdraws from the latter its very *raison d'être*.
He could do this the more easily that the Spirit was never
clothed with the attribute of personality, but remained what
it had been for the prophets, a divine energy, separable
indeed from God, but in no fashion distinct from Him.
Inevitably, one might say, it would retreat before or be
merged in the more definite and vivid figure of the living
Christ. Powerful forces were, however, operative to keep
this tendency in restraint. The idea of the Spirit was
deeply rooted in the sacred past and in the common
Christian faith. Paul's Christ-mysticism, on the other
hand, was hardly a common possession, hardly more than
the piety of a circle. Even had the Apostle wished to
substitute the indwelling Christ for the Spirit, he could not
have imposed his view on the Church. And there is no
sign that he did wish. Only in a single passage does he
expressly identify the two. On him too tradition was not
without its influence ; and while nowhere attempting to
define their mutual relations, he speaks in general as if
Christ and the Spirit were two distinct magnitudes. In the
Fourth Gospel the same tendency towards identification
and the same arrest of that tendency again meet us.

In attempting to trace the misery of the old age and
the glory of the new to their respective metaphysical
principles, Paul passes outside the domain of apocalyptic
and also of Hebraic thought and shows himself touched
by the Greek spirit. For philosophic construction was no

native product of the Hebrew genius; both in Judaism and in Christianity it was an import from Hellenism. What we have, therefore, in Paul's doctrines of the flesh and the Spirit is a Hellenistic stratum of thought superimposed on the primitive apocalyptic stratum. Do the conceptions themselves bear marks of Hellenistic influence?

In the case of the first conception, that of the flesh, the answer can scarcely be other than affirmative. It is true that it has in Hebrew and Jewish thought a certain point of attachment. Flesh frequently appears in the Old Testament as a synonym for man, and so used carries with it the suggestion of mortality and of physical and moral frailty (Gen. 6^3, Isa. 31^3 40^6 56^4). But further in the direction of Paul's doctrine the Old Testament does not go. Nowhere does it speak of the flesh as the seat of man's passions, or regard it as one among other elements in his being. Nowhere does it derive man's sinfulness from his fleshly constitution. And while un-Hellenised Judaism knows of the impulse to evil present in all men, it never connects this with the flesh. The Apostle's doctrine of an outer and an inner man, and of the former as the prison-house of the latter and the seat of sin, is not Hebrew or Jewish, but unmistakably Hellenistic. In the Hellenistic age psychology and not less religion and ethics were dominated by the antitheses of soul and body, reason and passion, the spiritual and the material. In comparison with the immaterial and rational element in man the body and its passions were despised, and virtue was made to consist in the complete subjection of the latter to the former. "The greatest cause of our ignorance," writes Philo, "is the flesh and our inseparable connection with it; and this Moses represents God as admitting, when He says that because men are flesh the spirit of God cannot abide in them. . . . But those souls which bear the heavy burden of the flesh, being weighed down and oppressed by

it, are unable to look upwards to the revolutions of the
heavens, but dragged downwards, have their necks forcibly
pressed to the ground like so many quadrupeds " (de Gig. 7).
Among the Mystery Cults the same opposition of flesh and
spirit obtained.   By mortification of the flesh and ecstatic
liberation from it the mystic sought to rise to the life of
the spirit.   This strain of thought was a heritage from the
East.   It is idle to ask the particular source from which
the Apostle derived it.   The atmosphere of the time was
impregnated with it.

That Paul's conception of the Spirit also bears upon it
the stamp of Hellenism is by no means so clear.   Attempts
have been made to connect it with the highly significant
conception current in Stoicism.   By $\pi\nu\epsilon\hat{\upsilon}\mu a$ or spirit the
Stoics understood the creative reason ($\lambda\acute{o}\gamma os\ \sigma\pi\epsilon\rho\mu a\tau\iota\kappa\acute{o}s$),
which as a vitalising breath or formative fire interpenetrated
the universe in all its parts, constituting the principle of its
activity, life and order.   Of this $\pi\nu\epsilon\hat{\upsilon}\mu a$—conceived as an
extended substance—the individual soul, or at least the
rational part of it, as opposed to its passions, was a particle.
Already in the Alexandrine Book of Wisdom this Stoic
conception is taken up into Jewish thought.   The writer
describes Wisdom as in its nature a spirit, thinking, holy,
loving the good, friendly to man, having power over all and
interpenetrating all spirits.   It is a breath of the power
of God, a clear effluence from the glory of the invisible
Ruler, and, remaining itself unchanged, it renews all things ;
and from generation to generation passing into holy souls
it endows friends of God and prophets with the Spirit
($8^{3\text{ff.}}\ 7^{22\text{ff.}}$).   But between such conceptions and that of
Paul there is but little in common.   Of an immanence of
the Spirit either in the universe or in the natural man the
Apostle knows nothing.   For him it is the exclusive possession of believers, and something distinct from their own
personality.   Nor can it be said that with the Stoics he

thinks of the Spirit as an extended substance. The formula " in the Spirit " can be appealed to in favour of this view only when it is interpreted as having a local reference; and, as we shall find later, such an interpretation cannot be maintained. Equally unconvincing is the appeal to the Pauline conception of a spiritual resurrection body (1 Cor. 15⁴⁴). The spiritual body need not be composed of spirit-material any more than the psychic (ψυχικόν) of psychic-material. All the Apostle means is a body appropriate to the new spiritual mode of existence. If he thinks of its composition, it is not spirit-substance, but light-substance that he has in view. That with antique thinkers in general he conceives the Spirit not as immaterial, but as a refined supersensuous matter is likely enough. None the less the Spirit is never for him the all-pervading element of Stoic philosophy, but always, as in the Hebrew and Jewish tradition, an energy proceeding from God and bearing within it something of the divine life.

Recently attention has been called by Reitzenstein and others to another conception of the Spirit current in the paganism of Paul's day. In such documents of Hellenistic religion as the so-called Mithras Liturgy, the Hermetic writings and the Oracula Chaldaica, the terms πνεῦμα and νοῦς with substantially the same meaning are of frequent occurrence. What they denote is a personally conceived, supernatural power different from anything in the natural man, a power which is a gift of grace to the pious, endowing them with right knowledge and the ability to control the lower bodily life. To receive the πνεῦμα or νοῦς into oneself is to be lifted to the life of God and deified.[1] In the Mithras Liturgy the mystic speaks of the Holy Spirit blowing within him as the effect of his initiation.[2]

---

[1] Reitzenstein, *Die hellenistischen Mysterien-religionen*, pp. 44, 136 ff. Bousset, *Kyrios Christos*, pp. 136 ff.

[2] Dieterich, p. 4.

That this Hellenistic doctrine has certain affinities with
that of Paul lies on the surface.   But it does not follow
that the former has to be regarded as the model of the
latter.   As we have seen, the Pauline conception can
be explained without the hypothesis of foreign influence.
Its roots lie in the Old Testament and in primitive
Christianity.   And in developing what was given to him,
the Apostle proceeds on genuinely Hebrew lines.   His
great achievement, the complete ethicising of the Spirit,
has but little analogous to it in Hellenistic religious
speculation, and takes us back to that ethical conception
of religion which was a heritage from the Old Testament
and above all from Jesus.

CHAPTER II.

Doctrine of Christ's Person : The Historical and Religious Basis.

The message of a Redeemer—that is the first article in Paul's gospel. Who is this Redeemer?

That the Apostle identifies Him with the Jesus whose words, deeds and fate are recorded in the Gospels is established on evidence that leaves no room for dubiety. The view advanced by Drews and others,[1] that while he thinks of Christ as having lived on earth and died on the Cross, he does not connect Him with any definite historical figure, that his Christ, therefore, belongs to the region of mythology, is too fantastic to require prolonged consideration. Paul describes Christ as of the seed of David according to the flesh, and refers to His betrayal, His institution of the Supper the same night, and to His rejection and crucifixion by the Jews (Rom. 1^3, 1 Cor. 11^{23}, 1 Thess. 2^{15}). Since he fixes His resurrection as having happened the third day after His burial, and mentions Peter as the first and himself as the last of those who had seen Him in His risen glory, he clearly regards Him as a contemporary (1 Cor. 15^5). On at least three occasions he appeals to words of Christ that we find recorded in the Synoptists (1 Cor. 7^{10} 9^{14} 11^{24}). He speaks of Christ's brothers and particularly of James, whom he had more than once met (1 Cor. 9^5, Gal. 1^{14}). He knows of the circle of the Twelve,

---

[1] *Die Christusmythe*, Zweiter Teil.

and mentions by name Peter and John. Whether in 2 Cor. 5[16] he implies that he had himself known Christ in the days of His flesh must be regarded as doubtful; but in any case he implies that there were men still living who could claim to have enjoyed that privilege. All this is sufficiently decisive on the point that Paul connects the Christ of his faith with a definite historical person who had lived and died in times within his own memory. With the hypothesis of a mythical Christ we need not longer concern ourselves.

Far more difficult to decide is the question as to the extent of Paul's knowledge of the evangelical history. In recent years the tendency among scholars of the liberal school has been to reduce such knowledge to the narrowest dimensions. Wrede cuts away all connection between the Apostle and the Master, declaring that the points of similarity in their teaching are due not to dependence, but to a common Jewish heritage. Even the ethical traits in the Christ of Paul do not take us back to Jesus, but are derived from the Apostle's own doctrine of redemption.[1] The question raised is a vital one, and demands the most careful consideration.

That Paul had the fullest opportunities for making himself acquainted with the story of Jesus is beyond dispute; and the presumption that he availed himself of them is well-nigh irresistible. Even before his conversion he must have learned something of the man whose followers he persecuted. After his conversion he had intercourse with Peter and with others prominent in the Church, like James, Barnabas, Mark and Luke. When we consider further that the bare existence of the Synoptic narratives supplies irrefutable proof that the Gospel story was treasured and preserved, we find it hard to believe that the Apostle,

---

[1] Wrede, *Paulus*, pp. 84 ff. See also Brückner, *Die Entstehung der Paulinischen Christologie.*

who journeyed through the length and breadth of the
Church, could possibly have escaped becoming acquainted
with that story. Were the matter to be decided on *a
priori* grounds, the decision would be prompt and un-
hesitating.

We have, however, to reckon with facts which, while
far from proving the Apostle ignorant of the Gospel story,
yet seem to reduce his knowledge to much narrower dimensions than has usually been assumed. His references to
the historical life of Jesus are meagre in the extreme.
Everywhere indeed the Cross is lifted high; but apart from
this culminating event we hear only of the betrayal, the
institution of the Supper and the burial. The things that
seem to us so infinitely significant, Jesus' attitude to
publicans and sinners, His freedom with respect to ceremonial observances, His communion with God in prayer,
His struggle and victory in Gethsemane—all these things
Paul, if he was familiar with them, passes in utter silence.
That Jesus claimed to be the Messiah and announced His
return in glory, that He healed the sick and cast out devils,
we find not the slightest hint.

This silence with respect to the great bulk of the
evangelical narrative comes out in a striking way when we
consider the illustrations he gives of the moral traits in
Jesus' character. For the grand trait of self-sacrificing
love, the solitary if overwhelming proof adduced is His
acceptance of the Cross. When the Apostle speaks of
Christ not pleasing Himself, he appeals, not to any incident
in His earthly life, but to an Old Testament prophecy, or
what he regards as such (Rom. 15³). And in entreating
his readers by " the meekness and gentleness of Christ " it
is again in all probability an Old Testament passage that
is in his mind (2 Cor. 10¹—Isa. 53⁷). Most significant of
all is the illustration he gives of Christ's humility and self-
renunciation. It is taken not from the historical, but from

3

the premundane life: "Being in the form of God, He emptied Himself, taking the form of a servant" (Phil. 2⁵).

And if Paul's references to the incidents of Jesus' historical career are scanty, those to His teaching are hardly less so. Only once, when communicating the ritual of the Supper, does he give what purports to be a direct quotation (1 Cor. 11²⁴). In two passages he enunciates with an appeal to the authority of the Lord laws which can be regarded as free reproductions of synoptic sayings: that the wife depart not from her husband, that they which proclaim the Gospel should live of the Gospel (1 Cor. 7¹⁰ = Mark 10⁹, 1 Cor. 9¹⁴ = Luke 10⁷). The Apostle also gives "by the word of the Lord" an intimation regarding the privilege of believers who have died before the Parousia (1 Thess. 4¹⁵). But the intimation has no parallel among Jesus' recorded words and could hardly have proceeded from Him. In this case we have to think not of a word handed down by tradition, but of an inner revelation from the risen Christ.

The slender list of Paul's direct references to sayings of Jesus is not, however, the only evidence of his acquaintance with the Synoptic tradition. We have also to take into account those passages which from their resemblance in thought or language to Synoptic sayings may claim to be regarded as echoes of them. With respect to the number of such echoes there is wide difference of opinion. Writers like Titius, Feine and Moe find them everywhere; others, like Brückner, whose demands are more stringent, will scarcely admit a single instance. We give below[1]

---

[1] Rom. 2¹—Matt. 7¹.
Rom. 2⁶—Matt. 16²⁷.
Rom. 2¹⁹—Matt. 15¹⁴ 23¹⁶.
Rom. 9³³—Matt. 21⁴².
Rom. 12¹⁴—Matt. 5⁴⁴.
Rom. 13⁷—Matt. 21²⁵.
Rom. 13⁸⁻¹⁰, Gal. 5¹⁴—Matt. 22³⁴ff.
Rom. 14¹³, 1 Cor. 8⁷⁻¹³—Matt. 18⁶⁻⁹.
Rom. 16⁹—Matt. 10¹⁶.

1 Cor. 1²⁷—Matt. 11²⁵ 16¹⁵.
1 Cor. 6²—Matt. 19²⁸.
1 Cor. 6¹⁷—Matt. 19⁵.
1 Cor. 13²—Matt. 21²¹.
Gal. 5¹³, 1 Cor. 9¹⁹—Luke 22²⁶.
Phil. 3¹⁰—Matt. 16²⁴.
Col. 3⁵—Matt. 6²⁴.
2 Thess. 3³—Matt. 6¹³.

a list of parallel passages in which the hypothesis of dependence is at least arguable. An examination of these passages will show that while the cases in which dependence is beyond dispute are comparatively few, there are a considerable number in which it can be affirmed with a fair degree of confidence.

But after the most liberal computation of such cases, it remains a matter of surprise that they are not more numerous and more unequivocal. And still more surprising are the infrequency of the Apostle's direct appeals to Jesus' teaching, and his silence with regard to all in His historical ministry prior to the events of the last night. The assertion often advanced that in his oral teaching he made much more copious use of the evangelical narrative is one for which no proof can be given. We have no reason to believe that the Gospel as preached by Paul differed in any material respect from that unfolded in his Epistles. We are face to face with one of the most serious and difficult problems which the early history of Christianity presents. How explain the fact that Paul makes so little use of the historical material, which we know was accessible to him, and of which we can hardly believe him to have been ignorant? There are three characteristics of his thought which, taken together, go far to provide a solution.

(1) The first is this, that Paul thinks of Christ almost exclusively as redeemer, and that he concentrates His whole redemptive significance in His death and resurrection. That Jesus communicated by His teaching and life a new moral ideal and a new conception of the divine love and mercy, is an idea that lies outside the Apostle's horizon. God indeed reveals His righteousness and grace in Christ, but only through the medium of the atoning death. Equally foreign to Paul is the notion of a redemption which is the result of the impression produced on receptive souls by Jesus' human personality. In the Cross alone

resides the power of God. It was inevitable that all
outside the Cross should be pushed into the background,
and that we should get a Christ who entered the world
with no other mission than to die.

(2) Similar in its tendency and action is this second fact,
that the Saviour of Paul's faith and proclamation is not so
much the Jesus who taught the multitude and healed the
sick by the shores of the Galilæan lake, as the risen Christ
exalted to God's right hand and invested with divine
power and glory. It is with this living Lord, who inter-
cedes for him and dwells in him, that he holds communion.
Of the days of Christ's humiliation he remembers practically nothing but the great sacrifice. These days pass out
of sight as a phase in His existence that has lost its
meaning.

(3) The effect of this absorption in the figure of the
living Christ in overshadowing the earthly career becomes
still more patent when we consider a third characteristic of
the Apostle's thought. As the source of his doctrine Paul
appeals, not to the words spoken by Jesus on earth, but to
revelations he had received from Him as the risen and
present Lord. In the most emphatic terms he repudiates
any dependence on tradition. "For I make known to you,
brethren, as touching the gospel which was preached by me,
that it is not after man. For neither did I receive it from
man, nor was I taught it, but it came to me through revelation of Jesus Christ" (Gal. 1[11ff.]). And he proceeds to
show that his movements after his conversion precluded
the supposition that he was indebted in any way to those
who were apostles before him. These original apostles
added nothing to him, but only acknowledged the validity
of the gospel he had received independently of them. It
would, I think, be illegitimate to press this denial of indebtedness, written in the heat of controversy, so as to
make it cover all information regarding Him who was

their common Lord and Saviour. What the Apostle has in view is the doctrine of Christ's redemptive work, more particularly in its relation to the Law. That doctrine constituted for him the Gospel; and it is quite credible that in asserting his independence of human instruction he should have left out of account, as not entering into the dispute, information regarding such secondary matters as Jesus' teaching and manner of life. One thing, however, this Galatian passage makes absolutely clear. Paul did not derive his gospel of the Redeemer and His work of redemption from sayings of Jesus communicated to him by Peter or another. As he himself tells us, it came to him as an immediate revelation from the indwelling Christ. And this testimony is in harmony with the whole habit of his thought. Although he treats the words of Jesus as authoritative, only in one or two cases, and then in matters of subordinate importance, does he appeal to them. His appeal is always to the indwelling Christ, or what is the same thing, to the inner witness of the Spirit (1 Cor. 2^{6-16}). When he affirms his authority as a teacher, it is not on the ground that he has access to the authentic tradition, but on the ground that he has the mind of Christ, that Christ speaks in him (1 Cor. 2^{16}, 2 Cor. 13^3). So profound and dominating is his sense of inner illumination, that everything traditional, outside the saving facts, appears to him as of comparatively little moment.

In the Second Epistle to the Corinthians there is a passage which, if our interpretation of it is correct, sums up Paul's attitude to the Jesus of history (5^{16}). After declaring that in Christ's death all died, and that He died for all that they should no longer live unto themselves, he continues: "Wherefore we henceforth know no man after the flesh : even though we have known Christ after the flesh, yet now we know Him so no more. Wherefore if any man is in Christ, he is a new creature : the old things are passed away; behold, they are become new." Once we have discovered the motive of this much-discussed passage its exegesis is comparatively simple. And the clue to its motive is almost certainly to be found in the preceding reference to certain men who gloried in appearance and not in heart. Who are these men? They can hardly be other than the Judaisers who in support of their views appealed to their superior opportunity of knowing the mind of the Master. Had they not followed His train while He was on earth? In maintaining the continued validity of the Law these men would inevitably emphasise the fact that Jesus had Himself observed the Law and spoken words that implied its eternal obligation. The Apostle cannot deny the facts, but he puts upon them his own interpretation. It is true, we may suppose him to have argued, that Christ was born under the Law, and was therefore under obligation to fulfil it. But if He was born under the Law it was in order to redeem men from it (Gal. 4^5). His death brought its reign to an end, and at the same time antiquated His own words and actions as a minister of the circumcision. The old things have passed away. The "Christ after the flesh," whom Paul no longer knows, is this minister of the circumcision whom the Judaising party claimed to know at first hand and to have on their side. And as he refuses to think of Christ in His temporal and transient relations, so does he of other men. That there were those who claimed superior authority on the ground that they had companied with Christ in the days of His flesh or were related to Him by ties of blood, is nothing to him. The verse must be regarded as parenthetical. What suggested the digression was his recollection cf his Judaising opponents, and the idea of Christ's death as having changed for believers the whole situation.

In accounting for Paul's perplexing silences, this additional fact must also be borne in mind, that in the other

New Testament writings, outside the Gospels, the same silences are just as marked. Do we learn more about the historical Jesus from the Book of Acts than we do from the Pauline Epistles? And yet that book was written by the author of the Third Gospel!

It might seem that the Apostle, both by his manner of conceiving Christ and His work and by his own express declarations regarding the source of his knowledge, so cuts himself loose from the historical basis as to render every hypothesis of dependence precarious if not untenable. The solution of the problem we believe to be this, that he was a thousand times more indebted to the earthly Jesus than he knew. Directly and indirectly, through the tradition of Jesus' life and words and through lives that were epistles of Jesus, the spirit and principles of the Master had access to his mind and soul. Received and assimilated, they reappeared in his consciousness, altered in form doubtless and stamped with his own individuality, under the guise of divine revelations. It is no disparagement of his revelations to treat them as psychologically mediated, and to trace them to a source of which he was himself only half aware.

Can we say that the essential traits of the historical Jesus have been carried over into the Apostle's conception of the living and exalted Lord? As the heart and soul of this conception we have the grand trait of forgiving, saving, self-sacrificing love. " He loved me and gave Himself for me." It has been asserted that for this he need not have gone to the historical life, that it lay to his hand in the Servant passages of the Second Isaiah, or again, was a deduction from his doctrine of redemption.[1] But such explanations are utterly inadequate. Not till Jesus had lived and died did the Servant passages begin to glow with life and meaning. And the love of Christ is for Paul too overwhelming a reality to admit of the idea that it was a

[1] Drews, *Christusmythe*, ii. 104. Wrede, *Paulus*, p. 85.

mere creation of dogma.   Let any one compare the bene-
volence of the gods of the Oriental cults with the love
which Paul adores in Christ, and he will hardly escape the
feeling that the gulf between them is that between the
mythical and the historical.   The Apostle's conception of
the love of Christ represents the impression produced on
him by the contemplation of Jesus' life and Cross.

When, however, we ask what other traits Paul appropriated from the historical life we cannot speak with the same
assurance.   It is true that he describes himself as an
imitator of Christ, as being under law to Christ, and that,
as we shall find later, his ethic is in all essential respects a
reproduction of that of the Master (1 Cor. 11¹ 9²¹, Gal. 6²);
true also that passages like Rom. 12 and 1 Cor. 13 seem to
embody not only echoes of Jesus' words but also reflections
of His personality.   And this must be regarded as afford-
ing a strong presumption that the Apostle had in his mind
a fairly detailed picture of Jesus' moral character.   But on
the other side has to be set the fact of the meagreness of
his references to historical words and incidents, and that,
when he appeals to Christ's example, it is invariably those
central traits of humility, unselfishness and self-renunciation that he has in view (1 Cor. 11¹ᶠᶠ· following 10²⁴· ³³,
1 Cor. 4¹⁶ᶠᶠ· following 4¹⁰ᶠᶠ·, Rom. 13³, Phil. 2⁵).   On the
whole one must conclude that what the risen Christ of Paul
represents is a generalised picture of the historical Jesus.
The central and the new fill the horizon to the overshadowing of much, the loss of which would have been an
unspeakable calamity.   In particular those features in Jesus
that make Him so human and so real pass out of sight.
Paul's Christ has not the inexhaustible richness nor the
human winsomeness of the historical figure.   While the
central traits are exhibited with surpassing force, the whole
vital content is not carried over.   Having apprehended
what seems to him the essential meaning of Christ, the

Apostle can dismiss the details as of but minor importance. We have only to compare the Christ of the Fourth Gospel with that of the Synoptists to see the inevitable outcome of such a conception. That the Synoptic Gospels were preserved meant nothing less than the saving of Christianity.

We take it, therefore, that into the living Christ of his gospel Paul has carried at least the central features of the historical figure. How does he conceive the Person of this Christ? What place and rank does he assign Him, and how does he relate Him to God and to man? Such are the questions that must now engage our attention.

The Apostle was not under the necessity of building a doctrine of Christ's person from the foundation. Already in Jesus' lifetime His disciples, under the impression produced by His commanding personality, had hailed Him as the Messiah of Jewish expectation (Mark 8[27]). Shattered for a moment by the tragedy of the Cross, this belief of theirs in His messianic dignity revived with redoubled force when the resurrection appearances confirmed His own assurance given in the last days of His life, that death would not be the end, that He would speedily return to accomplish His work of salvation.

For the early Christian community what Jesus' Messiahship meant was first and foremost an office. Jesus was exalted by God to be His vicegerent in the final act of the world-drama. The heavens had received Him until the times of the restoration of all things, but when that fateful day should dawn, He would return with His angels to judge the world and bring in the Kingdom. Meanwhile repentance and remission of sins were preached in His name. To such as acknowledged Him as the Messiah, ordered their lives by His teaching and waited for His coming, there was the assurance of salvation in the day of wrath (Acts 3[18-26]).

The messianic idea did not lend itself to speculative elaboration. Only one question of a speculative character seems to have emerged, the relation of Jesus' earthly life to His messianic office. From what hour was His dignity to be dated? According to the earliest view it was from the hour of the resurrection. During his earthly ministry He had been no more than " a man approved of God by mighty works and wonders and signs," or the great prophet foretold by Moses, or again the Servant described by Isaiah (Acts 2^{22} $3^{20ff.}$ 4^{27}). Although the significance of the Resurrection as marking His installation in office was never diminished, the later view pushed back His designation as Messiah to His baptism, and still further back to His conception. It has been customary to regard the idea of Christ's pre-existence as messianic in its origin. Appeal is made to the fact that in the apocalyptic Similitudes of Enoch the Messiah is spoken of as created before the sun and the constellations (En. 48^2). But it is improbable that the Christian idea was derived from this source. In the Synoptists and the Book of Acts, where the messianic theology has been best preserved, it is nowhere found; and its appearance in Paul, as we shall presently see, is in connection with other than messianic conceptions.

For Paul also Jesus is the messianic Judge and Saviour of the last day, whose coming may at any moment be expected. And the Apostle moves in this circle of ideas when he describes Him as of the seed of David according to the flesh, and regards the Resurrection as signifying His installation in office (Rom. $1^{3, 4}$). But such a conception of Christ hardly carries us beyond the confines of his religion and thought. Christ is far more to his faith than the Saviour for whose appearance from heaven he eagerly waits, and his conception of Him is incapable of being expressed in terms of messianic theology. Since it is the Apostle's religious attitude to Christ that is the fundamental thing, his christology having that for its basis, it is this attitude that first calls for consideration.

The primitive waiting for the Christ reserved in heaven has not disappeared, but to this there is added something new and distinctive. The Apostle looks to Christ as to one who is even now on the throne, and to whom all power in heaven and on earth has been entrusted. Equally with God He is the source of grace and peace (Rom. $1^{5.\ 7}$, 1 Cor. 1^3, 2 Cor. 1^2, Gal. 1^3). He disciplines and punishes the believer, averts trouble, directs the heart, establishes the heart in holiness, guards from the evil one, confirms in the way of God unto the end (1 Cor. 13^{29}, 2 Cor. 12^8, 2 Thess. 3^5, 1 Thess. 3^{12}, 1 Cor. 1^8). He is able to make His weak servant stand (Rom. 14^4). The providences of life are under His control: "I will come unto you shortly, if the Lord will" (1 Cor. 4^{19} 16^7, 1 Thess. 3^{11}). He dwells in the soul of the believer as a personal power, the source of every higher motion: "Christ in you the hope of glory" (Col. 1^{27} 3^4). Very striking is the way in which the Apostle alternates between God and Christ, attributing the same functions and attributes now to the one and again to the other. Sometimes he derives his apostolic office from the first, and sometimes from the second (Gal. 1^{16}, 2 Cor. 5^{18}, 2 Cor. 5^{12} 10^8 13^{10}). Now he speaks of God revealing His Son in him and again of Christ revealing Himself (Gal. 1^{16}, Phil. 3^{12}). The Holy Spirit is in one passage the Spirit of God and in another the Spirit of Christ (1 Cor. 2^{10}, 2 Cor. 3^8, Gal. 4^6, 2 Cor. 3^{17}). In view of all this it is not surprising that Paul should frequently transfer to Christ words spoken in the Old Testament of God: "Let him that glories glory in the Lord," "The same Lord is Lord of all and rich unto all that call upon Him" (1 Cor. 1^{31} 2^{16} 10^{22}, 2 Cor. 3^{16} 8^{21}, Rom. $10^{11.\ 12}$, Phil. 2^{10}).

One can say that in the Pauline Epistles Christ

exercises every function of Deity. He is still the Judge and Saviour of the last day, for whose coming eager hearts wait, but this messianic conception is no longer sufficient to express His significance. He has become a present God, able to help in every time of need. And Paul claims for Him and renders to Him the religious homage proper to God. He prays that the Lord Jesus Christ shall be glorified in believers, and declares that to Him every knee shall bow of things in heaven and things on earth and things under the earth, and every tongue confess that He is Lord (Rom. 10^{12}, Phil. 2^{10}). The homage that Jahveh claims for Himself in the Old Testament Paul claims for Christ (Isa. 45^{23}). That in such an atmosphere prayers should be addressed to Christ will hardly seem surprising. Believers are described as those who call upon the name of the Lord Jesus; and that such calling is indistinguishable from prayer one can see from the Apostle's words of encouragement, borrowed, be it noted, from an Old Testament reference to Jahveh: " The same Lord is Lord of all and is rich unto all that call upon Him, for whosoever shall call upon the name of the Lord shall be saved " (1 Cor. 1^2, Rom. $10^{12ff.}$). Paul tells us of a prayer he himself addressed to Christ. In the matter of the thorn in the flesh, he besought the Lord thrice that it should depart from him.

While these indications of prayer to Christ must be regarded as unambiguous, it has to be added that in general the assumption is that it is God who is the object of prayer. Referring to his Jewish countrymen the Apostle writes: " My heart's desire and my supplication to God is for them that they may be saved " (Rom. 10^1, cf. Rom. 1^9 15^{30}, 1 Cor. 11^{13}, 2 Cor. 13^7, Col. 1^3). And while he exhorts believers to do everything with an invocation of the name of the Lord Jesus, he bids them sing with grace in their hearts to God, and give thanks to God the

Father through Christ (Col. 3[16f.]). Christ is introduced only as presenting the prayer to God. In the New Testament the standing practice is not prayer to Christ, but prayer to God in Christ's name. The Fourth Gospel, evidently with a purpose, strongly emphasises this character of Christian prayer. Is the purpose to combat the perhaps growing practice of prayer to Christ? Not till a comparatively late period did this practice receive the sanction of the Church. Origen assumes that it is common but opposes it, insisting on prayer in the name.[1] The solution of the apparent discrepancy in Paul may perhaps be found, as Bousset[2] suggests, in the fact that while from the first there were brief ejaculatory prayers to Christ, cries of the full heart, the stated public prayers remained directed to God.

Notwithstanding this reservation, it is abundantly clear that in the Epistles of Paul we are face to face with a fully developed Christ worship. Christ has gathered to Himself the functions of Deity and become an object of religious homage. He is the centre of a cultus. Baptism is administered with an invocation of His name, and the baptized person enters into a mystic fellowship with Him in His death and resurrection (Rom. 6[3]). The Supper also becomes the medium of a like fellowship. How great is the distance between such a Christ-cult and the primitive waiting for the Messiah reserved in heaven, one does not need to say.

This change in the religious attitude to Christ is marked by a striking change in the title by which He is designated. The title Messiah retires into the background. For Paul it scarcely any more indicates Jesus' dignity, but has become a proper name. And the title Son of Man completely disappears. What is the new

---

[1] Bousset, *Kyrios Christos*, pp. 285 ff.
[2] *Ibid.* p. 102.

title? It is ὁ κύριος, the Lord. By this name Jesus is confessed and invoked in baptism : " If thou shalt confess with thy mouth Jesus as Lord, and shalt believe in thy heart that God raised Him from the dead, thou shalt be saved " (Rom. 10⁹). And it is the same name He bears in the salutation and benediction that opens and closes every Epistle.

Doubtless the title Kyrios or Lord carries with it a pronounced moral reference. It implies moral subjection to Christ and dependence on Him. Paul looks to Christ as the slave to his master. But this is far from exhausting its meaning. It marks out Jesus as an object of worship. It is as Kyrios that Paul prays to Him (2 Cor. 12⁸). This, the peculiar significance of the title, is clearly brought out in the great Philippian passage. The name which Jesus receives as the reward of His self-abasement and submission to death is the name Kyrios. " Wherefore also God highly exalted Him and gave unto Him the name which is above every name; that in the name of Jesus every knee should bow, of things in heaven and things on earth and things under the earth, and that every tongue should confess that Jesus Christ is Kyrios, to the glory of God the Father." God bestows upon Him the thrice-sacred name (κύριος in the Septuagint = Jahveh) which in the Old Testament He had reserved for Himself.

How is the rise of Christ-worship, and the parallel transition from the title Messiah to that of Lord, to be explained? We are here confronted with one of the most momentous questions in the history of Christianity. Nowhere in the Synoptic Gospels does Jesus ask of His disciples divine honour, and nowhere does He receive it. Nor is it possible to account for Christ-worship as a development of the messianic idea. Of a worship of the Messiah Jewish Apocalyptic knows nothing. If the

Messiah of Apocalyptic is God's chosen and filled with the Spirit, if he is sinless and mirrors God's glory, he still belongs to no higher circle than that of the angels. And to Judaism angel-worship is foreign. As little can the new cult be explained as the product of a growing insight into the moral glory of the historical Jesus, or of reflection on the experience made of His redeeming power. The cult attached itself, not to the historical Jesus, but to the risen and exalted Christ. One can say with all assurance that on the soil of a strict monotheism it did not and could not arise.

There is but one possible explanation, and it is to be found in the fact that, at an early period in its history, Christianity was carried from the soil of Judaism to that of Hellenism. In Antioch, Tarsus, Damascus and other Hellenistic centres, it came under the influence of an environment very different from that in which it had been born, the environment of Hellenistic mystery-religion. The various mystery-cults—that of Serapis, of Adonis, of Attis —had each its sacraments, and its patron divinity to whom prayers were addressed and from whom all help was expected. " I thank the Lord (κύριος) Serapis that, when I was in peril in the sea, he saved me immediately," " I make supplication for thee daily to the Lord Serapis," we read in papyri of the second century A.D.[1] Many of Paul's converts were recruited from the ranks of the cults. In such an atmosphere the primitive messianic conception could hardly maintain itself unmodified. It was in large measure foreign to the Gentile mind, and had none of the sacred associations it possessed for a Jew. How natural, how inevitable, that Christ should be conceived after the manner of the divinities the Gentile converts had been accustomed to adore! The Messiah reserved in heaven until the last days becomes the present God,

---

[1] Deissmann, *Light from the Ancient East*, pp. 169, 177.

who has all power in heaven and on earth, to whom worship is rendered and from whom all good is expected. Christ could occupy no lower rank in the faith of Gentile believers than the gods from whom they had turned. He was the true Lord and Saviour, and they but spurious pretenders.

This account of the origin of Christ-worship receives strong support when we fairly face the question how the name Kyrios came to be applied to Christ.

Various attempts at an explanation have been made. It has been suggested that the name came into use as the equivalent of the Aramaic *mar*, and at first meant nothing more than Rabbi. But apart from the fact that the form mar is not found, but only mari, maran (my lord, our lord), there is no bridge between the meaning Rabbi and the cultic meaning already present in the early formula, maranatha—Come, Lord![1] Again the title has been explained as a messianic name derived from one or two Old Testament passages, which could be regarded (mistakenly) as speaking of a second Lord side by side with the Lord Jahveh. So in Ps. 110, "The Lord said unto my lord." (Also Mal. 3[1]).[1] It is, however, hardly likely that a title carrying such a weight of meaning should have had its origin in a misinterpreted passage of Scripture. Before it was given to Jesus He must already in the faith of the Church have become the object of religious homage. If Jesus' interpretation of the 110th Psalm given in Mark 12[36] is historical and not a fragment of Church theology, it can mean nothing more than that a prince of the house of David is inadequate as a description of the Messiah. Still another line is to connect the title with the translation κύριος given in the Septuagint to the divine name Jahveh. And that in Paul Old Testament references to Jahveh are carried over to Christ has been

[1] Bousset, *Kyrios Christos*, p. 98.

already shown. But surely it is self-evident that this practice so far from explaining the origin of the title presupposes its currency. Only after Christ was worshipped and known as Kyrios or Lord, was it possible thus to identify Him with the Kyrios of the Old Testament. Finally, the suggestion has been made by Ramsay, Deissmann and others that in the Kyrios-title we have a silent protest against the worship of Cæsar, who was currently designated as *dominus et deus noster.* There is, however, little to show that in Paul's day Christ was set over-against the Cæsars; and it is highly improbable that His dignity would be defined in relation to theirs.

The question how the title Kyrios came to be applied to Christ can be answered only in one way. It was the title borne by the cult gods, the title that marked them out as objects of worship. Already we have quoted texts in which it is given to Serapis. It entered Christianity with the new attitude towards Christ, and is an index of the revolution. Paul himself sets the Lord Christ over-against the lords of pagan religion. "For though there be that are called gods, whether in heaven or on earth; as there are gods many and lords many; yet to us there is one God, the Father, of whom are all things and we unto Him; and one Lord, Jesus Christ, through whom are all things and we through Him" (1 Cor. 8[5f.]).

Was the introduction of Christ-worship and of the Kyrios-title the work of Paul? The supposition must at once be dismissed. Everywhere the Apostle assumes that his conception of Christ is that of the Church in general. While we read of a conflict of opinion regarding the Law, we read of none regarding the Person of Christ and the homage to be rendered to Him. In this matter James, Peter and Barnabas—all Jewish Christians—seem to have been at one with the Apostle. And Paul gives no hint of having once cherished a different view. When he speaks

4

of his conversion as a revealing of God's Son in him, he implies that the Christ of his vision was the Kyrios-Christ. From the beginning Paul stood on the ground of Hellenistic or Gentile Christianity. We may take it that a movement so widespread was not due to any one individual, but was the result of generally operative causes.

Against the view as to the origin of Christ-worship here advocated, two objections of a serious character can be urged. If there was a messianic Christianity anterior to Hellenistic, how could it have succumbed so quickly and left behind it so few traces of its existence? With respect to its rapid eclipse, this can be explained by the fact that the Jewish element in the Church was in the course of a very few years dwarfed by the Gentile, and that the Jewish element itself was largely made up of Jews of the Dispersion, open to Hellenistic ideas. Palestinian Jews like James, Peter and John were presumably drawn into the general movement. It is probable, however, that in the sect of the Ebionites we have a survival of the messianic Christianity of the early days. From Eusebius we learn that this sect rejected Christ's pre-existence and divinity—in other words, the Kyrios and Logos ideas, as also the Virgin-birth, dating His Messiahship from His resurrection or His baptism. And other relics of a messianic Christianity are not altogether wanting. The Book of Acts witnesses to a conception of Christ as the παῖς θεοῦ, the "Servant" of the Second Isaiah, and as reserved in heaven till the last day. That the relics are so few is sufficiently explained by the fact that heretical documents were allowed to perish, and that the older sources were worked over from the standpoint of the Church's later faith.

The second objection that can be urged against the existence of a primitive Christianity that knew nothing of Christ-worship is that the title Kyrios may with some plausibility be carried back to the very earliest days. It appears in Peter's speech at Pentecost as reported in Acts, and in all four Gospels. The Aramaic formula maranatha (Come, Lord!) has a primitive sound, and may seem to bear marks of a Jewish-Christian origin. What time is left, it may be asked, for a development such as we have assumed?

These objections must be met, and it is, I believe, possible to meet them. That the title should have found its way into the Gospels is not to be wondered at, since these were written at a time when it was in general use. And this highly significant fact has to be noted, that it is in the earliest strata of the evangelical narrative that its appearance is rarest, and that it becomes more frequent as we descend. In Mark, apart from the ungenuine conclusion, it is found only once, in the words "the Lord hath need of him." Q, the Logia-source common to Matthew and Luke, if we exclude the doubtful passage Matt. 8⁸— Luke 7⁶, does not contain it at all. In Luke it occurs some dozen times.[1] Against such evidence of a growing use of the title the Book of Acts cannot be allowed to weigh. The primitive sources on which it undoubtedly founds have been modified by the influence of later ideas. There remains the formula maranatha. Unquestionably this formula, which is known to Paul, carries us far back, and is most naturally explained as a product of Jewish Christianity. But its Gentile origin in a bilingual community like that of Antioch is by no means impossible; and in any case our inability to trace it to a Gentile source cannot be set against the body of evidence we have adduced that it was through the influence of Hellenistic religion that the title Kyrios was adopted by the Christian Church as the designation of its Head.

To many, doubtless, these conclusions will seem to menace the very foundations of our Christian faith. But

[1] Bousset, *Kyrios Christos*, pp. 94 ff.

a little reflection will show that they affect rather the traditional categories of our thought about Christ than our fundamental attitude to Him. It is true that we cannot to-day, in Hellenistic fashion, think of Christ as a second God and duplicate the object of our worship. We cannot to-day worship God and Christ; but we can worship the God who in Christ has come to us in the might of His holiness and His love. We cannot divide our prayers between God and Christ, but we can pray to the God who in Christ has revealed Himself to us. We cannot think of God as having surrendered for a period the government of the world into the hands of a regent, but we can believe that the power that is over us and over all things is the same power that appeals to us in Jesus' life and Cross. The categories of our religious thought are subject to constant change. There is no such thing as a revealed theology. And that the Pauline categories are for the most part derived from a source outside the Old Testament and Judaism is a fact that need not disquiet us. The conception of Christ as Lord is not less but much more adequate as an interpretation of the historical reality than the primitive conception of Him as the Messiah of Apocalyptic. The advance from Jewish to Hellenistic Christianity justifies itself at the bar of history.

CHAPTER III.

DOCTRINE OF CHRIST'S PERSON: THE SPECULATIVE ELABORATION.

THE conception of Christ as Kyrios or Lord with all of religious homage it implies was no product of theological reflection; it arose spontaneously as a result of the trans-ference of the Gospel from its native Jewish into a Hellenistic atmosphere. Reflection came in time; it arrived with Paul, but it had that development as its presupposition and starting-point.

The position which Christ had assumed in Christian faith rendered some work of reflection imperative and inevitable. How was the worship rendered Him to be reconciled with belief in one God? In what relation did He stand to God? What was His precise rank in the scale of being? Such questions Paul nowhere explicitly formulates; but they were in his mind, for he attempts to give them some kind of answer.

One obvious way of safeguarding monotheism was to insist on Christ's subordination to the Father, and this Paul consistently does. Nowhere does he call Him God. Not till a later day did the Church cast aside this reserve.[1] In bringing together God and Christ, he explicitly affirms that there is but one God, and plainly assumes that the Lord Christ stands on a lower level. "For though there be that

---

[1] John 20²⁸, Tit. 2¹⁶, 2 Pet. 1¹. Ignatius speaks quite frankly of "our God, Jesus Christ."

are called gods, whether in heaven or on earth; as there
are gods many and lords many; yet to us there is one
God, the Father, of whom are all things and we unto
Him; and one Lord, Jesus Christ, through whom are all
things and we through Him" (1 Cor. 8⁵ᶠ·). God is the
origin and goal of creation, the author of salvation; and
Christ the instrument through whom He accomplishes His
will (2 Cor. 5¹⁸). As the head of every man is Christ, so
the head of Christ is God; and Christ belongs to God as
the believer belongs to Christ (1 Cor. 11³ 3²³). In the
classical Philippian passage, where the Apostle describes
Christ as receiving the homage of every created being, he
ends with the declaration that all this is to the glory of
God the Father. The view that the opening verse of that
passage asserts an equality with God is absolutely untenable. Christ's self-renunciation consisted in the fact that
He did not, like Adam or Satan or some other mythical
rival of the Almighty, aspire to a higher honour than He
already possessed, but on the contrary emptied Himself,
accepting the humble lot of a child of man and submitting
to a shameful death. Most uncompromising in its assertion
of subordination is the passage in which Christ's authority
as Lord is described as being no more than temporary, to
be retained only until His work of redemption and conquest has been carried to completion. "When all things
have been subjected to Him, then shall the Son also be
subjected to Him that did subject all things unto Him,
that God may be all in all" (1 Cor. 15³⁸). These assertions
of subordination are unambiguous and deliberate, and one
and all they relate not to Christ as the subject of a
voluntary humiliation, but to Christ in His dignity as
Lord.

The idea of subordination does not, however, carry us
far. Christ's essential nature remains undetermined. Are
we to think of Him as a man exalted to divine power,

or as an angelic being, or, again, as in some real sense divine?

Founding on the Second Adam passage and on one or two others in which Christ is designated as man, scholars like Baur, Beyschlag, Pfleiderer, Schmiedel, Holtzmann and J. Weiss have concluded that in the last resort Paul thinks of Him as human (1 Cor. 15⁴⁵, Rom. 5¹⁵, 1 Cor. 15²¹). Is this view tenable?

In the passage in question, Adam as the founder and head of the old humanity is set over-against Christ as the founder and head of the new. The first was a mere living soul (ψυχὴ ζῶσα, ψυχικός), a creature of the flesh with nothing spiritual in his constitution. The second is not only a spirit, but a life-giving or quickening spirit. Again, while the first belonged to earth, to the natural order, the second has a heavenly origin. In all this there is nothing but contrast. But, it may be argued, the two progenitors have at least this in common, that they are both men. The inference is unjustifiable. The conception of a heavenly archetypal man was a traditional one. Philo[1] speaks of an ideal, generic man, incorporeal and imperishable, who was created before the progenitor of empirical humanity; and the myth of an *Urmensch* was current in paganism.[2] From what source the Apostle derived the conception may be doubtful, but the fact that he works with it as something given forbids us to take it as the key to his christology. And there are still stronger reasons against such a course. The conception of Christ as human, even with the qualification that He is the man from heaven and a life-giving spirit, would have supplied no basis for the Christ-cult, would in fact have condemned it. And to this we have to add the Apostle's express declaration as to Christ's affinities. In the great Philippian passage the pre-

---

[1] *Leg. allegor.* i. 131.
[2] Bousset, *Kyrios Christos*, p. 159.

existent Christ is described as being " in the form of God " (ἐν μορφῇ θεοῦ). He is classed not with humanity, but with Deity. That He stooped to a human lot involved a process of self-emptying and a descent to a mode of existence foreign to His real nature.

The same considerations are decisive against the view that Paul thinks of Christ as an angelic being. And this other may be added, that when he brings Christ into connection with the angels it is to set Him over-against them as their creator, lord and redeemer (Col. 1^{16} 2^{10}, Phil. 2^{10}). Unquestionably for Paul, Christ belongs to the side of reality we call divine. And His pre-existence would seem to him an inseparable concomitant of His divinity. His divinity is the primary fact to which every further determination or limitation attaches itself.

The conception of Christ as divine and yet as subordinate to God forms the main content of the title, Son of God (Rom. 1^{3} 4^{9}, Gal. 2^{20}). In the Old Testament this title is applied sometimes to Israel and sometimes to the theocratic or messianic king. As thus used it carries no suggestion of a metaphysical relation to God, but connotes merely a position of dignity, and a relation, on the one side of love and favour, and on the other of trust and obedience. In the later Jewish literature it appears more than once as a title of the Messiah (En. 105^{2}, 4 Esd. 7^{28} 13^{27}); but whether it was ever current in the Church with a purely messianic sense must be regarded as doubtful. Certainly as used by Paul the messianic meaning is lost in a higher. That Christ is the Son of God means that He stands to God in an aboriginal and metaphysical relation. As God's first-born, He is anterior to and separate from all created beings (Col. 1^{15}). The assertion that He was " marked out as Son of God with power by the resurrection of the dead " is not to be taken as meaning that He was then for the first time elevated to that dignity (Rom. 1^{4}). He was Son

during His earthly life, though He bore the form of a
servant (Rom. 5^{10} 8^{32}). And He was Son in His pre-
existent state: "God sent His own Son in the likeness of
sinful flesh" (Rom. 8^{3}). Of an adoptionist christology we
find no trace.

The title Son of God must therefore be regarded as a
product of reflection and as serving mainly a theological
interest. Indicating as it did divinity and also subordination to God, it supplied some sort of solution to the problem
which the elevation of Christ to the throne of Deity raised
for the Apostle's monotheistic faith. That it could hardly,
without further development of its meaning, be regarded
as a philosophical solution will at once be evident. Not
till the idea of an eternal Son of God was grounded in
some general conception of God and the world could such
a claim be made for it. Does the Apostle make any
attempt to develop it in this direction?

To his hand there lay the conception of the Spirit.
The Spirit is for Paul a divine magnitude, the creative
source of the new life in man. Already in popular thought
it had been brought into close connection with Christ:
through the Spirit Christ had been equipped for His
messianic task. How natural if the Apostle should regard
Christ's divinity as constituted by the fact that the Spirit
formed the essential element in His being. Approaches
to such a construction we do as a matter of fact find. The
Spirit of God is for Paul also the Spirit of Christ, and in
at least one passage, as we have seen, Christ and the Spirit
are expressly identified. Further, he can speak of deliverance from the law of sin and death as effected through the
agency of the Spirit of life in Christ Jesus (Rom. 8^{2}), and
describe Christ as spiritual ($\pi\nu\epsilon\nu\mu\alpha\tau\iota\kappa\acute{o}\varsigma$) and a life-giving
spirit (1 Cor. 15$^{45ff.}$). It was in virtue of His connection
with the Spirit that Christ was marked out by the resurrection as the Son of God with power (Rom. 1^{4}). But if these

passages may be regarded as showing an approach to such
a theory as we have indicated, certainly they do not
amount to it.   Nowhere does the Apostle contemplate a
view of Christ's divinity that would make it dependent on
His possession of the Spirit or on His identification with
it.   All that the passages quoted really prove, is that Paul
in describing Christ's renewing activity was almost inevitably led to do so in terms of the Spirit.

A speculative construction of Christ's divine Sonship,
based on the conception of the Spirit, Paul does not
possess.   This, however, does not end the matter.   Such
a construction, though on another basis, meets us in at
least two passages, the first from one of his earlier, the
second from one of his later, Epistles.   Let us bring the
passages together.   Contrasting the objects of Christian
with those of pagan worship, the Apostle writes : " For
though there be that are called gods, whether in heaven or
on earth ; as there are gods many and lords many ; yet for
us there is one God, the Father, of whom are all things
and we unto Him (ἐξ οὗ τὰ πάντα καὶ ἡμεῖς εἰς αὐτόν), and
one Lord, even Jesus Christ, through whom are all things
and we through Him (δι' οὗ τὰ πάντα καὶ ἡμεῖς δι' αὐτοῦ) "
(1 Cor. 8⁶).   " In Christ we have our redemption, the
forgiveness of our sins : who is the image of the invisible
God, born first before all creation : for by Him (ἐν αὐτῷ)
were all things created, in the heavens and upon the earth,
things visible and things invisible, whether thrones or
dominions or principalities or powers ; all things have
been created by Him and for Him (δι' αὐτοῦ καὶ εἰς
αὐτόν) ; and He is before all things and by Him all things
hold together (καὶ τὰ πάντα ἐν αὐτῷ συνέστηκεν) "
(Col. 1¹⁴⁻¹⁷).

Everywhere in Paul Christ appears as the mediator of
salvation, but in these two passages His mediatorial office
is widened out into a universal and cosmic fact.   God,

Christ and the world are brought together, and God and Christ are distinguished with respect to the relation in which they severally stand to the world. God is the ultimate source of things and also their final goal. Christ, on the other hand, is the agent who calls them into existence. To His agency the world, whether of angelic powers or of men or of material objects, owes its being. These cosmological determinations are common to both passages. But in the second several new ones are added. Not only is Christ the mediator of creation, He is also the power that holds it together, sustains its order, and for whose sake it exists. The last determination may seem to contradict the statement in the Corinthian passage and elsewhere (*e.g.* Phil. 2¹¹) that it is God who is creation's goal; but doubtless the Apostle would hold it with some unexpressed limitation. New also is the determination that Christ is the first-born before all creation and the image of the invisible God.

To the same circle of ideas belongs what Paul, in Col. 1¹⁹ 2⁹, says of Christ as the mediator of the divine Pleroma or Fulness. "For it was in Him that the divine Fulness (πλήρωμα) willed to settle without limit, and by Him it willed to reconcile in His own person all on earth and in heaven alike, in a peace made by the blood of the cross." "It is in Christ that the entire Fulness of deity has settled bodily, and it is in Him that ye reach your full life, and He is the head of every angelic Ruler and Power." [1]

It is of the utmost importance that we make clear to ourselves the world-view in which these determinations of Christ's place and office in the universe have their setting. What we have is a thoroughgoing dualism. God is withdrawn from all direct contact with the world. He did not create it directly, but only through an intermediary. And

[1] Moffatt's translation.

it is the intermediary who orders and sustains it. Still further, God being transcendent is inaccessible to human thought. Man cannot know Him immediately or come into immediate contact with Him. He can know Him only through His image, the intermediate being. And he is dependent on the same source for participation in the life-potencies of the divine Pleroma.

We are now in possession of what may be called a philosophical answer to the question as to Christ's essential relation to God and His rank in the scale of being. He is God's intermediary in creation and redemption. As such He stands with God over-against the world, though subordinate to Him, and partakes of His nature. He is God's image, and in knowing and receiving Him men know and receive God.

Whence did Paul derive this conception of a being who mediates between the created world and the invisible, transcendent God? Not from the Old Testament and not from Jesus. For both alike God is the Creator and Pre-server, in whose hand is the life of every living thing. There is, however, one saying attributed to Jesus, which, if it were genuine, could be quoted on the other side. It is the well-known saying on which so much christological speculation has been built: " All things have been delivered unto Me of My Father: and no one knoweth the Son save the Father ; neither doth any know the Father save the Son, and he to whomsoever the Son willeth to reveal Him " (Matt. 11^{27} = Luke 10^{22}). Here undoubtedly we have the idea of the transcendent God, hid from human knowledge, whom only the Son knows and can reveal. Externally the saying is well authenticated, having been taken from the very early logion-source common to Matthew and Luke. But both its language and its content speak decisively against it. "The Son" and "the Father" are character-istically Johannine terms. And nowhere else in the

Synoptic Gospels does Jesus speak of God's fatherhood as hidden from human knowledge and disclosed for the first time by Himself. That great fact is for Him no secret supernaturally revealed; it is written on the face of creation and on the heart of man. " If God so clothe the grass of the field, which to-day is, and to-morrow is cast into the oven, shall He not much more clothe you, O ye of little faith." " If ye, being evil, know how to give good gifts unto your children, how much more shall your Father which is in heaven give good things to them that ask Him."

It has been argued that in universalising Christ's mediatorial office Paul is but drawing a logical conclusion from his experience of redemption through Christ. Since the world is one, the mediator of redemption must also be the mediator of creation. But what we have to explain is not simply the extension of an idea from one field to another, but a developed philosophy of an exceedingly characteristic type. Such a philosophy no experience of Christ's redemptive power can by itself account for. We are driven therefore to look for its source outside Paul's experience and outside his heritage of Hebrew and Jewish ideas. And such a source is known to us.

Substantially the same world-view as that to which Paul's conception of a mediating being belongs meets us in the Hellenistic thought of the time. Oriental religion had wedded itself to Greek, more particularly to stoical, speculation, and the product of the union was a gnosis half mythological, half philosophical, in character, and that ministered to an interest that was much less speculative than religious. This gnosis was rooted in pessimism and dualism. The world of sense was regarded as inherently evil, the creation not of the highest, but of a subordinate god, who in creating it himself became entangled in the meshes of the material. Dualism has as its correlate a

transcendent conception of God; and Norden [1] has shown
that the idea that the highest God lies beyond the reach
of human thought, that He is an unknown God, but wills
to be known by men and reveals Himself to them in a
supernatural way, was widely current.

Already in Philo we have a gnosis of the type described.
There is the same dualistic opposition between God and
the world. To bridge the gulf Philo introduces the great
conception of the Logos, which plays at once a cosmogonic
and soteriological part. The Logos is the agent of God in
creation and the power by which the world is held together
and preserved from destruction. In him the world in idea
is contained. God and the Logos are related to the world,
the one as its originative and final, the other as its instrumental cause. "He by whom a thing originates," Philo
writes, "is the cause, that by means of which ($\delta\iota'$ $o\tilde{v}$) it was
made is the instrument, and why? is the object. Now of
this world the materials are the four elements, the instrument
the Logos of God, and the object of the building you will
find to be the display of the goodness of God" (*de Cherub.*
35). Further, the Logos is the divine agent in revelation and redemption. The Old Testament theophanies are
explained as his manifestations. He is described as the
image of God, the intercessor, the high priest of the universe
and as such sinless. God is his father and he is the object
of God's love, His first-born son. He is constantly called
the Divine Logos ($\acute{o}$ $\theta\epsilon\hat{\iota}os$ $\lambda\acute{o}\gamma os$), and sometimes even the
second God.

The kinship of Paul's conception of the cosmic significance of Christ with these conceptions of Hellenistic gnosis
is too patent to be denied or explained away. When the
Apostle distinguishes between ultimate, efficient and final
causes—of whom, through whom, to whom—when he sets
forth Christ as the agent of God in creation and as

[1] *Agnostos Theos*, pp. 67 ff.

mediating to men the knowledge and the life-potencies of
the Being who lies beyond the world and beyond human
thought, he is on Hellenistic ground and operating with
the categories of Hellenistic thought. From the passages
themselves, indeed, one can see that he is developing his
conception of Christ in opposition to current beliefs in
mediating divinities. There were those in the Church who
sought to participate in the divine Pleroma through other
mediums than Christ. The only question open for discussion is whether Paul has in the background of his mind
the Logos speculation in some such form as we find it in
Philo. Considering the many points of contact with that
speculation, it is difficult to refuse an affirmative answer.
The Apostle, it is true, nowhere calls Christ the Logos, but to
the explicit declaration of the Fourth Gospel is only a step.
He would have the less scruple in attaching his thought to
the Logos-idea since that idea was already prefigured, not
only in Jewish writings like the Wisdom of Solomon, but
in the Old Testament itself. The passages that speak of
Wisdom as brought forth before the hills and present with
God as a master workman when He established the
heavens, that describe it as a clear effluence of the glory of
the All-ruler, a stainless mirror of the divine working and
an image of His goodness, and as renewing all and endowing friends of God and prophets with the Spirit, such
passages might well appear to him as prophecies of Christ
(Prov. 8^{21-31}, Sap. Sol. $7^{21.26}$ 8^1, Sir. 1^4 24^3).

That Paul borrows certain categories from Hellenistic
gnosis does not mean that he appropriates the whole world-
view to which they belong. In cosmological speculation
he has no interest, and he betrays no sense of a gulf
dividing God from the world. Though he refuses to man's
natural powers anything but the rudiments of a knowledge
of God, he cannot be said to regard God as a transcendent
Being. In the passages under consideration the Apostle's

interest and view are limited to two points. He will claim for Christ the place and functions of the spurious mediators of Hellenistic religion. It is Christ and not another who is the image of the invisible God, the first-born of all creation, the maker and sustainer of the universe; Christ and not another who mediates to men the Fulness of Deity and the knowledge that saves. And we may also take it that in fitting Christ into a cosmic scheme and distinguishing His relation to the world from that of the Father, he is feeling his way towards some conception that will exhibit Christ at once in His divine nature and functions, and in His subordination to the God who is supreme over all. The Logos-idea presents itself as a solution of the problem raised for a monotheistic thinker by the elevation of Jesus to a place of divine honour.

The doctrine of the Trinity as formulated in the Greek creeds has filled so large a place in Christian theology that it is inevitable we should ask how far Paul anticipates it or provides for it points of attachment.

Everywhere, as we have seen, God and Christ are set side by side as the two great objects of Christian faith and worship. "Grace be unto you and peace from God our Father and from the Lord Jesus Christ," is the opening salutation of almost every Epistle; and the Apostle gives as a summary of the Christian creed, that there is one God, the Father, of whom are all things, and one Lord, Jesus Christ, through whom are all things. In a few passages we find the Holy Spirit associated with God and Christ as a third divine actor. "Now there are diversities of gifts, but the same Spirit; and there are diversities of ministrations, but the same Lord; and there are diversities of workings, but the same God who worketh all things in all" (1 Cor. 12⁴⁻⁶). A similar conjunction is found in the benediction which closes the second Corinthian epistle : " The grace of our Lord Jesus Christ and the love of God and the communion of the Holy Ghost be with you all." We have thus a recognition of God, Christ and the Spirit as the three great divine actors in the world-drama. But how are they interrelated?

At the outset we have to reckon with the fact that the Apostle, in transferring to the exalted Christ the functions of the Spirit, in effect merges the latter in the former. Nowhere in his speculative thought does he contemplate more than a duality.

How Christ stands related to God we have just considered. Never is He placed on an equality with God, whether as pre-existent or as exalted. Can we speak of an eternal and immanent relation? The idea lies outside the Apostle's horizon, but there are elements in his thought that are hardly reconcilable with it. Christ is from beginning to end a fully personal being. We can detect no tendency to sublimate Him into a hypostasis in the divine substance. Still more decisive is the fact that the Apostle contemplates a time when Christ, His work completed, shall surrender His delegated power that God may be all in all (1 Cor. 15^{24}). Christ's office and dignity belong to the world-era that opens with creation and closes with the gathering of God's elect into the Kingdom.

One other christological question of capital importance has still to be considered. It is that of the Incarnation.

What was involved in Christ's passage from heaven to earth is most fully described in Phil. 2$^{5\text{ff.}}$: " Though He was divine by nature, He did not snatch at equality with God, but emptied Himself by taking the nature of a servant ; born in human guise and appearing in human form, He humbly stooped in His obedience even to die,

5

and to die upon the cross."[1] When we endeavour to determine the precise meaning of these words two questions at once present themselves.

The first relates to the exact force of the expression, " He emptied Himself." What was it Christ surrendered in becoming man ? Evidently it was the " form of God," native to Him ; He exchanged this for the " form of a servant." In modern kenotic theories Christ's self-empty-ing is interpreted as self-limitation with respect to such divine attributes as omnipotence and omniscience, a solution being thereby found for certain familiar problems presented by His earthly life. But such an idea is as foreign to Paul as are the problems it is supposed to solve. Probably he had nothing more definite in his mind than the idea of glory, the glory that is the garment and evidence of Deity. Christ was rich and for our sake became poor (2 Cor. 8[9]).

Much more fundamental in its bearing upon the Apostle's theology is the second question, what was involved in Christ's assumption of the form of a servant? Christ, we are told, was found in fashion as a man. To understand what this assertion means we must go outside the Philippian passage to other passages in which the Incarnation is treated in a more dogmatic way. The idea not only implied in the Apostle's whole doctrine of redemption but also clearly stated, is that Christ assumed our human flesh. God sent Him " in the likeness of sinful flesh " (Rom. 8[3]). This means much more than that He was a god walking the earth in a human body. One must remember what the flesh signifies for Paul. When we have described it as the vestment and the prison-house of the soul that inhabits it we have not yet touched the vital point. It is the element of the passing world and its institutions, the element of sin, the element of death.

[1] Moffatt's translation.

Christ's assumption of flesh involved His subjection to the Law, which, as we shall find later, is connected in the closest way with man's fleshly being (Gal. 4⁴). Further, it involved His subjection to the power of death. Most important fact of all, it brought Him into immediate contact with sin. Some, indeed, have taken the phrase " in the likeness of sinful flesh " as indicating an element of difference as well as an element of similarity ; and it is probably true that the Apostle shrinks from an unqualified identification of Christ's flesh with the sinful flesh of humanity. None the less this is what his doctrine of redemption presupposes and what he certainly means. If Christ is to execute a judgment of condemnation on sin in the flesh of His body, and if this judgment is to be effective for the race, His flesh must be one with that of the race ; it must be sinful flesh.

It will be evident that this account of the constitution of the incarnate Christ differs in important respects from the doctrine formulated later at Chalcedon. Paul does not think of an assumption of human nature or of a union of two natures in one person. All that Christ has in common with men is the body of flesh, and flesh does not for the Apostle constitute the essence of the human soul, but is only the seat and source of the sin that enslaves it. As regards His inner being Christ remained after the incarnation what He was before it, divine and sinless. The difference between the two conceptions—that of Paul and that of Chalcedon—rests ultimately in a difference in the conception of redemption. Behind the Chalcedon formula lies the idea that Christ received our human nature into union with His own divine nature and thereby divinised it. To the Apostle such an idea is entirely foreign. If Christ clothes Himself with our human flesh it is only that He may destroy the sin that has there its seat. The incarnation is not itself the redeeming fact ; it is but the pathway to the Cross.

CHAPTER IV.

REDEMPTION FROM THE DEMONS.

THE longing for redemption lies deep in the human heart.
That man's life is full of miseries and wrongs, that a wide
gulf separates him from his ideal, are facts too peremptory
and exigent to permit of a placid acceptance of things as
they are. Man sighs for deliverance from the evils that
oppress him, looks for a new heaven and a new earth; and,
taught by hard experience the limitations of human power,
he builds his faith not on his own feeble efforts, but on the
working of Almighty God.

In all the great religions this longing for and belief in
redemption have found some kind of expression. Zoroaster,
Buddha, the prophets of Israel, John the Baptist, Jesus
were one and all preachers of redemption. It was as a
religion of redemption that Christianity entered the world,
and it shared this character with the Oriental cults in
which it found its most formidable rivals.

In the Hellenistic age the longing for redemption was
widespread. It was intensified by a deeply pessimistic
conception of the existing order. In the eyes of apocalyptic writers the world was demon-ridden, given up to
wickedness and the prey of mortality. And the pagan
estimate was hardly less unfavourable. On paganism too
the belief in demonic beings weighed like a nightmare.
From the East had come astrological fatalism, and men
felt themselves to be in the hands of dark world-powers—

εἱμαρμένη, τύχη—with which it was hopeless to contend. To this there was added a profound sense of the tyranny of the material over the spiritual. The old Platonic myth which told of the failure of the soul to attain the vision of truth and its consequent fall from heaven to earth, of its imprisonment in a human body, and of its long and arduous endeavour in successive incarnations to free itself from the material and ascend to its true home, was widely current. Men sought deliverance from the tyranny of astral powers, from the flesh and its passions, from death; they sought elevation to the pure, blessed and immortal life of the gods. And the hunger and thirst for righteousness and the God of righteousness was not altogether absent, though it was rather in the background than in the foreground. When Paul carried his gospel of redemption to the Gentile world he found minds prepared to receive it, found also formidable rivals already on the field.

In preaching the Christ-redemption Paul presents it under three relatively distinct aspects. It appears in the first place as a victory won over the demons, a deliverance of men from their power. It signifies also a deliverance from the Law and its curse. Lastly, it signifies a deliverance from the power of sin seated in the flesh. These three presentations are only in part complementary. In part they cross, representing, as we shall find, different strands in the complex structure of the Apostle's thought.

We begin with the conception of redemption as a deliverance from subjection to the demons, not because that aspect of it is first in importance, but because it goes farthest back and forms the most obvious link of connection with the doctrine of the early Christian community.

For Jewish Apocalyptic redemption meant the great deliverance of the last days, when the Messiah, with His holy angels, would descend from heaven to destroy the enemies of God and bring in the Kingdom. And in the primitive

Christian community it was this redemption that was the object of faith and longing. It knew of no other. From the very beginning doubtless Jesus' death was regarded as a sacrifice for sin; but, as we shall find later, it was not until Paul took it up that the idea was developed into a scheme of redemption. The eyes of the first disciples were turned not backward, but forward to the grand consummation of the End. They waited for God's Son from heaven.

For Paul too this redemption of apocalyptic expectation is a mighty reality dominating his whole outlook. "Now is salvation nearer to us than when we first believed. The night is far spent and the day is at hand" (Rom. 13^{11}). In 1 Cor. $15^{24ff.}$ the Apostle gives a brief account of the struggle and conquest that must precede the resurrection of believers and their reception into glory. "Then cometh the end, when Christ shall deliver up the Kingdom to God even the Father: when He shall have abolished all other rulers, all other authorities and powers. For He must reign till He hath put all His enemies under His feet. The last enemy that shall be abolished is death." What is here described is not a figurative but a real battle. The foes that Christ will meet and vanquish are the angel-powers that dominate the existing age and hold the human race in bondage. Here, as in Jewish Apocalyptic, the messianic war with earthly kings and empires of which we read in the Old Testament, is transformed into a war with demonic principalities. To this final struggle belongs the figure of the man of sin whom the Lord shall slay with the breath of His mouth, and bring to nought by the manifestation of His coming (2 Thess. 2^8). To it also the Apostle refers when he declares that the saints will sit in judgment upon angels (1 Cor. 6^2).

So far Paul is on traditional ground. But it is something new when he introduces a triumph over the demons on the cross, prior to that triumph of the last days. This

he does in an extremely loosely constructed sentence in
the Epistle to the Colossians, where God is described as
having cancelled the indictment based on the ordinances of
the Law that was against us, nailing it to the cross, and as
having disarmed the principalities and powers, making an
open show of them and triumphing over them in the Cross
(Col. $2^{14f.}$). The principalities and powers referred to are
obviously those that presided over the Law and had a
malicious interest in enforcing its curse to man's undoing.
God triumphed over them, reduced them to impotence,
through the abrogation of the Law effected by Christ's
atoning death. In this passage there is no hint of a
personal struggle of Christ with these sinister figures. Nor
is there anything to justify the view taken by Bousset[1]
that the ransom which Christ paid was paid to them.
Such a method of buying men out of their power could
scarcely have been described as a disarming of them and
triumphing over them. But it is not the angels of the
Law only that Paul thinks of as having been reduced to
impotence by Christ's death on the cross. In 1 Cor. 2^8
the same thing is asserted of the angel-powers that rule
the existing age. These compassed the death of Christ in
ignorance of the fact that they were in reality preparing
their own discomfiture. No more here than in the previous
passage is there any suggestion of a personal combat with
the demons or of a ransom paid to them. The truth is,
that while the Apostle everywhere assumes that the death
of Christ had as one of its results a deliverance from the
angel-powers, he does not attempt to describe the how
(cf. also Gal. 4^{8-11}, Col. 1^{13}). In such a region of thought
theory could hardly move with secure steps. The great
thing of which he is indubitably certain is that the Lord
Christ is mightier than all the demons, that His Cross has
broken their power and brought their reign to an end, and

[1] *Kyrios Christos*, p. 161.

that believers need stand in no fear of them (Phil. 2¹⁰).
For yet a little while they will continue their baleful
activity, but in Christ's keeping believers are safe (2 Cor. 12⁹).
" For I am persuaded that neither death, nor life, nor angels,
nor principalities, nor things present, nor things to come,
nor powers, nor height, nor depth, nor any other creature,
shall be able to separate us from the love of God, which
is in Christ Jesus our Lord."

For us all this lies in the region of mythology. But in
the Apostle's day the dread of demonic powers constituted
a real bondage, and deliverance from that dread a real
redemption. And all about him Paul could see facts that
seemed to point to a retreat of the spirit hosts before the
advancing kingdom of Christ. In the rescue of men from
the toils of idolatry and vice and in the miracles of healing
and exorcism wrought in Christ's name, Christ was proving
Himself master of the demons.

In an isolated Colossian passage another fate is contemplated for the demonic powers than that of subjugation
and destruction. They are brought within the scope of
Christ's reconciling work. " For it was in Christ," we read,
" that the divine Fulness willed to settle without limit, and
by Him it willed to reconcile in His own person all on
earth and in heaven alike, in a peace made by the blood
of His cross " (Col. 1¹⁹ᶠ·, cf. Eph. 1¹⁰). It is natural to
connect the heavenly beings referred to with the thrones,
dominions, principalities and powers of verse 16. One
must remark that the motive behind this novel idea is not
the human sympathy with Satan expressed by our Scottish
poet. Paul will glorify Christ by attributing to His death
a cosmic significance; he will leave nothing standing that
may throw any shadow over the brightness of His triumph.
The passage is not without interest as showing with what
unfettered wing the Apostle can pursue his speculative
flights.

CHAPTER V.

REDEMPTION FROM THE LAW.

" WHEN the fulness of time came, God sent forth His Son, born of a woman, born under the Law, that He might redeem them that were under the Law, that we might receive the adoption of sons." " Christ redeemed us from the curse of the Law, having become a curse for us." " Him who knew no sin He made to be sin for us, that we might become the righteousness of God in Him." Of the three aspects under which Paul presents Christ's redemptive work that formulated in these verses is not only the most carefully elaborated, but incomparably the richest in significance. It is in connection with the doctrine of redemption from the Law that the majority of the Apostle's most characteristic ideas—grace, reconciliation, vicarious suffering, justification, liberty, sonship, a universal gospel—are developed. So far as his religion is concerned with the present rather than with the future, and moves in ethical rather than in mystical thoughts, its centre lies here.

That this doctrine in anything like the developed form in which we find it in Galatians and Romans was present to the Apostle from the outset of his ministry, is in the highest degree improbable. From the first doubtless he preached a free gospel, refusing to impose upon his Gentile converts the burden of the Levitical law. Even this tacit setting aside of the Law awoke resentment in the stricter circles of Jewish Christianity and in time led to organised opposition. Still the fact remains that for some fourteen years Paul was allowed to prosecute his Gentile mission in comparative peace. Is it credible that the Judaising party would have held its hand so long, if during all these years the Apostle had been proclaiming the uncompromising and highly provocative doctrine that Christ was the end of the Law, that the Law had never been given as an instrument of salvation, and that to subject oneself to it was to fall from grace and be severed from Christ? The thing is unthinkable. Such a doctrine could have been formulated only in the thick of the fight, and after every idea of compromise had been thrown to the winds. Nor is it necessary to assume that prior to that the Apostle must have had at least the outline of the argument in his mind as a justification to his own thought of his conduct in preaching a free gospel. Almost invariably in such matters practice precedes theory; and the Apostle's practice is sufficiently explained by the fact that there were liberal Christians such as Stephen before him, and by his own independent insight into the Gospel's spiritual and universal character. The scheme of redemption from the Law through the death of Christ was a product of the legal controversy, and only in the light of that controversy can it be rightly understood.

But before proceeding to discuss the genesis of this scheme, it may be well to consider what basis it had in the common Christian faith. That the Apostle in his argument would start from an idea accepted by the whole community may be taken as self-evident. His argument would otherwise have possessed no cogency for his readers. And doubtless he was convinced that he was doing nothing more than working out to its logical issues a fundamental and unquestioned truth (Gal. 2[15ff.]). What this common ground was is not difficult to determine. It was the idea that Christ died for our sins, according to the Scriptures.

That this idea belonged to the primitive tradition which he had received the Apostle himself expressly asserts (1 Cor. 15³).

The conception of an atoning virtue attaching to the martyr death of the righteous carries us far beyond the Christian community, and in order to understand the place it held in that community it is necessary to glance at its previous history. It emerges for the first time in the great Servant passage of the Second Isaiah, of which we may say that it represents the culminating point of Old Testament thought. Speaking of the unexampled sufferings of the Servant, the writer declares that they were not inflicted on him on account of his own sins, but on account of the sins of others, and that through his vicarious sin-bearing salvation would accrue to many. "Surely he hath borne our griefs and carried our sorrows : he was wounded for our transgressions, he was bruised for our iniquities, the chastisement of our peace was upon him, and with his stripes we are healed : all we like sheep have gone astray, and the Lord hath laid on him the iniquities of us all : he shall see of the travail of his soul and shall be satisfied : by his knowledge shall my righteous servant justify many, and he shall bear their iniquities" (Isa. 53). The idea running through these verses is unmistakable. God imposes upon the innocent Servant the sufferings deserved by the guilty many, and accepting as sufficient the penalty thus vicariously endured, restores the many to His favour, turns to them with forgiveness and healing.

Whence did the Prophet derive this idea? Not from the institution of sacrifice, though the verses may contain a sacrificial reference. He went back to the time-honoured conception, which we know had still vitality, of corporate responsibility. In one of its aspects this conception frequently meets us in the Old Testament. For the sin of Achan not merely Achan himself, but the whole congregation of Israel was held responsible. But while that story shows us the many suffering for the sins of the one, it does not show us the complementary idea, that the punishment of the one may be accepted as an equivalent for that of the many. It was this complementary idea that the Prophet seized and put to such noble use.

But another and far more vital question has to be considered. What was the motive that led the Prophet to grasp at the idea of vicarious punishment? What was the problem for which it offered itself as a solution? Usually it has been assumed that he was wrestling with the question, How can God remit penalty and yet be just? How is divine forgiveness possible? But nowhere in the Old Testament do we find the slightest indication that forgiveness or the remission of penalty ever presented itself in the light of a problem. Always God's sovereign right to forgive appears as a thing self-evident. Quite other is the problem with which the Second Isaiah stands confronted. It is that of Israel's bitter fate. Was Israel worse than her neighbours that she had been singled out by God for unexampled calamity, her cities laid waste, her people scattered among the heathen? The Prophet cannot believe it. But calm returns to his troubled spirit, nay a thrill of exultation runs through him, as the idea becomes clear to his mind, that what his people has suffered has been the penalty not of her own but of others' sin, and that in making her an offering for sin God is preparing the way for the world's salvation. The conception of vicarious sin-bearing, taken from the vanishing notion of corporate responsibility, became the means through which the Prophet's faith in the justice of God's dealing with men and in the ultimate victory of the good was able to assert itself against the staggering facts of experience. And surely the Prophet was substantially in the right. It was in large measure through her sufferings that Israel rose to

the height of her mission as the mediator of God's revelation
to mankind. What has fallen away is nothing more than
the time-garment of the great conception.

The Old Testament supplies us with no second instance
of this line of thought, but we meet with it again in the
post-canonical Fourth Book of the Maccabees. About to
die for his faith, Eleazar gives utterance to the following
prayer: "Thou, O God, knowest it, I could have saved
myself, but I die under the fire's torture for the sake of
Thy Law. Be gracious to Thy people : let the punishment
which we have endured for them content Thee. Let my
blood serve as a purification for them ($\kappa a\theta\acute{a}\rho\sigma\iota o\nu$), and as
an equivalent for their souls take my soul" ($6^{27f.}$, cf. $17^{21f.}$).
Here we have the same interpretation of undeserved suffering as vicarious punishment, and the same motive behind
the employment of the conception.

The genuineness of Jesus' saying about giving His life
as a ransom (Mark 10^{45}, Matt. 20^{28}) is often contested on
the ground of its absence from the parallel passage in
Luke $22^{24ff.}$ and its supposed affinities with Pauline doctrine.
But the former reason is hardly decisive, and the latter
has no force whatever, since neither in language nor in
thought is the saying really Pauline. Rather does it
attach itself, as the words "for many" show, to the Isaianic
passage. How natural that Jesus, with the staggering
tragedy of the Cross in front of Him—how staggering we
can see from His prayer in Gethsemane—should have
found support for His faith in the sublime conception of
the sin-bearing Servant! The conception was to Him
precisely what it had been to the Second Isaiah. And in
the primitive Christian community this was still the part
which the atonement idea played. The first disciples laid
hold of it as bringing the offence of the Cross under the
divine plan and filling it with a splendid meaning. This
was for them its significance, that it enabled them to think

of the Cross as ordained by God, and ordained as the means of the world's salvation. That it was the solution of the problem, How is forgiveness possible? how can God remit punishment consistently with His penal justice? never crossed their minds. Such a problem had no existence for them, as it had no existence for the Hebrew prophets, or for Jewish thought, or for Jesus. Whether it was present to Paul will be considered by and by.

If this account of the part which the atonement idea played in religious thought prior to Paul be correct, we can understand how that idea should never have been elaborated into a scheme of redemption. And that it never was so elaborated is a demonstrable fact. Nowhere do we find its logical presupposition, that in the absence of an equivalent God must exact the penalty even where the sinner repents, drawn out or contemplated. Neither by the Hebrew prophets nor by the later Jewish writers, nor by Jesus, nor by the early Christian community, so far as its scanty records permit us to judge, is God's sovereign right to forgive subjected to any limitation. When the early disciples preached forgiveness and salvation, it was in the name of the exalted Christ (Acts 5[30] 13[13], Matt. 28[18ff.]). Forgiveness and salvation, that is to say, were grounded not in Jesus' atoning death, but in the authority and power belonging to Him as Messiah and Lord.

We take it, therefore, that the common Christian foundation on which Paul built his scheme of redemption from the Law was not anything that could be called a theory of salvation. It was nothing more than this, "that Christ died for our sins, according to the Scriptures" (1 Cor. 15[3]).

The legal controversy was not of Paul's seeking, but was forced upon him. So long as no obstacle was put in

the way of his Gentile mission with its free gospel, he was
content to refrain from overt attacks on the Law. The
real aggressors were the Jewish-Christian zealots. It does
not appear that this party objected to the Gentile mission
in itself, or even that they wished to impose on Gentile
converts the full rigour of Pharisaic legalism. But clinging
as they did to the belief that the community of salvation
must be fundamentally Jewish, and that Gentile converts
could obtain a place in it only through incorporation with
the people of promise, they were adamant on the point
that such converts should observe at least the cardinal
ordinances of the Law, and in particular submit themselves
to the typical ordinance of circumcision. To the Apostle
it was clear that such a demand struck at the very root of
his gospel, and he met it with an unqualified refusal.
Speaking of the Jerusalem council, where the battle was
fought out, he declares, " But not even Titus, who was
with me, being a Greek, was compelled to be circumcised :
and that because of the false brethren privily brought in,
who came in privily to spy out our liberty which we have
in Christ Jesus, that they might bring us into bondage : to
whom we gave place in the way of subjection, no, not for
an hour : that the truth of the Gospel might continue with
you " (Gal. 2³ᶠᶠ·). More clearly than any of his contemporaries he understood how far-reaching were the principles
involved and how big the issues at stake. We need not
follow the course of the controversy. It is enough to note
the position which Paul was led to take up. He sets the
Law and the Gospel over-against each other as absolute
contraries. A man cannot have part in both, but must
make his election between them. " Behold, I Paul say
unto you, that, if ye receive circumcision, Christ will profit
you nothing : ye are severed from Christ, ye who would be
justified by the Law : ye are fallen away from grace "
(Gal. 5²ᶠᶠ·). The Apostle does not deny that the Law was

God-given and had its day of validity. But that day is past. With the death of Christ the reign of the Law ended and the reign of grace began.

It is in establishing these positions that Paul develops his scheme of redemption from the Law. That scheme cannot be understood as a solution of the problem, How is forgiveness possible? The Apostle has no such problem before him. His problem is to demonstrate the sole right of the gospel of grace as over-against the religion of the Law. Nor can we understand his scheme as the product of a process of reflection on the significance of Christ's death. Nowhere do we find any indication that Christ's death formed for him a subject of independent reflection. Where one or other aspect of its meaning is brought forward it is always in connection with some question of the Christian life.

When Paul speaks of the Law, what he has in his mind is Jewish legalism, the religion which his opponents wished to fasten on the Christian Gospel as an integral part of it, the religion which he himself had once professed. This religion he subjects, for purposes that will appear later, to careful analysis. On its objective side, that is as a divine revelation, it can be resolved into two elements—the first, commandment; the second, recompense. In legal religion God comes to men with a bare " Thou shalt," and stands over-against them as the supreme Judge who, without partiality but also in the case of transgression without mercy, will render unto every one according to his works. Forgiveness in this revelation has no place, and as little the quickening activity of the Divine Spirit. Commandment and recompense—these two principles sum up its character (Gal. 3, Rom. 4). And the piety—the subjective aspect of legal religion—that corresponds to such a revelation can be nothing else than a legal piety. To his own deeds and not to the favour of God a man must look for salvation. Of the faith that rests on God he can know nothing. His piety is and must be a piety of "works." "To him that worketh, the reward is not reckoned as of grace, but as of debt" (Gal. 3, Rom. 4). How antithetical the Law and the Gospel are the Apostle shows by setting their respective principles over-against each other. On the one side we have commandment, on the other the quickening activity of the Spirit; on the one side recompense, on the other grace; on the one side works, on the other faith.

Jewish legalism is what Paul really means by the Law. But to his Jewish and Jewish-Christian opponents he makes this amazing concession, that the legalism for which they stand is the genuine interpretation of Old Testament religion. Unlike Jesus, the Apostle never accuses the Jews of corrupting the Law by their traditions. While reproaching them with their failure to observe it, he never hints that their conception of it is other than true. The Law, accordingly, uniformly appears as the revelation of the divine will contained in Scripture. No distinction is drawn between what is ethical in it and what is ceremonial, or between the Law and the prophets (Gal. $3^{10.\ 17}\ 4^{24}$, Rom. $2^{17-20}\ 3^{19}$). All form part of a single, indivisible, divinely given system, and the system bears the characters we have seen. One reservation has, however, to be made. In the Old Testament Paul recognises an element that transcends the legal economy in which it is embedded and looks forward to the economy to come, the element, namely, of promise (Gal. 3^8). But this element is not to be taken as affecting the unity of Old Testament religion, or its divine authority. Up to the hour of Christ's death, the Law was the one true religion, and that under which God meant His people to live. It was the religion of the evil age (Gal. $3^{22ff.}$).

The Law had stood since Moses; it formed the content

6

of an inspired book and still retained the allegiance of the vast bulk of the Jewish people. Why had it to go? In order to demonstrate its inadequacy the Apostle subjects it to a searching criticism.

In one or two passages he treats the Law as if it stood on practically the same level with the religions of paganism. Adopting a Jewish tradition that it was delivered to Moses by angels, he makes use of the tradition to disparage it, as not having come like the Gospel directly from God (Gal. 3^{20}). And he goes still further on the same line when he stigmatises the conduct of the Judaising Galatians in observing days and months and seasons and years as a return unto bondage to the weak and beggarly star-spirits, evidently on the ground that these festivals, being fixed by the stellar motions, subject such as observe them to the stellar powers (Gal. 4^9). Col. 2^{14-17} may even suggest that it was from these sinister beings the Law derived its authority. But in view of what the Apostle says elsewhere, such a depreciatory judgment can hardly be regarded as deliberate. Nor can we attach much importance to the rabbinical proof of the Law's merely provisional character, drawn from the fact that in its promulgation it was posterior to the promise of grace given to Abraham (Gal. 3^{15}). More to the point is his characterisation of legalism as a religion of servitude (Gal. $4^{1\text{ff.}}$ 5^1). Governed like slaves by commandment and threat, those under the Law can know nothing of the spontaneous obedience of sons. And what sort of commandments are they which the Law imposes? For the most part a useless and burdensome system of rites and ceremonies, a system that belongs essentially to the domain of the flesh (Gal. 5^3). Its regulations regarding sacred days, clean and unclean meats, its great ordinance of circumcision, do not touch the moral nature but only the fleshly, and are therefore morally indifferent (Gal. 6^{15}). The true circumcision is that of the heart. Paul also criticises the Law as an institution powerless to achieve the end it proposed; though the modern idea that it was wanting in any sufficient moral dynamic hardly represents his standpoint. For him its weakness consists in its inability to effect that destruction of the sinful flesh which Christ effected in His death, and in the fact that it is unaccompanied by the working of the Spirit, a working which he uniformly limits to the new age and the Christian community (Rom. $8^{3f.}$). All this, however, is only preliminary to his crowning demonstration of the Law's insufficiency and futility when viewed as an instrument of salvation.

The point on which Paul rests the burden of his case is that the Law, while it offers salvation, attaches to its offer a condition which no human being can possibly fulfil. Its promise of life is only to those who render to its commandments a perfect obedience; and to man's moral impotence experience and Scripture alike bear irrefutable testimony. From the beginning until now there has been no child of Adam that has not been convicted of sin (Rom. 1–2). The salvation which the Law offers being thus illusory, men are left face to face with its curse as the one operative element in its central principle of recompense. " For as many as are of the works of the Law are under a curse: for it is written, Cursed is every one which continueth not in all things that are written in the book of the Law, to do them " (Gal. 3^{10}).

The conclusion to which the Apostle is led is that the Law could never have been designed by God as an instrument for justifying or saving men. It was not without its use, but its use was not to save, but only to create and deepen within men the sense of sin, to ripen lust into conscious transgression and so make its real character apparent, to demonstrate to men their utter helplessness in the face of the divine demands, in fine, to prepare men for the redemption to come by convincing them of their need of it (Rom. $7^{7.\ 13.\ 19}\ 5^{20}$). It was the divinely appointed tutor to lead reluctant humanity to Christ. As serving this great end the Apostle can describe it as holy, righteous and good (Rom. $7^{7ff.}$).

In this analysis and criticism of legal religion there is much that is of deep and permanent value. The salient features both of Judaism and of the Gospel are seized and exhibited with penetrating insight. Judaism was really in the main a religion of statute, recompense and works. And Paul's demonstration of the inadequacy of such a faith holds good for all time. A God who is known only as the eternal power behind Law—whether natural law or moral law—is not a God that can bring to the human heart either inspiration or peace. And recompense is not the ultimate principle of the world's moral order. The greatness and the power of the Christian Gospel consists above all in this, that it establishes grace, mercy, love on the throne of the universe.

But while we recognise the substantial truth of the Apostle's criticism, we cannot wonder that few of his Jewish opponents found it convincing. The analysis on which it rests must have seemed to them at many points unfair. No Jew would have admitted that God's grace and mercy were foreign ideas to him, or that he looked for salvation to his own works alone. Dominant as are the ideas of recompense and merit in the later Jewish literature, that literature also contains not a few utterances of heartfelt penitence and humble trust in the divine mercy. "In truth," says the writer of 4th Esdras, "there is no one born of woman who has not sinned, no one of the living who has not gone astray; for in this, O Lord, is thy righteousness manifest, that thou hast mercy on those who have no treasure of good works" (8^{31-36}). And the Gospels themselves may be cited as witnesses to the fact that there

were many among the Jews who nourished their faith on
the Prophets and the Psalms. What Paul really does is to
abstract the dominant principles of Judaism from their
concrete setting and press them to their logical conclusion.
His criticism shows clearly enough the influence of the two-
age doctrine. As the old age and the new are set over-
against each other in sheer opposition, so also are their
respective religious institutions, the Law and the Gospel.
On the one side lies the reign of recompense and the flesh;
on the other the reign of grace and the Spirit. There, we
have a ministration of condemnation; here, of righteousness. There, all is bondage, and here all is liberty; there
the passing and here the abiding. But momentous as was
the change from Judaism to Christianity, it cannot be
described in terms so sharply antithetical. History shows
no such absolute cleavages. It sets all clear-cut schemes
at defiance.

Paul's criticism of Jewish legality prepares the way for
the one inevitable conclusion. The Law has served its
purpose in preparing the world for Christ and, like all outworn things, must take itself off the stage. In the new
age it has neither place nor right. Sometimes the Apostle
speaks as if the presence of the higher revelation was of
itself sufficient to release men from their obligation to the
lower. "Now that faith has come," he declares, "ye are no
longer under a tutor; for ye are all sons of God through
faith in Jesus Christ." And when he disparages the Law
by connecting it with angels of more than doubtful
reputation, relegates it to the sphere of the flesh, and
asserts that it was never meant to be other than a provisional institution, he cuts the ground from any possible
objection that might be urged against its summary
dismissal. This, however, cannot be taken as his considered view. Paul concedes to the Law a right which God
himself was under obligation to recognise. Through its

central principle of recompense it had a claim on the sinner that could not be simply set aside, an account against him that could not be simply cancelled. The sinner's life was forfeit to the Law; and until the Law's demand for the exaction of the penalty had been met, the sinner could not be lawfully withdrawn from its jurisdiction. Paul can also state the situation from the historical standpoint, and indeed this is the standpoint most organic to his thought. Not till the Law's account against sinful humanity had been finally squared could its reign be brought to a termination and the way cleared for the reign of grace. If the Apostle does not say all this in so many words, it forms the necessary presupposition of his redemptive scheme.

Such being the situation, it is obvious that release from the Law could come only by way of redemption. If the sinful race was not to go down to destruction under the Law's curse, another qualified to satisfy its demand must interpose. And now we come to what is for the Apostle the greatest and most wonderful of facts. Christ did for our guilty race what it could not do for itself. Himself sinless, He consented in His wondrous love to endure the penalty of death that hung over it. He was made sin for us, in the sense that for our redemption He was treated as a sinner : He became a curse for us, in the sense that He bore the curse that would otherwise have lighted on our head (2 Cor. 5²¹, Gal. 3¹³). Through His vicarious death the Law's claim on man was met and man for ever released from its dominion. His death was its end, its abrogation (Gal. 4⁵ᶠ·, Rom. 7⁴· ⁶).

So far our reproduction of the Apostle's argument has encountered no very serious difficulty. His scheme is really simple and intelligible enough. It is when we ask how he came to concede to the Law a right which even divine grace had to reckon with that our difficulties begin.

We are here confronted by one of the most disputed points in the interpretation of his theology, and it is necessary to consider it with the utmost care.

So long as we limit our attention to the scheme and its logic, the conclusion seems inevitable that the right which Paul concedes to the Law is that of God's retributive justice. It is true that in Galatians this identification hardly seems to be contemplated. There it is the institution that is in the foreground, the abstract principles embodied in it scarcely coming into view. When the Apostle contends that those under the Law are under a curse, and that it was this curse Christ bore, he appeals in support of his view not to the principle of justice, but to the Law's own statements: "Cursed is every one which continueth not in all things that are written in the book of the Law, to do them"; "Cursed is every one that hangeth on a tree" (Gal. 3$^{10ff.}$). But in Romans the scheme is presented in a distinctly more developed form, the Apostle operating not so much with the Law's own statements as with the abstract principles embodied in it. What pursues men to their merited doom is the "wrath of God," in other words, the principle of retributive justice in God's nature (Rom. 1^{18}). And it was to satisfy the claims of this justice that Christ died. God, we read, "set forth Jesus to be a propitiation, through faith, by His blood, to show His righteousness, because of the passing over of the sins done aforetime, in the forbearance of God; for the showing, I say, of His righteousness at this present season; that He might Himself be just, and the justifier of him that hath faith in Jesus" (Rom. 3$^{25ff.}$). There are points in this passage to which we shall return presently. Here we simply note its unambiguous statement, that the propitiation which Christ offered was offered to divine justice, and that without such a propitiation God could not, consistently with His justice, have justified the believer.

Is this then the answer to the question proposed, How did Paul come to concede to the Law a right which God Himself was under obligation to recognise? Was the necessity for an atonement based by the Apostle from the first on God's retributive justice? Was it his conviction that until God's justice had been satisfied remission of penalty was morally impossible—was it this conviction that led him to formulate his atonement scheme? An affirmative answer would mean that the real aim of the Apostle in Galatians and Romans is not as we have stated it, to demonstrate that the old dispensation of the Law has yielded its place to a new and better dispensation, but rather this—to prove to the conscience-stricken soul that every obstacle in the path of God's forgiving grace has now been removed. The historical institution might then be eliminated from his scheme as having no essential place in it, or a place only in so far as it was an historical embodiment of eternal principles. As a matter of fact this is the view taken by exponents of the traditional doctrine of the atonement. The Apostle is regarded as operating with abstract and eternally valid principles. But against such a view decisive objections can be urged.

Jewish scholars of the present day have confessed themselves at a loss to discover where Paul found his principle that God's right to forgive is limited by His retributive justice. As we have shown, such a principle is unknown to the Old Testament and to the later Jewish writings. These last do indeed witness to a belief in the propitiatory efficacy of suffering, particularly undeserved suffering, and of various pious practices. But never is it implied that God cannot forgive until a propitiation has first been provided. The truth is that, apart from the logic of his redemption scheme, the principle is as foreign to Paul as to Hebrew and Jewish writers in general. Anticipating our final conclusion we may say, that it cannot be regarded as the starting-point and basis of his scheme, but only as the product of its logical working out.

Even in the Epistle to the Romans, where the conception of the Law is to some extent universalised, the Apostle never quits the ground of the historical institution. No more than in Galatians is his purpose to reassure troubled consciences. It is to prove against Jew and Judaiser that the reign of Jewish legalism has ended and the reign of the gospel of grace begun. The very passage in which Paul comes nearest to operating with an abstract principle shows on closer examination that it is still the historical institution that is in his mind (Rom. 3$^{25ff.}$). What made it necessary for God to demonstrate His justice, we are told, was His forbearance in passing over the sins done aforetime. Why this temporal limitation? The forbearance the Apostle has in view is that exercised while the Law was still in force. Though under the old dispensation God's one principle of action had been recompense, He had in His forbearance refrained from carrying out this principle in its rigour. His justice or consistency was therefore open to question. It was to place it above question that He set forth the propitiation. Not till He had as it were squared the account of the legal economy could He bring it to an end and introduce the economy of grace. Sins committed under this new economy do not need to be atoned for, since in it recompense has neither place nor right. From this standpoint we can understand why the Apostle, when dealing with the sins of believers, should never ground the hope of forgiveness in Christ's atoning work. When he thinks of the final reckoning to which believers and unbelievers will alike be called, he connects salvation, not with the atonement, but with the interposition of the living Christ (Rom. 5$^{9. 10}$). From this standpoint also we can understand his apparent inconsistency in speaking of a judgment of believers, and a judgment by works, while almost in the same breath proclaiming the Law for ever abolished.   What makes him unconscious of any inconsistency is the fact that the Law he thinks of as abolished is not any abstract principle of recompense, but the historical institution.

We take it, therefore, that in conceding a right to the Law which God Himself could not override Paul was not moved by any antecedent conviction as to the absolute inviolability of the principle of retributive justice.   How then is his action to be explained?   By Pfleiderer and others a solution has been sought in the consideration that for Paul the Law was Scripture and not to be lightly set aside.   But this does not carry us far.   The Apostle's action becomes intelligible only when we suppose that he took as the starting-point and basis of his scheme the common Christian idea that Christ died for our sins. Confronted by the task of rebutting the demands of Judaising Christians, and of vindicating the sole right of the gospel of grace, he brought this idea into connection with the Law in order to prove through it the Law's abrogation.   Christ's death becomes a debt vicariously paid to the Law's central principle of recompense.   Since atonement had always been related to God's anger against sin, this step would hardly strike the Apostle as a departure from traditional lines.   In thus connecting Christ's death with the Law, he necessarily concedes to the latter an independent right ; for if God could have simply brushed the Law aside there would have been no necessity for Christ to die.

The primitive idea of Christ's death for our sins is thus developed by Paul into a scheme of redemption.   That Christ died for our sins receives the interpretation, He paid our debt to the Law that He might rescue us from the Law's clutches and bring its reign to an end.   It may well have seemed to the Apostle, that in giving to the primitive notion this interpretation he was doing nothing more than making explicit what was already implied in it. None the less an idea is introduced that had never before been contemplated, the idea, namely, that until an atonement had been provided it was impossible for God to manifest His grace. But as has already been remarked, this idea is not present to Paul as an axiom ; it emerges as a necessary implication of his scheme, a product of its logical working out.

In connection with this scheme of redemption from the Law two or three subsidiary questions have still to be considered.

(1) In what capacity did Christ suffer for the sins of the race ? The answer frequently given, that it was as our substitute, scarcely reproduces the Apostle's idea. Christ acted not as man's substitute, but rather as his head and legal representative. If the death of one on behalf of all can be described as the death of all, it is because the act of the head is conceived as legally binding the members and as being equivalent to their act (2 Cor. 5^{14}). The same idea, which was familiar to Hellenists as well as to Jews,[1] is employed to explain the transmission of Adam's guilt and punishment to his posterity (Rom. 5$^{12ff.}$). In neither case is there any question of physiological or psychological mediation. The category is purely forensic.

(2) Always it is with the death that the idea of atonement is connected. That the death should have been brought about by violence is presupposed as necessary ; its penal character would not otherwise have been manifest. And in the further fact that it was by crucifixion the Apostle sees a precise carrying out of the Law's sentence (Gal. 3^{10}). At the same time it is not the incidents of the

---

[1] Deissmann, *Light from the Ancient East*, p. 339.

death, but the death itself that is the essential fact.   The Genesis story that death entered the world as the divine judgment on Adam's transgression is taken with a seriousness unknown in the Old Testament or in Judaism.   For Paul death is the king of terrors, of which he cannot think without a shudder, the last enemy to be destroyed, and, for the sinner, final and irretrievable ruin (2 Cor. 5^1).   It is in fact sin's specific penalty: " The wages of sin is death " (Rom. 6^{23}).   Such a conception of it is neither Hebrew nor Jewish, but Hellenistic.   In Hellenistic religion mortality uniformly appears as the radical evil of our human lot, and immortality as the chief religious good.

While regarding Christ's death as the equivalent of that deserved by the sinful race, Paul is at no pains to establish an exact equation between the two.   The obvious difficulty that the first was speedily followed by resurrection, while the second was eternal, does not occur to him.

(3) Does Paul anywhere present the idea of redemption from guilt and its penalty under another aspect than that of redemption from the Law?   In not a few passages the efficacy of Christ's death is expressed not in forensic terms, but in terms borrowed from the institution of sacrifice. Wherever we find a reference to Christ's blood, or to propitiation, the sacrificial system is obviously running in the Apostle's mind (Rom. 3^{25} 5^9, 1 Cor. 5^7 10^{16} 11^{25}, Col. $1^{14.\ 20}$).   Do these references carry with them any other conception of redemption than that we have already considered ?

For the piety of the later Judaism the institution of sacrifice possessed but little significance.   That it still survived was due less to any living idea embodied in it than to the fact that it formed part of the Law.   When a Jew brought his sin-offering to the altar it was probably in most cases with no other thought than that he was fulfilling a statutory obligation.   If there was more than this in his mind, it would be one of two ideas—either he would ascribe to the sacrificial blood a mystic purificatory virtue, or he would regard the victim as a means of appeasing the anger and securing the favour of God. That the former idea, which was also widely current in paganism, was carried over into Christianity is witnessed by more than one New Testament passage (Heb. 9^{14}, 1 John 1^7, Rev. 7^{14}). The Apocalypse speaks of the saints as having " washed their robes and made them white in the blood of the Lamb." But there is no trace of such an idea in Paul. When he speaks of a purificatory washing, it is not the blood of Christ, but the water of baptism that is the medium (1 Cor. 6^{11}).

With respect to the idea of propitiation, it might at first sight seem to be otherwise. Christ is described as having been set forth in His blood as a propitiatory offering ($ἱλαστήριον$) ; and there are frequent references to the wrath of God as pursuing the sinner (Rom. 1^{18} 2^8 4^{15}, Col. 3^6). This might seem to imply that God's wrath needed for its placation a bloody atonement. And it would be a confirmation of this view if we had to read the term enemies applied to sinners in Rom. 5^{10} in the passive sense, as equivalent to hated of God. Such an interpretation, however, though exceedingly common, is hardly correct. The analogy of other passages in which the term occurs in a similar connection is all against it. When in Rom. 8^7, Phil. 3^{18}, Col. 1^{22} sinners are spoken of as enemies, it is in the sense of being hostile to God. Moreover, had Paul in Rom. 5^{10} been thinking of sinners as God-hated, we should have expected him to say that through the death of His Son God was reconciled to them. What he does say is something very different : sinners were reconciled to God. And whenever the idea of reconciliation occurs, it is always with man as the object (2 Cor. $5^{18ff.}$, Col. $1^{20f.}$). God is not reconciled to men ; He reconciles men to Himself. We are not indeed to suppose that the atoning efficacy of Christ's death is found in its ethical appeal, the demonstration of God's love on the Cross winning man to a better frame of mind. Always redemption is for Paul a purely objective fact, in the accomplishment of which neither man nor his faith plays any part. When he describes Christ's death as the means through which God reconciles the world to Himself, we must suppose that he is thinking, not of its proximate, but of its ultimate object and effect. At the same time the fact that he deliberately avoids saying that God was reconciled to man is a strong proof that he does not intend his words about the wrath of God and a propitiatory offering to be taken literally. Indeed, by making God Himself provide the propitiation, he breaks through the idea in the very moment of adopting its terminology (Rom. 3^{25}). As we can see from the passage in question, the thought of Christ's death as a propitiatory offering is one and the same with the thought of it as a debt paid to the Law. The sacrificial ritual is in fact nothing more for Paul than vivid symbol. When he uses its language he reads into it his forensic idea. Nowhere does he attribute any efficacy to the old sacrifices, or speak of them as pointing forward to the great sacrifice on Calvary. That the death of Christ effected a change in God's disposition toward our race is an idea out of harmony with the whole complexion of his thought. From first to last redemption is exhibited as God's work. "All things are of God who reconciled us to Himself through Christ." It is God's love that is commended to us in Christ's death (Rom. 5^8). One may, however, speak of a change in God's attitude. While the Law stood, God was bound by it, and could show Himself to men only as the avenger of sin. What first opened a way for His activity as a God of grace was the Law's annulment; though, indeed, it has to be added that this annulment was itself an act of His grace, and had been in view throughout the whole legal dispensation.

Summing up this whole chapter, we can say that one of the great things that Paul found in Christ was deliverance from the burden of his ancestral religion. Not infrequently a degenerate or outworn faith has been felt by ardent spirits as a burden and a fetter, and emancipation from it been hailed as a veritable redemption. The Roman poet Lucretius could regard even a crass materialism as a haven of refuge from the paralysing fears fostered by the popular belief in the gods and a life to come. Hardly less revolutionary and to far grander issues was the redemption of which Paul made experience. From a religion of subjection to ordinances and ceremonies he passed into one in which the service of God was in the freedom of a filial spirit. Formerly he had thought of God mainly as the almighty Lawgiver and Judge before whom the sinner must tremble, whose favour he must earn, if he can, by punctilious obedience. What was true in that conception he did not part with, nay, he retained it in a purer form ; but into his horizon there burst the glorious assurance that not law or recompense is the ultimate reality in the universe, but mercy and love, that the God with whom we have to do is a God who forgives our sins and has made our salvation His own problem and endeavour. This more than anything else created for the Apostle his new world, this more than anything else was what redemption essentially signified for him. How such redemption was mediated to mankind by Christ he tells in his own language, using the categories at his disposal. His categories are not ours, cannot be really appropriated by us. But this we can say, that in its essential meaning his gospel of redemption from the Law is as true to-day as when it was first proclaimed.

That Paul took his scheme, or even the suggestion of

it, directly from Jesus few will assert. Jesus has neither his narrow legalistic conception of the Law, nor does He for a moment contemplate its abrogation. Interpreting it not from the standpoint of the Pentateuchal code, still less from that of Pharisaism, but from the standpoint of the prophets and psalmists, He regards it as the one guide to salvation. " If thou wouldest enter into life keep the commandments " (Matt. 19[17]). And so far from relegating its principle of recompense to the evil past, He keeps it continually in the foreground (Matt. 7[21-27]). In every formal respect, the Apostle's doctrine of the Law stands in diametrical opposition to that of the Master.

When, however, penetrating beneath the surface, we compare Master and Apostle with respect to the essential import of their teaching, we find not contradiction, but deep and far-reaching agreement. If Jesus does not proclaim the Law's abrogation as a statutory system, by tacitly dropping whatever in it is without moral significance, by bringing into the foreground the spiritual principles underlying it and by giving to these principles a larger and finer application, He really makes of it something new. The Law as the Pharisees understood it is abolished. This new conception reappears in Paul under the guise of the law of Christ or of the Spirit. And notwithstanding his polemic, the Apostle can speak of even the Mosaic law as fulfilled in the one word, Thou shalt love thy neighbour as thyself (Gal. 5[14]).

Again, while Jesus nowhere contemplates a dispensation in which the principle of recompense has lost its validity, He is far indeed from treating that principle as the ultimate and inviolable rule of God's action. His God is not the God of Pharisaic legalism. He is, indeed, the righteous judge whom men must fear ; but He is far more the sovereign giver who bestows, not according to the measure of man's merit, but with royal generosity. He is kind to the unthankful and the evil, merciful and forgiving. The lives of men are precious in His sight; the very hairs of our head are numbered. He does not willingly consent to lose even a single soul. In His great love He goes out to recover the lost, and there is joy in His presence over one that repenteth. It is impossible not to see in all this the ultimate source of the Apostle's conception of the reign of grace that supersedes the reign of the Law. To explain, as Wrede does, the points of community between Paul and Jesus as due to their common Jewish heritage is preposterous. It is precisely in matters that involve a breach with that heritage that the agreement lies. If Paul's construction must be pronounced his own, the motives behind it, the ideas embodied in it, the spirit that animates it, take us back to Jesus. The new conception of God and of religion which Jesus taught in words and embodied in His life and Cross laid hold of Paul and was mighty enough to revolutionise his life and create for him a new heaven and a new earth.

7

CHAPTER VI.

REDEMPTION FROM THE TYRANNY OF SIN.

By some exponents of the Pauline theology it is denied that the Apostle teaches an objective redemption from the bondage of sin, an objective destruction or laming of sin's power, parallel and co-ordinate with that redemption from the Law already described. The former redemption is represented as the subjective result of the latter. Subdued by the demonstration of divine love in Christ's vicarious death, the believer turns from sin to righteousness, finding in his faith and his gratitude a force mighty enough to release him from the tyranny of his fleshly nature. In the words of Professor Denney: "It is Christ dying for sin, dying our death on the tree, who evokes the faith by which we become right with God; and the faith which He evokes answers to what He is and to what He does: it is faith which has a death to sin in it." [1] That the Apostle occasionally uses language that points in this direction must be admitted. The greatest of preachers, he could not but be familiar with the power of the Gospel message as an ethical appeal. In a well-known passage he speaks of the moral constraint which the thought of Christ's wondrous love lays upon the believer. "For the love of Christ constraineth us: because we thus judge, that one died for all, therefore all died; and He died for all that they which live should no longer live unto themselves, but unto Him who for their

[1] *The Death of Christ*, p. 183.

sakes died and rose again.   Wherefore if any man is in
Christ he is a new creature ; the old things are passed
away, behold they are become new " (2 Cor. 5$^{14ff.}$).   But
though here and in other passages Paul thinks of deliverance from sin's power as effected through the operation of
new motives, this is far from being a complete statement of
his view.   When he deals with the subject in a dogmatic
way, the categories of psychology retire into the background
and redemption is presented as a predominantly objective
process.   That this is so a study of that section of the
Epistle to the Romans which extends from the beginning
of the sixth to the middle of the eighth chapter will place
beyond doubt.

Having established his great doctrine that justification
is not to be obtained through the works of the Law but
only through faith in Jesus Christ, the Apostle sets himself
in the above passage to vindicate the ethical character
of the Christian salvation.   By some this character had
been called in question, by others it had been ignored.
Jewish opponents had argued that if in justification faith
is everything and works count for nothing, a righteous life
must be a matter of indifference.   And there were those
among Paul's own followers, as we can see from his fervent
appeals, who conceived salvation in an unethical fashion.
How does the Apostle meet these misconceptions ?   Not
in our modern way by showing that the faith that justifies
is an ethical magnitude with a death to sin and a resurrection to righteousness at the heart of it.   Throughout
the section the word faith does not once occur.   Appeal
is made, not to the nature of faith as expounded in the
preceding chapters, but to the nature of the baptismal
experience.   " Are ye ignorant," Paul asks, " that all we
who were baptized into Christ Jesus were baptized into
His death ?   We were buried therefore with Him through
baptism into death : that like as Christ was raised from

the dead through the glory of the Father, so we also might walk in newness of life. For if we have become united with Him through the likeness of His death, we shall be also by the likeness of His resurrection : knowing this, that our old man was crucified with Him, that the body of sin might be done away, that we should no longer be in bondage to sin : for he that hath died is justified from sin " (Rom. 6³ff·). The precise character of the experience here described, whether it is nothing else than faith, is a question which we shall not at the present point consider. It will come up again in a later chapter. What we have to note here is that the believer's experience of death and resurrection points back to prior acts of Christ in which that experience has its possibility and ground. Something happened when Christ died and rose again that so altered the moral situation as to make a righteous life on the part of man for the first time possible. What precisely was effected the Apostle throughout the section in question struggles to tell us, and hardly succeeds in telling us. With regard to the significance of Christ's resurrection, it is true, his thought is sufficiently clear ; but it is otherwise when he deals with His death. Here he is manifestly groping his way, at a loss to discover the fitting formula. And he ends by presenting us, not with one formula but with three, and these mixed up in the most perplexing fashion. The causes of his embarrassment will be indicated presently.

(1) In one or two passages Christ's death appears as a price or ransom paid to sin in order that sin might consent to release its bondservants (Rom. 6⁷⁻¹¹· ¹⁸· ²²). Sin, it is assumed, had a certain legal title to the obedience of the race enslaved by it, a title which could not be cancelled without the payment of an equivalent. Christ died unto sin in the sense that He surrendered His life as an equivalent for man's life. Through His vicarious death,

or through a mystical dying with Him—the Apostle vacillates between the two conceptions—believers are justified or made free from sin. Sin ceases to be their legal master, and they are no longer under any kind of obligation to obey it. While formerly they were "free" with respect to righteousness and under law to sin, now the order is reversed (6^{15-23}). The outcome, it will be observed, is meagre and dubious, not a redemption from sin's power, but only from its legal right. Such as it is, the Apostle founds on it an earnest ethical appeal.

It is not necessary to read into this formula the idea which gained currency at a later date, that the ransom paid by Christ was paid to the devil. Paul is evidently trying to express the fact of redemption from sin's thraldom in terms of his forensic theory, sin being substituted for the Law as the power whose right has to be recognised and satisfied. He is conscious of indifferent success, and warns his readers that his words are not to be read in too literal a fashion (6^{19}).

(2) Much more organic to his thought is Paul's second attempt to formulate the redemption from sin's power which Christ achieved in His death. Already we have encountered the idea that the Law was in some sense responsible for the hold which sin had on the race. Though the lusts of the flesh were from the first evil, it was not until they were confronted by the Law's "Thou shalt not" that they assumed the character of deliberate transgression and were imputed as sin (Rom. 5^{20} 7^7). Still further, the Law acts upon lust as a direct provocative (Rom. $7^{5,\ 8}$). But what if the Law is abolished or a man withdrawn from its jurisdiction? Will the lusts of the flesh in such case lose their malignant power? So the Apostle assumes. "Sin shall not have dominion over you, for ye are not under the Law but under grace." "For when we were in the flesh, the sinful passions, which were through the Law,

wrought in our members to bring forth fruit unto death.
But now we have been discharged from the Law, having
died to that wherein we were holden; so that we serve in
newness of the Spirit, and not in oldness of the letter"
(6^{14} 7^{5-6}). Redemption from the power of sin is thus
exhibited as to some extent the direct result of the Law's
abrogation. Not altogether. For in being delivered from
the Law, the believer is at the same time brought under
the reign of grace and of the Spirit. It is the activity of
the Spirit that enables him to render to God the new and
spiritual service ($7^{4.\ 6}$).

(3) There remains to be considered the third of the
Apostle's formulas. It is contained in a single verse.
"The law of the Spirit of life in Christ Jesus made me free
from the law of sin and of death. For what the Law
could not do in that it was weak through the flesh, God,
sending His own Son in the likeness of sinful flesh and in
connection with sin (περὶ ἁμαρτίας), condemned sin in the
flesh (κατέκρινεν τὴν ἁμαρτίαν ἐν τῇ σαρκί), that the
requirement of the Law might be fulfilled in us who walk
not after the flesh, but after the Spirit" (8^{3-4}). The point
of this passage lies in the assertion that God in Christ's
death condemned sin in the flesh. What meaning are we
to attach to such words? Approaching them with our
modern presuppositions we naturally read into them a
purely ethical meaning. We think of a moral condemnation. In Christ's death, we say, sin was confronted with
the divine holiness, the divine displeasure and sentence:
it was held up to moral reprobation and in this sense
condemned. But if such were the Apostle's thought, how
could he assert that the Law had no power to effect this?
Was not this moral condemnation the one thing the Law
could and did effect? To the sinful lusts it opposed the
divine commandment and threat. The flesh made it
impossible for the Law so to strike at sin as to bring its

reign to an end, but it did not make it impossible for the
Law to brand it as sin. What the Apostle has manifestly
in view is not any moral condemnation of sin, but such a
crippling of its power as shall open the way for a fulfilment
on the part of the believer of the Law's demand for righteousness. That God condemned sin in the flesh means that
He carried out on it a judicial sentence of execution. The
death of Christ signified an act of judgment in which God
struck at sin as seated in Christ's fleshly body. Flesh and
sin are thought of after the manner of Platonic realism as
single, indivisible magnitudes. Smitten in the flesh of
Christ, sin was smitten in all flesh. By one stroke God
could wound it to death. We have also to keep in view
the Apostle's doctrine of the inseparable connection between
sin and the flesh.

In this third formula as in the other two, Paul's
starting-point is the common Christian idea of Christ's
death as a propitiatory offering. But in adapting it to his
purpose he has to modify it almost beyond recognition.
The notion of an equivalent or ransom disappears ; and it
is no longer on Christ, but on sin seated in His flesh that
the death-sentence is carried out. We are thus justified in
saying that at bottom the Apostle has only one doctrine
of Christ's death, the common Christian doctrine that
Christ died for our sins. This doctrine is, however,
variously modified in the attempt to make it cover the
different aspects of redemption that come up for explanation.

But the death of Christ, however important, represents
but one side of His redemptive working. Equal significance
is ascribed to His resurrection. Risen from the dead,
Christ entered on a life different in essential respects from
that which He lived on earth. For one thing it is a life
above the reach of death. Raised from the dead, Christ
dieth no more : death hath no more dominion over Him

(Rom. 6⁸). Further, it is a life cut loose from that contact with sin which His assumption of our flesh involved. " For the death that He died, He died unto sin once for all; but the life that He liveth, He liveth unto God " (Rom. 6¹⁰). All this, however, is but preliminary to the main thing, which is that He entered through the resurrection on a new career of saving activity not less vital and necessary than that He completed on the cross. As the risen Lord, a quickening, life-giving Spirit, He unites Himself with believers to create within them the life that is life indeed. To the working of the exalted Christ, or the Holy Spirit— the two are for the Apostle identical—every motion of the redeemed soul is traced. It is the law of the spirit of life in Jesus Christ that makes us free from the law of sin and of death (Rom. 8². ¹⁰, Gal. 5²²). If by His death Christ destroyed the old, as the risen Lord He creates the new.

It was a real and splendid fact which Paul undertook to explain. Something of infinite moment had happened in the history of the race. The gospel of the Cross and the Kingdom, preached by devoted disciples, was kindling a fire of religious enthusiasm throughout the length and breadth of the Roman world. And the new movement was authenticating its divine origin by the noblest ethical fruits. Paul had before him men and women whose lives Christ had transformed, working in them what could be truthfully described as a death to sin and a resurrection to righteousness and God (1 Cor. 6¹¹). And in his own soul he had made experience of Christ's liberating and renewing power. The redemption he essayed to explain was a palpable, indubitable fact.

In showing how Christ had effected this redemption, the Apostle had necessarily to operate with the categories of his time. That these categories are not such as are in use to-day, that they have in large measure become foreign to us, is only what was to be expected. No less than those of philosophy or science, the conceptions of theology change with the changing years. Consider this one fact that in accounting for the moral revolution wrought by Christ, Paul allows nothing for the influence of Christ's transcendent personality, nothing for the influence of the new revelation of divine truth, the new faith and hope and love, embodied in Christ's teaching and life. The category of personal and moral influence, so prominent in the religious thought of our time, finds in Paul practically no dogmatic employment. His way of looking at things is realistic, one might say mythological. Christ buys men out of the power of sin, or He inflicts on sin, as if it were a personal being, a mortal wound. It is the hopeless inadequacy of the Apostle's forensic and mythological categories that is largely responsible for the embarrassed character of his argument in Rom. 6. Largely but not wholly. Another fact has to be taken into account. The construction that has occupied our attention in this chapter is not a primary, but only a secondary creation of Paul's thought. Outside Rom. 6–8 hardly a trace of it is to be met with. What is primary for the Apostle is the conception of death and resurrection with Christ. As we shall find later, this conception dominates his piety. And it forms his starting-point in the construction in question; the construction is only a working out of the presuppositions of that conception. If the believer dies with Christ to sin and rises with Him into a new life of righteousness, then must Christ also in an archetypal way have passed through the same experiences. One sees the difficulties in the way of establishing between the experiences of the redeemed and those of the redeemer anything like an exact parallelism. How was a death to sin and a resurrection to righteousness possible for a sinless being? The attempt to equate the two inevitably ends in a construction more or less artificial.

Surveying Paul's doctrine of an accomplished redemption in all its branches, we are arrested by the fact that uniformly and exclusively it turns on the two great events of Christ's death and resurrection. So far as dogmatic theory is concerned nothing else in Christ's earthly ministry comes into account. How are we to explain this concentration of interest? It cannot be regarded as a heritage from the primitive community. While the primitive community looked to the resurrection as a fact of cardinal importance, it found its significance not in any redemptive efficacy attaching to it, but in this, that it was the divine authentication of Jesus' messiahship and the pledge of His return in glory. Nor did the Cross occupy in its faith the central position which it occupies in that of Paul. Not yet had the doctrine of Christ's death for our sins been elaborated into a scheme of redemption. The redemption towards which the early disciples looked lay not in the past, but in the future. For an answer to our question we must go outside the primitive tradition.

Something, surely, must be set down to the Apostle's rare spiritual insight. Far more than any of his contemporaries he had an eye for the moral glory of the Cross. His perception, it is true, has its limits. Of the Cross as the symbol of moral heroism, of uttermost fidelity to the divine will and of calm trust and submission in the face of the darkest mysteries of existence we hear little or nothing. But there are two aspects of its significance which chain his thoughts and stir him to the innermost fibre of his being. The Cross stands out before him as the grand demonstration of the divine love that stoops to the lost to forgive and save. "Scarcely for a righteous man will one die; though, perhaps, for the good man some might even dare to die; but God commended His love toward us, in that while we were yet sinners Christ died for us." "He loved me and gave Himself for me." The second aspect of the Cross that captivates him is the self-renunciation of which it speaks. So far from grasping at a new dignity and power, Christ " emptied Himself, taking the form of a servant, being made in the likeness of men ; and being found in fashion as a man He humbled Himself, becoming obedient even unto death, yea, the death of the cross " (Phil. 2⁵ᶠᶠ·). It is Paul's highest glory that he can in this imitate Christ, turning his back on the world and its goods, and filling up his particular share of the afflictions of Christ for His body's sake, which is the Church (Col. 1²⁴). When he speaks of fellowship with Christ in His sufferings and of bearing about in his body the dying of the Lord Jesus, it is this self-renunciation in the service of the highest cause that he has in view. If the Cross had not been thus radiant for the Apostle with the noblest religious and ethical meaning, he could never have made it the basis of his redemption theology. That he couples the resurrection with the death may be accounted for by the place which the risen Christ holds in his faith.

It is difficult, however, to accept this as a full explanation of Paul's exclusive concentration on the two great facts. Why should everything else in Christ's life—His teaching, His miracles, His ministry of healing, His personal dealing with men and women — have been so completely overshadowed ?

The attempt has been made to show that in making redemption turn on Christ's death and resurrection, Paul was dominated by the redemption theology of the Hellenistic cults. One and all these cults attached themselves to the myth of a saviour-god (θεὸς σωτήρ), subordinate to the supreme God and often his son, who descended to earth, died and rose again, opening to men by His death and resurrection the way to immortal and divine life. Such a saviour-god was the Greek Dionysos, the Phrygian Attis, the Egyptian Serapis and the Persian Mithra. While the myth varies, the underlying ideas are everywhere the same, and one story may be taken as typical of all.   Attis, who was miraculously born of a virgin, appears as a young and beautiful hunter, the husband of Cybele, the great mother of the gods.   Two different accounts are given of his death. According to the Lydian form of the myth, he was slain by a wild boar; according to the Phrygian, he mutilated himself in a fit of madness with which Cybele in a moment of jealousy had struck him, and expired under a pine tree. With passionate outcries Cybele lamented her dead lover. But after three days the god returned to life and Cybele's mourning was changed into joy.   So runs the myth;[1] and its original significance is clear.   It carries us back to the days of nature-worship.   Like the other saviour-gods, Attis was originally an astral or vegetation divinity, his death representing the decay that falls upon nature at the touch of Winter, and his resurrection the revival of Spring.   But in Hellenistic times this primitive meaning of the myth had fallen into the background.   It was no longer nature but human destiny that was the centre of interest.   What the worshipper found in the story of Attis and similar stories was a type of the fall of the human soul from the ideal world and its entanglement in the lower world of sense, a type also of its deliverance and reascent.[2]

That there is a certain resemblance between the part played by these pagan divinities and that which Christ plays in the theology of Paul cannot be denied.   In both cases there is a death and a resurrection to which saving significance is ascribed.   But here the resemblance ends. The pagan divinities do not really accomplish anything for man's redemption, unless it be to establish the sacraments through which it is effected.[3]   They are not historical

---

[1] Hepding, *Attis, seine Mythen und sein Kult*.
[2] Bousset, *Kyrios Christos*, pp. 165 ff.
[3] Dieterich, *Eine Mithras-liturgie*, p. 14.

actors, but at the best typical figures. Far other is the Christ of Paul. He enters into history in a decisive way and changes its course. The workings attributed to Him are real and historical—the liberation of the human spirit from an outworn religion, the introduction of the reign of grace, a shattering blow dealt at the power of sin, a new impulse towards goodness and God. That in construing Christ's redemptive work the Apostle should have been in any way influenced by the crude and in part repulsive myths of a dying and rising saviour-god is unthinkable.

From another side, however, it is not so easy to deny Hellenistic influence. As we have just seen, the Apostle's construction of Christ's work in redeeming from the power of sin seated in the flesh is moulded on his conception of Christian piety as a dying and rising with Christ. And this conception, as we shall show in our next chapter, is in its origin Hellenistic, however much Paul may have purified and elevated it. Here, then, at one point we can adduce an influence that does something to explain the exclusive significance attached to Christ's death and resurrection. That this influence was also active in the Apostle's construction of redemption from the Law it would be hazardous to assert. In this case we have to reckon with a starting-point in the primitive tradition.

In estimating Paul's doctrine of redemption one must not forget that it was the first attempt to exhibit in a systematic way what Christ had done and was doing for the world. While the early community looked to the earthly Jesus as its teacher and to His life as an example, while it spoke of His death as an offering for our sins, it had but little conception of the difference which His sojourn on our earth had made. It was preoccupied with the risen Lord and with the redemption He would achieve at His second coming. Christ's real messianic work was regarded as still lying in the future. Paul too believed in the risen Lord and in the events of the last days ; but he saw, as none of the original apostles did, that redemption was already an accomplished fact. Far better than any contemporary or any other New Testament writer he understood the true character of Jesus' contribution. In formulating the significance of Jesus' ministry in our world he rendered a splendid service to religion ; and if those elements in his thought which represent the fruit of direct insight into spiritual reality have proved more permanent than his theological constructions, it is only what happens in the case of every great religious genius and teacher.

PART II.

THE LIFE IN SALVATION.

CHAPTER I.

Faith and Mystical Union.

Pressed to its logical conclusion, Paul's doctrine of an objective redemption would seem to involve the immediate and unconditional salvation of the whole human race. If the demons have been overthrown, how should they any longer have power to harm? If the reign of recompense has been replaced by the reign of grace, what is left for man to fear? If the fleshly body of sin has been done away, how should man continue to be in bondage to sin? That the Apostle does not contemplate any such conclusion hardly needs to be said. Though in the work of redemption man has no part, that work becomes effective for his salvation only when he has fulfilled a certain divinely attached condition. He must meet the Gospel message with belief. Between the two great facts of redemption and salvation faith is the absolutely indispensable connecting link.

Long before Paul had developed his doctrine of salvation through faith, faith had come to be recognised as one of the great factors in religion. What first brought it into the foreground was the loosening of the bond between religion and nationality and the rise of a propaganda. When Judaism entered with a claim to universal acceptance into competition with other religions and became a matter of personal choice, the question whether a man believed in the one God and accepted as true His laws

8

and promises inevitably advanced into a position of cardinal importance. Faith was seen to be the initial and grounding act of religion. Accordingly we find that in the later Jewish writings this conception has a position assigned to it which it is far from possessing in the Old Testament (En. 46[7] 58[5], Bar. 54[5. 16. 21], 4 Esd. 5[1] 9[7f.]). Philo in particular lays upon it the greatest stress and subjects it to minute psychological analysis. For him it is the most perfect of the virtues and the basis of man's higher life (*Quis rer. div. hær.* 91 ff.; De Abrah, 268 f.).[1] Though coloured by Platonic idealism, his conception of faith is not really intellectualistic, but genuinely religious. In faith a man turns away from the passing things of sense, to build his confidence on the unseen and eternal realities, on God and His promises. For Philo as for Paul, Abraham is the hero of faith.

From the first the character of the Christian movement was such as to bring faith into the foreground. The gospel was preached not primarily as a law to be obeyed, but as a message to be believed. Jesus, risen from the dead, had been exalted as Messiah to God's right hand, and in a brief space would reappear in glory to judge the world and establish the Kingdom. Whoever accepted this message was assured of salvation. "Believers" was amongst the 'earliest names given to the disciples of the crucified. In his controversy with Peter at Antioch, Paul could assume the doctrine of salvation through faith in Christ as ground common to all Christians (Gal. 2[16]).

But though Paul found this doctrine already in practice established, his importance in its history is nevertheless immense. He was the first to carry it out in its stringency and to set it on a reasoned basis. Through him it was that the Church was brought to a clear consciousness of the significance which faith had come to possess for it.

[1] Bousset, *Religion des Judenthums*, 2nd ed., pp. 235 ff., 514 f.

What led the Apostle to formulate his doctrine of salvation through faith was the attempt of the Judaising party to impose upon Gentile converts, as a condition of salvation more or less co-ordinate with faith, an observance of the main prescriptions of the Levitical law. This attempt he met with the watchword, not faith and works, but faith only. In vindicating faith's title to be the sole and sufficient condition of salvation, his main argument is its congruence with the nature of the Christian gospel (Gal. 3, Rom. 4). Since the gospel comes as a revelation of divine grace and of a righteousness freely offered to guilty men, the fitting response on man's part can be nothing else than humble and thankful acceptance of the gift. Putting away the proud thought that we can stand on our own merits, secure justification by our own works of righteousness, we must believe in Him who justifies the ungodly. To build anything on works is to withdraw from the dispensation of grace to that of recompense; it is to lapse from the gospel into legalism.

From this it will be seen that the proper object of faith is for Paul the revelation of divine grace, the offer of salvation, in Jesus Christ. It is true that his description of the object varies. While in some passages it is given as God, the grace of God, the word or saving truth of God, in others it appears as the working of God who raised Jesus from the dead, the blood of Christ, Christ's death for our sins, His resurrection, His messianic dignity and power and, most frequently of all, Christ. In the latter series of passages it might appear as if the Apostle presents for belief something much more doctrinal than the simple message of divine grace. It has, however, to be remembered that the modern distinction between fact and speculative construction lies outside his horizon, and that the grace of God has no meaning for him apart from the drama of redemption in which it exhibits itself to his imagination and thought. Every fact or doctrine proposed for belief carries with it the whole gospel. Especially is this true when the fact is Christ.

That the Apostle has no thought of identifying faith with a mere intellectual assent to doctrine is evident also from another side. When he declares that " whatever is not of faith is sin " he reveals clearly enough his conception of faith as steadfast conviction as to what is true, but also that such conviction relates to matters of conscience (Rom. 14[23]). Elsewhere he speaks of it as a function of the heart : " With the heart man believeth unto righteousness " (Rom. 10[10]). Everywhere it implies moral earnestness, the sense of sin and of need, openness and submissiveness towards God. One can say that faith as conceived by Paul is indistinguishable from that trust in God's grace and care of which Jesus has so much to say.

In developing his doctrine of faith as the sole condition of salvation, Paul limits his attention to justification and views faith under the one aspect of receptivity. Does he anywhere regard it as productive as well as receptive, a power that wills and achieves the good, the inner spring of the new life ? In one or two passages he approaches this idea, as when he speaks of the Thessalonians' work of faith, and of faith as working through love, and declares that whatever conduct is not of faith is sin (1 Thess. 1[3], Gal. 5[6], Rom. 14[23]). But the idea remains undeveloped. In general the activities of the new life are traced not to faith but to the supernatural working of the Holy Spirit (Gal. 5[22], Rom. 8[2]). It is not to Paul but to the writer of Hebrews—following in the wake of Philo—that we owe the conception of faith as the principle of all right and heroic action.

More far-reaching in its importance is another question regarding the place which faith occupies in Paul's religion and thought. As defined in Rom. 4, Faith, whether its object be God or Christ or Christ's work of atonement, is a personal and moral relation. It is trust in the sin-forgiving, salvation-bringing grace of God revealed to men in Jesus Christ. To believe in Christ is to rely on the gracious purpose of which He is the mediator. As we have seen, the Apostle establishes such trust as the condition of salvation and therefore as the fundamental principle of Christian piety. And as a matter of fact, much of his piety has no other root than this. It is grounded in a personal and moral relation to God, a personal and moral relation to Christ. And in his doctrine of justification the Apostle builds upon such a conception of the fundamental religious relation. But is this true universally? Does his piety everywhere exhibit itself as a faith-piety? Does his doctrine of salvation, in all its branches, presuppose no other relation of the soul to God and to Christ than that of faith? The truth is, that in the piety of the Apostle and not less in his thought we meet with a strain which assumes a union, not indeed with God but with Christ, more intimate and close than can be described in personal and ethical terms. Believers are in Christ. They have put on Christ. They have died with Christ and risen with Him. Christ lives in them, and His indwelling is the great Christian mystery. It is not possible to find in these formulas merely an explication in figurative language of the inner nature of faith. They point to a relation that reaches far beyond the faith-relation. And on such the Apostle builds at least one of the main sections of his doctrine of salvation. The strain of feeling and thought here indicated is perhaps the most characteristic thing in Paul and it is necessary to subject it to careful examination.

Of the three main formulas in question—in Christ, Christ in the believer, fellowship with Christ in His death and resurrection—the first, though by far the most frequent, stands lowest in definiteness and importance. Since the publication of Deissmann's monograph, it has been pretty generally assumed that it must be read in a local sense. The believer is in Christ, or in the Spirit, as the element or atmosphere of his life; the pneumatic Christ, or the Spirit, being thought of as an extended supersensuous substance. But a careful examination of the many relevant passages will show that it is not possible to regard the formula as conveying everywhere a single uniform idea. Hellenistic Greek was notoriously lax in its use of prepositions, and Paul can use the preposition ἐν to denote a variety of relations. In many passages "in Christ" can hardly mean anything else than "through Christ," ἐν carrying the instrumental force of διά (Rom. 6[11], 1 Cor. 15[22], 2 Cor. 2[17], Col. 1[14] 2[6]). In others the formula is most naturally interpreted as equivalent to "in fellowship with Christ" (Rom. 16[7, 8], 1 Cor. 1[2, 30], 2 Cor. 1[21] 5[17], Gal. 3[27]), and in still others as equivalent to "under the power of Christ." The following passage from the Epistle to the Romans is an instance in which the last-named meaning seems the appropriate one: "They that are in the flesh cannot please God. But ye are not in the flesh but in the Spirit, if so be that the Spirit of God dwelleth in you. But if any man hath not the Spirit of Christ he is none of His. And if Christ is in you, the body is dead because of sin" (Rom. 8[9f.]). What is it to be in the flesh but to be under the power of the flesh, to be in the Spirit but to be under the power of the Spirit? And this passage throws another light on our formula. It shows that in the Apostle's mind it is connected in the closest way with the second formula, Christ in the believer. That a man is in the Spirit or in Christ means that the Spirit or Christ dwells in him. Whether the formula ever carries the local meaning contended for by Deissmann, Holtzmann and others must be pronounced highly doubtful. The Book of Acts puts into the Apostle's lips the words, "In God we live and move and have our being," but this Stoic and pantheistic conception of God as the universal life-element finds no support in his Epistles. And the probabilities are that if God is nowhere thought of in this way neither is Christ nor the Spirit.

On the whole one may conclude that the formula " in Christ " commends itself to the Apostle largely on account of its elasticity, and that while now one relationship and now another may be in the foreground, the meaning is in most cases left more or less vague. It is enough for him that the relation indicated is one of closest union and absolute dependence. And since such union and dependence is bound up in his mind with the idea of Christ's indwelling, we may safely assume that it too contributes its quota to the formula. To this last idea, which is embodied in the second of the formulas, we now turn.

Christ in the believer—that may be described as the signature of the Apostle's piety. In a former chapter we have seen how his sense of being dominated by the supernatural might of the Spirit merges itself, though without altogether losing its independence, in the sense of being dominated by the indwelling personal Christ. " I have been crucified with Christ," he can say, " yet I live ; and yet no longer I, but Christ liveth in me " (Gal. 2^{20}). " For to me to live is Christ " (Phil. 1^{21}). Christ speaks in and through him, directs him in his undertakings and communicates to him revelations of truth (2 Cor. 13^3, Gal. 2^2, Gal. $1^{11f.}$). And this indwelling of Christ is not a privilege peculiar to the Apostle ; it accomplishes itself in every genuine believer. " Know ye not as to your own selves, that Jesus Christ is in you unless indeed ye be reprobates ? " (2 Cor. 13^5). " He that is joined to the Lord is one Spirit " (1 Cor. 6^{17}). It is this sacred presence within the believer that is the spring of every motion of his higher life. "And if Christ is in you, the body is dead because of sin ; but the spirit is life because of righteousness" (Rom. 8^{10}). This is the great Christian mystery, "Christ in you, the hope of glory " (Col. 1^{27}).

Clearly we have something here which is not capable of being described in purely ethical terms. That the Apostle means that Christ's disposition and will are reproduced within the believer is true ; but he means much more than this. In language that leaves no room for misunderstanding, he asserts an indwelling of the personal Christ, a union with Him which can only be described as mystical. This mystical union precedes the moral renovation and is its cause. It is an accomplished fact even while yet the believer is far from being conformed to Christ's image (Rom. 6, 1 Cor. 13^3).

And now we come to the third formula of the Pauline mysticism, that of union or fellowship with Christ in His death and resurrection. Space forbids us to quote more than one or two of the many passages in which this conception comes to expression. "Are ye ignorant that all we who were baptized into Christ Jesus were baptized into His death? We were buried therefore with Him through baptism into death : that like as Christ was raised from the dead through the glory of the Father, so we also might walk in newness of life. For if we have become united with Him by the likeness of His death, we shall be also by the likeness of His resurrection ; knowing this that our old man was crucified with Him, that the body of sin might be done away, that so we should no longer be in bondage to sin" (Rom. $6^{3ff.}$). " I have been crucified with Christ ; yet I live ; and yet no longer I, but Christ liveth in me " (Gal. 2^{20}). Death and resurrection with Christ thus appears as the grounding experience of the Christian life, the experience in which a man is renewed inwardly. But the process is also regarded as repeated so long as a man lives, until the final goal of the resurrection of the dead is reached (Phil. 3¹⁰). " We are pressed on every side," the Apostle says, " yet not straitened ; perplexed, yet not unto despair ; pursued, yet not forsaken ; smitten down, yet not destroyed ; always bearing about in the body the dying of Jesus, that the life also of Jesus may be manifested in our body. For we which live are always delivered unto death for Jesus' sake, that the life also of Jesus may be manifested in our mortal flesh " (1 Cor. 4⁸ᶠᶠ·).

Here again it has to be said that Paul's thought is radically ethical. To die and rise with Christ is to renounce sin and surrender oneself to righteousness, cheerfully accepting whatever hardship and sacrifice that process may involve. And were attention to be limited to the continued dying and renewal, one might judge that nothing more than this is in view, unless indeed a vivid sense of companionship with the crucified and risen Lord. But, as will be shown more fully in a later chapter, the grounding baptismal experience cannot be exhaustively described in ethical terms. Christ's archetypal experiences—the condemnation of sin in the flesh and the resurrection to a new life with God—automatically reproduce themselves in the believer who is united with Christ. The body of sin is in some sense done away, its might is in some sense broken ; and there is a rebirth into a mode of existence in which the indwelling Christ or the indwelling Spirit is the all-controlling power. Behind the ethical revolution and as the ground of its possibility the Apostle places these two wholly supernatural processes. A union with Christ that involves such a death and resurrection is obviously something more intimate and mysterious than the personal relation of faith or trust. It is in fact a mystical union, and as such incapable of being made clear to thought. And we may add that the piety rooted in the consciousness of such a union is mystical piety.

Like poetry, mysticism has been found hard to define. We may take it that the goal which in all ages it has set before itself is union with God. In some sense, it is true, this is what not merely mysticism but all living religion strives after. But in a religion that moves in ethical and personal relations, such union is conceived as effected in the region of thought, feeling and will. To be one with God or with Christ is to think His thoughts, to love and to hate what He loves and hates, to act as He acts. Mysticism too in its nobler forms has included this in its conception. But—and herein lies its peculiarity—it regards the ethical and personal union as only preliminary to something deeper and more intimate. The mystic contemplates God's eternal being as the real substance of his own soul, and his own upward aspirations and endeavours as the motions of the universal Spirit. In the highest moments of his religious life all personal and moral relations, all "my, mine and me," are swallowed up in the rapturous consciousness of immediate contact with and absorption in the Deity. It is no longer himself that lives, but God. "If I am to know God directly," says Eckhart, "I must become completely He, and He I."

Now it is true that Paul's mysticism is not a God but a Christ mysticism. The conception of God as in the believer, or as the element of His life, hardly emerges. When he speaks of the believer as the temple of God, he explains this as meaning that the Spirit of God dwells in him—which is not a mystical thought. It has, however, to be remembered that for the Apostle Christ is in fact equivalent to God. And the union with Christ he contemplates has all the characters of that *unio mystica* which is the goal of mystic piety. Christ and the soul are no longer distinguishable. Christ has become the believer's life, and His archetypal experiences complete themselves automatically in the believer's soul. And as in all ages mystic piety has been combined with experiences of an ecstatic kind, so is it also in the case of Paul. He spoke with tongues, and he can tell of a vision in which he was caught up into paradise and heard unspeakable words, which it is not lawful for a man to utter (2 Cor. 12^2).

How the mystical union is related to faith Paul nowhere considers. The question in all probability never presented itself to him, for he can pass from the one to the other without betraying any sense of their difference. " I have been crucified with Christ; yet I live; and yet no longer I, but Christ liveth in me: and that life which I now live in the flesh I live in faith, the faith which is in the Son of God, who loved me, and gave Himself for me." Whether he regards the mystical union as established by baptism is a question that will be considered in our discussion of that sacrament.

How are we to account for this mystical strain in the religion of Paul? That it formed no part of his Hebrew or Jewish heritage may be taken as certain. To the Old Testament the idea of a divine indwelling or of a relation to God that transcends all personal relations is altogether foreign; and it is equally foreign to Jewish Apocalyptic. In the later Jewish writings we find mysticism only when, as in Philo, there has been influence from the side of Oriental religion. It is true that both the Old Testament and the literature of the later Judaism are familiar with the prophetic ecstasy and with the idea of an internal working of the Divine Spirit; but ecstasy is not treated as the culminating experience of religion, and that God by His Spirit acts on the human soul is not in itself a mystical thought. In the teaching of Jesus one will look for any mystical touch in vain. Jesus contemplates no closer relation to God than that of obedience, trust and moral likeness.   His piety is through and through a faith-piety.

Was Paul's mysticism, then, a creation of his own, an experience that came to him unmediated by any outside influence?   Fatal to that hypothesis is the fact, were there nothing else, that the Apostle shared it with believers who had not received their Christianity from his hands. Writing to the Roman Church, he assumes that the conception of a fellowship with Christ in His death and resurrection is one familiar to it.   "Are ye ignorant," he asks, "that all we who were baptized into Christ Jesus were baptized into His death?"

We are driven therefore to assume an influence that acted on the Church in general, and proceeded from a source outside both Judaism and the mother community in Jerusalem.   Such a source of mystical thought and feeling is known to us.   It is that of Hellenistic religion.

Time and again we have had occasion to refer to Hellenistic religion as affecting at vital points the structure of the Apostle's thought.   To this source we have traced the dualism he establishes between the flesh and the Spirit, his conception of Christ as Kyrios and as the Logos, and his concentration of the significance of Christ's historical life in the two cardinal events of the death and the resurrection. And in succeeding chapters, when we come to speak of his doctrine of regeneration, of pneumatic gifts and of the sacraments, it will be necessary to recur to it.   It may be well, therefore, at this point to give some account of Hellenistic religion not only on its mystical side, which is that which immediately concerns us, but as well in its general features.   Such an account, brief though it must necessarily be, may serve to link up the scattered allusions that have preceded; and it can be referred to in the chapters that follow.

Hellenistic religion stands out as the classical example

of syncretism. It was the product of an interchange of ideas and sentiments between the East and the West continued through many centuries. What the East—Asia Minor, Syria, Persia, Egypt—contributed was a highly characteristic type of religion, a type very different from that native to Greece and Rome. Unlike the faiths of these lands, Oriental religion, completely detached from the State and its interests, made its appeal to men not as citizens, but as individuals conscious of personal need and desirous of personal salvation. And further, its pre-occupation was not with the present life, but with a life beyond the grave. The great boon it offered was a blessed immortality. With respect to the present life and the existing world its view was deeply pessimistic. As material, the existing world is evil; and the soul is shut up in the body as in a prison-house, its connection with the material being the source of all its miseries. What redemption meant was deliverance from that bondage; and it was effected through a mysterious new birth in which the soul became itself a god. In its piety Oriental religion was ascetic, enthusiastic and mystical. It taught contempt for the things of the body, and found in ecstatic union with the divinity the crowning religious experience.

As early as the sixth century B.C. the Orphic and Dionysic cults had found their way from the East into Greece. Not, however, till the victories of Alexander the Great and the establishment of the Roman Imperium had levelled the barriers that separated peoples and races, did the invasion assume considerable proportions. From the second century B.C. onwards wave after wave of Oriental religion—the Phrygian Attis cult, the Syrian Adonis cult, the Egyptian Serapis cult and, last of all, the Mithras cult —swept over the Roman Empire, withdrawing in large measure the devotion of the masses from their ancestral divinities.

If the contribution of the East to the new religious era was a type of religion individualistic, otherworldly, orgiastic, dualistic, ascetic, redemptive, mystical, that of the West can be summed up in the word Greek philosophy. In the amalgamating process it was philosophy that took the initiative and that played the leading part. Already in Plato we see the process begun. His conception of the soul as a stranger from a higher realm immured in the body, his teaching with respect to immortality, his doctrine of an inspired madness that releases from the tyranny of custom and fills the soul with love and yearning for divine beauty must all be traced back to Oriental sources. The later Stoicism, as represented by Posidonius and Cornutus, shows further progress in the same direction. Allying itself with popular religion and, it must be added, with popular superstition, philosophy assumed a preponderatingly religious character. Belief in the gods was harmonised with a philosophical conception of the universe, the gods being interpreted by means of the allegorical method as aspects or manifestations of the one universal rational principle. It was thus that conceptions like the Logos and the Nous, identified now with Hermes or again with the Egyptian Thoth, received the half-mythological character which they bear in Hellenistic thought. Of the earlier Hellenistic religious philosophy or gnosis the classical example is provided by the Alexandrine Jew Philo. Much as Philo borrowed from Plato, from the Stoics and from the Old Testament, his cardinal religious ideas are at bottom Oriental. To the same stream belong the Hermetic writings, the many Gnostic sects and the Neoplatonic philosophy.

Hellenistic gnosis represents, however, only one of the two lines of syncretistic development. If philosophy was permeated by Oriental religion, it is also true that the Oriental cults were to some extent modified in their turn

by contact with Greek thought. It was as partially
Hellenised that they conquered the West. How far the
Hellenising went beyond a mere elimination of elements
offensive to Western feeling is not easy to say. Certainly
their Oriental character was not materially altered. We
may take it perhaps that the gnosis associated with the
mysteries of the various cults, when it was more than a
knowledge of mere magic formulas and passwords, was
borrowed from the religious philosophy rather than
developed from within.

In attempting to describe with some detail the cardinal
features of Hellenistic religion we shall draw on both
streams—that of the religious philosophy and that of the
Cults.

Already in an earlier chapter we have referred to the
significance attached by the Cults to the myth of a god
who died and rose again. In their public festivals, which
were celebrated annually and lasted some thirteen days,
the death and resurrection of the saviour-god—Attis,
Serapis, Adonis, etc.—were dramatically exhibited before
the eyes of the assembled worshippers with every circumstance that could touch the imagination and excite the
feelings. The worshippers on their part followed the
spectacle with frenzied demonstrations now of grief and
again of joy, the devotees of Attis sometimes carrying their
sympathy to the point of imitating the god in his act of
self-mutilation. We read of an Attis celebration in
which the image of the god was first buried and then,
when the lamentation was at its height, brought out of the
grave, a light being at the same moment kindled. Having
anointed the lips of the worshippers with holy oil, the priest
pronounced over them the consoling words, " Take courage,
ye pious ones, your god is saved ; so shall ye also be
saved from your trials." [1]

[1] Hepding, *Attis, seine Mythen und sein Kult*, p. 167.

But far more important for an understanding of Cult religion than these public rites are the rites to which none were admitted save those who had passed through a severe probation and taken an oath of secrecy. This secret worship was known by the name of the Mysteries, and those who took part in it were called mystics (μύσται). Every cult had its Mysteries; we read of the Mysteries of Orpheus, Cybele, Isis, Mithras and many more. In them the popular rites and beliefs were refined and elaborated; and they may be taken as representing the faith of the more earnest and enlightened followers of the Oriental gods. To Apuleius we are indebted for a graphic descrip-tion of the chief Mystery rite, that of initiation, as it was practised in the Mysteries of the Egyptian goddess Isis.[1] The description belongs to the middle of the second century A.D., but the ceremonies of which it tells are of course much older. The candidate Lucius is represented as earnestly and often beseeching the high priest that his desire for initiation should be fulfilled. But the high priest restrains his impatience, and requires him to wait sub-missively for the sign of the goddess' will. To approach her unbidden might entail the penalty of death. "For the portals of the nether world," he admonishes him, "and the guardianship of salvation are in the hands of the goddess, and the initiation itself is solemnised as the symbol of a voluntary death (*ad instar voluntariæ mortis*), and a salvation given in answer to prayer. For the god-dess is wont to choose such as, having fulfilled a course of life, stand at the very threshold of the departing light, to whom nevertheless the great mysteries of religion can be entrusted. And after they have been by her providence in a sense born again (*quodam modo renatos*), she places them again in the course of a new life in salvation." Not till after repeated instructions and a prolonged discipline

[1] Metamorphosis XI.

of prayer and fasting is Lucius' desire gratified. Covered
with a coarse linen cloth, he is taken by the hand and
led into the most holy place. What happens there?
Lucius, who is made to tell the story, draws a veil over
the scene. It is not permissible to disclose its secrets.
But he consents to give a certain symbolical description
of his experiences. " I penetrated," he says, " the boundaries
of death; I trod the threshold of Proserpine, and after
being borne through all the elements I returned to earth;
at midnight I beheld the sun radiating white light; I came
into the presence of the gods below and the gods above,
and did them reverence close at hand."

After his initiation, Lucius is arrayed in the robe of
Olympus; a flaming torch is put in his hand and a crown
of spotless palm on his head. In this guise, "set up like
the image of a god," he is exhibited to the people, and
receives from them religious homage. The account ends
with Lucius' impressive prayer of thanksgiving to the goddess, reproduced probably from some liturgy. " Thou
who are the holy and eternal saviour of mankind, ever
bountiful to the mortals who cherish thee, thou bestowest
thy gracious mother love upon the wretched in their
misfortunes. No day . . . no brief moment ever passes
without thy benefits. On land and sea thou watchest
over men and holdest out to them thy saving right
hand, dispelling the storms of life. Thou dost undo the
hopelessly ravelled threads of fate and dost alleviate the
tempests of Fortune and restrainest the hurtful courses
of the stars. . . . As for me, my spirit is too feeble to
render thee worthy praise, and my possessions too small
to bring thee fitting sacrifices. I have no fluency of speech
to put in words that which I feel of thy majesty. . . .
Therefore will I essay to do that which alone a poor but
pious worshipper can : thy divine countenance and thy
most holy presence will I hide within the shrine of my

9

heart : there will I guard thee, and continually keep thee before my spirit."[1]

This highly important document, written evidently from inside knowledge, may serve as a starting-point for our discussion. We begin with the conception of redemption or regeneration.

The drama enacted before the eyes of the candidate for initiation was in all probability substantially that of the public celebration. Scenes from the history of the god, particularly his death and resurrection, were impressively presented.[2] To such scenes Lucius' veiled reference points. They had as their purpose to work on the feelings of the neophyte. Under their influence he passed through a real religious experience. With respect to the interpretation put on the experience we are not left in doubt. It was a repetition of that of the god. The neophyte died with the god to his material and mortal existence, and rose with him to a new life divine and immortal. As the priest in Apuleius' account says, the initiation is solemnised as the symbol of a voluntary death, and the initiates are by the providence of the goddess in a sense born again. To the same effect is a passage in the so-called Mithras Liturgy. " Gaze upon the god," so the neophyte is instructed, " and greet him thus : Hail, Lord, ruler of the water . . . potentate of the spirit, born again I depart life (πάλιν γενόμενος ἀπογίγνομαι), being the while exalted ; and having been exalted I die : born of the birth which is the parent of life, dissolved in death (or released into death) I go the way as thou hast appointed it for a law and created the sacrament."[3]

In the Taurobolium, another initiation rite which

----

[1] The translation is Dr. Kennedy's, *St. Paul and the Mystery Religions*, pp. 100 ff.

[2] Anrich, *Das antike Mysterienwesen*, p. 30. De Jong, *Das antike Mysterienwesen*, p. 30.

[3] Dieterich, *Eine Mithrasliturgie*, p. 14.

obtained wide currency, similar ideas were embodied. To the accompaniment of a dirge the neophyte descended into a latticed pit as into a grave. Above him a steer was killed; and when he emerged bespattered with the sacrificial blood, he was greeted as a god. He was *renatus in æternum,* born again into eternity.

No less than the Cults the religious philosophy bears witness to this idea of a regenerative change. Philo's prophetic intelligence through which alone a man is capable of knowing God and exercising worship is the product of a spiritual and mysterious birth.[1] In the Hermetic writings the need for regeneration (παλιγγενεσία) is strongly emphasised. A passage quoted by Dr. Kennedy,[2] tells how Tat became the subject of such a transformation. Set free from the twelve evil propensities, and endowed with the ten divine powers, he can say of himself, " My spirit is illumined. . . . To thee, O God, author of my new creation, I, Tat, offer spiritual sacrifices."

Regeneration as conceived in Hellenistic religion went far beyond anything that can be described in terms of psychology. The moral element, at least in the case of the Cults, when contemplated at all was in the background. The vital thing was that a man became a partaker of the divine nature. Lucius, as we have seen, on the completion of his initiation was greeted as a god. In the Compagno tablet the neophyte receives the assurance, " Happy and blessed one, thou shalt be god instead of mortal." Usually he assumed the god's name. The Attis mystic became himself an Attis. " Methought in a dream that I had become Attis, and that the festival of the so-called Hilaria was fulfilled to me by the great mother, which manifested the salvation from Hades which had become ours." [3]

---

[1] Bréhier, *Les idées philosophiques et religieuses de Philon d'Alexandrie,* p. 246.
[2] *Op. cit.* p. 107.
[3] Quoted by Bousset from Damaskios, *Kyrios Christos,* p. 150.

Frequently the process is described as one of deification (θεωθῆναι, ἀποθεωθῆναι). One may doubt, however, if much more was meant than that transformation from mortal to immortal substance which Athanasius had in view in his famous formula, " God became man that man might become God."

From the subject of regeneration we turn to that of mystical union. The two are closely connected, for in general the second is regarded as the condition and cause of the first.

We have seen that in the public festivals of the Cult gods the worshippers accompanied the drama with frenzied demonstrations of sympathy. What was the idea behind this orgiastic outburst? Undoubtedly it was that of union with the divinity. Always the primitive interpretation of ecstasy was this, that a god had entered into the man, that the man was god-possessed, ἔνθεος.[1] Thus united with the god, the worshipper would regard himself as sharing, like the neophyte in the initiation rite, the god's experiences of death and resurrection. " As truly as Osiris lives," so runs an Egyptian text, " he also shall live: as truly as Osiris is not dead shall he not die: as truly as Osiris is not destroyed shall he not be destroyed." The purpose of the sacred drama alike in the public rites and in the Mysteries was to excite the ecstasy in which the mystic union was consummated.

In this interpretation of ecstasy as the sign of divine possession we have the primitive root of all mystical conceptions of the relation of the human soul to God. But already in Hellenistic religion the primitive notion of the mystical union is subjected to important modifications. We can trace three lines of development.

In the first place we find a strain of thought in which the divine indwelling appears not as the mere experience

[1] Rohde, *Psyche*, II. 11 ff.

of a rapturous moment, but as an abiding condition. Lucius' prayer of thanksgiving ends with the words: " Thy divine countenance and thy most holy presence will I hide within the shrine of my heart ; there will I guard thee, and continually keep thee before my spirit." " Abide with me in my soul, forsake me not," is the petition of the mystic of the Mithras Liturgy.[1] To the same effect is a prayer found in a Greek papyrus: "Come to me, O Lord Hermes, as the fœtus into the womb of woman."[2] Sometimes the *unio mystica* is pushed to the point of identity : " Thou art I, and I am thou (σὺ γὰρ ἐγὼ καὶ ἐγὼ σύ)."[3] Side by side with this we set three passages from the Hermetic literature.[4] " Thy name and spirit are upon the good. Enter into my mind and my heart all the days of my life and fulfil all the desires of my soul. For thou art I, and I thou ; what I say may it always come to pass. For thy name I hold as a charm in my heart, and no menacing hand shall have power over me, and on account of thy name which I hold in my soul no spirit or demon or phantom or any other evil presence from Hades shall rise up against me." " I know thee, Hermes, and thou me. I am thou, and thou I." " Thy name is mine, and mine is thine. I am thy image." One can see that the experience of God's presence in the soul has in large measure been loosed from its primitive connection with the ecstatic rapture and has come to be regarded as a normal feature of piety.

The second line of mystical development shows a more radical breach with the past. In this case the notion of ecstasy is retained, but it is interpreted from the standpoint of a metaphysical opposition between the body and the soul, the material and the spiritual. Leaving the

---

[1] P. 14. [2] Kennedy, *op. cit.* p. 201.
[3] Dieterich, *Eine Mithrasliturgie*, p. 97.
[4] Reitzenstein, *Poimandres*, pp. 17, 20, 21.

material world far beneath him, the ecstatic wings his way into the intelligible world, the region of immortal light, where the soul comes face to face with the divine. "Where the knowledge and vision (γνῶσις καὶ θέα) of the divine light is attained, all the bodily senses are lulled into silence."[1] Of this sort is the vision of the mystic in the Mithras Liturgy. "For to-day I, a mortal born of mortal womb, exalted by almighty power and incorruptible right hand, with immortal eyes shall behold by immortal spirit the immortal æon and lord of the crowns of fire—I who have been sanctified by sacred rites, while for a little my natural human faculties stay behind, which I shall again resume, having been severed from defilement with respect to the present bitter fate that weighs me down. . . . For it is not possible for me, a mortal born, to rise up on high to the golden splendours of the immortal light. Stand still, my corruptible human nature, and relieve me with respect to the inexorable and crushing weakness."

This mode of conceiving ecstasy as a supersensible and superrational apprehension of the divine has as its correlate a transcendent conception of God. God is no longer thought of in a personal way, but as the Being that lies beyond all rational determinations. Union with Him is therefore something inexpressible. It is effected through a gnosis in which the knower in some mysterious way becomes one with what is known. Such a conception of the relation of the soul to the divine meets us in Philo—to know the Logos the soul must become one with the Logos, to know the ineffable God, one with Him—in the Fourth Gospel, and also here and there in the Hermetic writings.

In the third line along which the mystical idea developed the conception of divine possession was rationalised, being interpreted in terms of the Stoic philosophy. When Seneca declares, "God is nigh thee, God is with thee, God is with-

[1] *Corpus Hermetic.* x. 4.

in thee," " a holy spirit dwells within us to mark our evil and good," what he means is that our rational nature is a spark or manifestation of the universal reason that penetrates and orders the universe. From the same standpoint a still later Stoic, Marcus Aurelius, speaks of God as the Being from whom and in whom and unto whom are all things (ἐκ σοῦ πάντα, ἐν σοὶ πάντα, εἰς σὲ πάντα). Wherever a Pantheistic metaphysic is made the basis of religion this mystical feeling for the One in the many, the Eternal in the temporal, the Infinite in the finite, is the form which piety assumes.

Among the most characteristic conceptions of Hellenistic religion is that of GNOSIS. Every Mystery Cult had its secret knowledge which it imparted to its initiates. Such knowledge consisted in part at least in an interpretation of the inner meaning of its ritual, the interpretation amounting probably to a more or less developed theory of the universe and man's place in it. Hippolytus, one of the Church Fathers, tells us that the Gnostic sect of the Naassenes " frequent the so-called Mysteries of the Great Mother, thinking that through what is performed there they see clearly the whole mystery."[1] The Mystery gnosis was not, however, all of this character. Much of it consisted in mere magical formulas and passwords designed to secure a safe passage for the soul after death in its ascent through the planetary spheres to the realm of light. The papyri and the Mithras Liturgy supply us with copious examples of these dubious instruments of salvation.

Where Hellenistic gnosis reached its full development was not, however, in the Cults—there it was overshadowed by ritual and sacrament—but in the religious philosophy, if such a name can be applied to the strange mixture of mythology, theosophy and rational principles in which for the most part it consisted. The following prayer, quoted

[1] *Refutation of all Heresies*, book v. chap. iv.

by Reitzenstein from the papyrus Mimaut, will indicate the place which gnosis occupied in Hellenistic religion and also something of its character:[1] "We render thee thanks, Most High, for by thy grace we have received this light of knowledge (γνῶσις), namely, the unutterable name honoured by the appellation, God, and blessed by the invocation, Father. For to all men and women thou hast exhibited a fatherly goodwill and affection and friendship and most sweet influence. For thou hast graciously bestowed upon us mind, reason, knowledge (νοῦν, λόγον γνῶσιν)—mind that we may know thee, reason that we may take account of thee, knowledge that having discerned thee we may rejoice. Having been saved by thee, we rejoice, for thou hast fully shown thyself to us. We rejoice that thou hast made us, while in bodies, to be partakers in the divine nature (ἐν σώμσιν ἡμᾶς ὄντας ἀπεθέωσας) through the vision of thyself. Thanks of man be to thee for our knowledge of thy greatness. We have known thee, O light discernible, by intelligence alone: we have known thee, O life of man's life: we have known thee, O fertile womb of all things. Having worshipped thee, we have asked no boon of thy goodness except this—be pleased to preserve us in the knowledge of thyself, be entreated that we should not be turned aside from this way of life."

From this prayer it is clear that the knowledge which makes man a partaker of the divine nature is no product of philosophical speculation, but a gift of Heaven. To the human understanding God is inaccessible, an unknown God; but He desires to be known, and reveals Himself through inner revelation. In the Hellenistic age philosophy had fallen into discredit; the conflict of opinions had undermined faith in the ability of human reason to reach truth, and men sought for a surer word. This craving Hellenistic religion in its fashion met.

[1] *Die hellenistischen Mysterienreligionen*, p. 113.

For the reception of the saving knowledge the typical condition is ecstasy; illumination comes as an ecstatic vision. "The knowledge and vision of God," says a passage in the Hermetic writings already quoted, "involves the silence and abeyance of all the senses. For he who perceives this can perceive nothing else. . . . Forgetting all bodily perceptions and movements he keeps still." We also read of the gift of gnosis as following a baptism in the νοῦς or Spirit.[1] If ecstasy in the strict sense is not always presupposed, there is always the idea of a detachment of the mind from the visible and temporal and an ascent to the world of pure intelligence. We can thus understand why ascetic discipline should usually appear as an indispensable preparation for the mystic vision: the soul must cut itself loose from its entanglement in the things of sense.

With respect to its content, gnosis supplied some sort of answer to the great religious questions as they presented themselves to the thought of that age. Two such questions stand out above all others. The first relates to the origin of the existing order of things. A metaphysical and moral dualism between spirit and matter being assumed, it is asked, how account for the creation of the evil material world, above all how account for the fact that the human soul, whose true home is elsewhere, finds itself entangled in that world? This question is preliminary to the second: by what means can the soul be delivered from its bondage and win its way back to the intelligible world to which it properly belongs? For our present purpose it is unnecessary to linger over the fantastic myths and the hypotheses of creation by powers lower than the highest through which the attempt is made to solve the riddle of the universe. What concerns us is the answer given to the second question, which is that gnosis itself is the way of salvation.

[1] Norden, *Agnostos Theos*, p. 102.

The supreme importance thus attached to gnosis is one of the most outstanding features of Hellenistic religion. A passage in the Hermetic writings defines piety as "the knowledge of God," and another declares that in this alone is salvation for man.[1]   If we ask how precisely gnosis is effective for salvation it would no doubt be a partial answer to say that it is "a way of life."   It instructs a man with respect to the true nature of the soul—its origin, its bondage, its destiny; it points him to God as the goal of his being, and shows him how by mortification of the flesh and a life of virtue he may tread the upward path.   All this, however, conducts only to the threshold of the inner shrine. What works the regenerative change is not instruction and not self-mortification and virtue—these are only preparatory —it is immediate contact or mystical union with the ineffable God.   Gnosis culminates in the ecstatic vision ($\theta \acute{\epsilon} a$) in which the soul touching the divine receives the "powers" of God and is itself divinised.   "That which is beheld illumines the whole inner life, drawing the soul out from the body and transforming it into $o\mathring{v}\sigma\acute{\iota}a$ (the divine supersensible substance).[2]   The place given to gnosis in Hellenistic religion can be understood only when we keep in view its connection with the mystic vision; and it is in the light of this connection that we must interpret the statement in the Hermetic writings : " This is the blessed issue for those who have attained gnosis, that they are transformed into the divine ($\theta \epsilon \omega \theta \hat{\eta} \nu a\iota$)."   From Dr. Kennedy we quote the account of a dialogue between Hermes and his son Tat on the subject of regeneration and the manner in which it is effected.   Tat reminds his father that he had told him that no one could be saved without regeneration.   Regeneration was only possible to one who had cut himself loose from the world.   Tat has renounced the world and entreats his father, who has himself been regenerated, to

---

[1] *Corpus Hermet.* x. 4, x. 15.   [2] *Ibid.* x. 4.

communicate the secret. Hermes replies that this must be a revelation to the heart by the divine will. By the mercy of God he had seen an immaterial vision inwardly, and had passed out through his body into an immortal body. He is no longer what he was. While Hermes speaks, Tat becomes conscious of a transformation. He is set free from the twelve evil propensities, which are replaced by the ten powers of God. He can now declare: " My spirit is illumined. . . . To thee, O God, author of my new creation, I, Tat, offer spiritual sacrifices. O God and Father, thou art the Lord, thou art the Spirit, accept from me the spiritual sacrifices which thou desirest ! " [1]

We come in the last place to the subject of SACRA-MENTS. Neither in Philo nor in the Hermetic literature does ritual play any real part; the one way to redemption lies through gnosis. But in the Mystery Cults it is other-wise. There the notion of salvation through gnosis is not indeed absent, but it is overshadowed by that of salvation through sacraments and magic formulas.

The initiation rite itself was a sacrament, and that in the strictest sense, a sacrament of regeneration. It is true that it could be interpreted allegorically, and that it was designed to excite the ecstatic rapture in which union with the god was effected; but neither of these view-points nor both taken together exhausted its significance. That an *ex opere operato* virtue was ascribed to it may be taken as certain, the precise mode of its action being probably left in obscurity. The sacramental character of the blood-bath of the Taurobolium from which the neophyte emerged a new creature, " reborn into eternity," lies on the surface.

The Cults had also their regularly recurring sacra-mental meals. " Chairemon," we read in a papyrus, " invites

[1] *Op. cit.* p. 107.

you to dinner at the table of the Lord Serapis, in the
Serapæum, to-morrow." While these meals would serve a
social end, bringing the members of the cult together, the
fellowship with one another would have as its basis a
common fellowship with the god. How precisely communion with the god was thought of as mediated is a
question not easy to answer. Dr. Kennedy's suggestion
that the participant looked upon himself as the table
companion of the god, who presided as host, fails to
do justice to the mystical character of Mystery religion.
Founding on certain primitive religious rites in which the
animal representative of the god was devoured, Dieterich [1]
and Heitmüller [2] contend for the view that in the Cult
meal the worshipper sought to unite himself with the
god by feeding upon him. That such an interpretation
may turn out to be correct is not impossible, but
certainly no definite proof has so far been produced in
its favour.

Among the Mystery sacraments lustration or baptism
has also to be numbered. To such a rite Lucius sub-
mitted prior to his initiation. The water would be regarded
as a mystic means of purification, and there is evidence to
show that the all-dominating idea of regeneration was also
connected with it.

In concluding this sketch it must be said that what
we have tried to reproduce is Hellenistic religion in its
general features rather than any particular cult or system
in which it found expression. It is just those general
features that must chiefly come into consideration in any
attempt to estimate Paul's indebtedness to it. That the
sources from which we have drawn represent different strata
and belong to different dates, often later than that of the
Apostle, is not really a valid objection; for the various

---

[1] *Eine Mithrasliturgie*, p. 100.
[2] *Taufe und Abendmahl bei Paulus*, p. 40.

Cults and systems, with whatever difference in detail, all conformed to the same type; and if we must reckon with the fact of development, it can be added that the type remained substantially unaltered.

There are points in the foregoing account—the conception of regeneration and of the sacraments, for example —to which we shall have to return later; our immediate concern is with the mystical side of Hellenistic religion. Does Hellenistic mysticism exhibit affinities with that of Paul close enough to warrant us in regarding it as the source of the Apostle's inspiration?

As we have seen, the Pauline mysticism moves in two great conceptions—that of death and resurrection with Christ, and that of Christ's presence and activity within the soul of the believer. With respect to the first of these it has to be admitted that nowhere is the Pauline formula to be found in any pagan source. Nowhere is it said that the neophyte dies and rises with the Cult divinity. None the less, every element in the conception was undoubtedly familiar to the pagan world of Paul's day. Both in the Cult festivals and in the Mystery initiation, the worshipper followed the drama of the god's death and resurrection with a rapture of responsive feeling; and there are the strongest reasons for believing that he looked upon this rapture as the occasion or the sign of union with the god. And in the Mysteries, as in Paul, the result of the experience was a radical transformation: the believer died to his mortal life and was reborn as a child of eternity. In both cases, moreover, the experience stood in close connection with a sacrament—in the one case with the sacrament of initiation, in the other with that of baptism (Rom. $6^{3ff.}$). These are no casual resemblances; and it is impossible to resist the conclusion that in this matter the Apostle was a debtor to the pagan religion of his time.

It may be remarked that the idea of death and resurrection with Christ was not taken up by the Church generally. In the New Testament, outside the Pauline Epistles, we find only one solitary echo—" It is a faithful saying: For if we be dead with Him, we shall also live with Him " (2 Tim. 2¹¹).

The second conception of the Pauline mysticism—Christ in the believer—has also its parallel in Hellenistic religion. There too the mystical union is sometimes conceived as a divine indwelling. And on the authority of Reitzenstein we may add, that in pagan literature as in Paul the expressions to enter into God, to be in God, and to receive the Holy Spirit or God into the soul interchange with one another.[1] Paul, however, nowhere pushes the mystical union to the point of identity, as the Attis and Serapis mystic did. Nowhere does he say, " I am Christ, and Christ is I "; his assertion, " For me to live is Christ," falls far short of this. From such a mode of expression his reverence and sobriety restrain him.

That Paul, a native of a Greek city and a traveller whose journeys led him through Syria, Asia Minor and Macedonia, had ample opportunity of making himself acquainted with pagan religion hardly needs to be insisted on. As a proof of his familiarity with the Mystery Cults appeal might be made to his not infrequent use of their distinctive terminology. Words like μυστήριον (mystery), τέλειοι (those fully initiated), μυεῖσθαι (to learn the secrets imparted in the Mysteries), ἐμβατεύειν (to enter the higher stages of initiation), γνῶσις (knowledge), ψυχικός (psychic), πνευματικός (spiritual), had come to carry mystery associations; and the Apostle could scarcely have employed them in the way he does without being aware of the fact (1 Cor. 2²⁻¹⁰, Col. 1²⁵, 1 Cor. 2⁶, Phil. 3¹⁰ 4¹², Col. 2³, 1 Cor. 15⁴⁶).

[1] *H.M.R.* p. 45.

But the decisive proof of his acquaintance with Hellenistic religion does not lie in his vocabulary, but in the fact that almost everywhere his thought bears unmistakable marks of its influence. Mysticism was in the air he breathed, and he could absorb it without being conscious of its ultimate source.

All this, however, is not to be taken as meaning that the mysticism of Paul is on the same level with that of the Mystery Cults or the Hermetic writings. In absorbing it the Apostle in large measure transformed it. The chief thing is this, that he suffused it with the ethical spirit of Hebrew piety. To describe Hellenistic mysticism as morally indifferent would certainly be unjust, as witness the following quotation from the Hermetic writings : " I mind (νοῦς) myself am present with holy men and good, the pure and merciful, men who live piously. To such my presence doth become an aid, and straightway they gain knowledge of all things and win the Father's love by their pure lives and give him thanks." [1] But in general what union with the Deity signifies for Hellenistic religion is summed up in the word Immortality. For Paul also immortality is a vital interest ; only, in his case it is an interest inseparable from that of moral renewal and moral fellowship with God. If death and resurrection with Christ means for him a transformation from the corruptible to the incorruptible, it means still more fundamentally a transformation from unrighteousness to righteousness. And the indwelling Christ, whom he recognises as the life of his life, is no half-ethicised nature-power like the saviour-gods of the Cults, nor a pale abstraction like the Hermetic νοῦς. He is the embodiment of the highest religious and moral ideal.

Mysticism was not introduced into the Church by Paul. He found it already established and in a form, if we may

[1] Mead, *Thrice Greatest Hermes*, II. 4.

judge from his references to it in Rom. 7, but too like that which prevailed outside. That he baptized it into Christianity, made of it something genuinely Christian, must be judged one of his greatest achievements.

What is the permanent value of the Pauline mysticism? In its original form, as a Christ-mysticism, it can scarcely be said to be any longer living, unless indeed as a dogma in minds that fail to understand its true meaning. Who to-day distinguishes between the presence and activity of the risen Christ within the soul and the presence and activity of the Holy Spirit or of God? The mysticism of to-day, like that of the Middle Ages, is a God-mysticism. Is it not, however, the case that the association of mystical religion with Christ is the one effective guarantee of its Christian character? Our modern world is familiar with a mysticism—Rabindranath Tagore is its most recent representative—that seeks immediate contact not with the God of grace, but with the God of nature. Far be it from us to contest its right and value. At the same time it must be said that no mysticism has a title to be called Christian in which the Eternal Spirit, whose presence is recognised in the workings of nature or in the inner motions of the soul, is not one with the God whom Jesus reveals.

But has mysticism of any description a valid title to a place in our Christian religion? Certainly the claim sometimes made for it, that it represents a more intense and spiritual piety than the Hebrew type, must be unhesitatingly rejected. The *unio mystica* of its aspiration is far from being a deeper or more intimate relation to God than the ethical and personal relations of trust and obedience in which the piety of Jesus moves. Nevertheless, it must be conceded that Christian mysticism has proved its vitality by its constant resurgence. It will never, one may confidently affirm, become the dominant type of piety, never be more than the piety of a circle. But its circle it will always have. Always there will be those for whom religion means above all else a feeling for the universal Spirit that touches them in the great universe and that manifests its presence in the secret motions of their own soul.

CHAPTER II.

JUSTIFICATION.

GREAT and wonderful is the salvation, as Paul conceives it, in which through his faith the believer becomes a partaker. It is not only that he obtains assurance of deliverance in the day of wrath and of an inheritance in the Kingdom that is to come. All the conditions of his present life are revolutionised, and he himself is made nothing less than a new creature. He enters into a new relation to God. Delivered from the terrors of the Law, he can look up to God as a God of grace, and with the confidence of a son commit his life to the divine Providence. No longer need he tremble before the might of the demons; in Christ's keeping he knows himself safe. The world with all its fell powers lies behind and beneath him. Through the Cross the world has been crucified unto him, and he unto the world. And within the depths of his being he has experienced a renewing change. The law of the Spirit of life in Christ Jesus has made him free from the law of sin and of death; and his life is no longer an unavailing struggle with the flesh, but a free and glad service of righteousness and God. We can say that he has passed from the old age into the new, from the kingdom of darkness into the kingdom of light. With respect to his outer life, it is true, the evil age still in some sense obtains. For a brief transition period he must consent to endure the buffetings of Satan and carry about with him the burden of his mortal and sinful flesh. But inwardly he is emancipated ; even now his citizenship is in heaven.

In nothing is Paul's greatness more evident than in the rich and to a considerable extent new content he introduces into the idea of salvation. To him there was given an experience of extraordinary range and intensity, and what was also indispensable for his task, the ability to bring it to utterance.

In the Epistles to the Romans and the Galatians Justification stands in the very foreground as the great gift offered by the gospel. In the fact that the gospel reveals to men the one way to justification the Apostle sees the secret of its power. The prominence of the conception in these Epistles is doubtless in part due to the central position it had assumed in the controversy with the Judaisers. But certainly not altogether. Justification represents a vital element in the Apostle's religion ; and if the term is of less frequent occurrence in the later Epistles, written when the legal controversy had died down, what it stands for is by no means forgotten (Phil. 3^9, Col. 1^{14}).

What Paul means by justification and its equivalent " the righteousness of God " is scarcely any longer a matter of dispute. We are to think not of a process of inward renewal, but of a judicial sentence. The believer is acquitted at God's judgment bar, declared to be just or righteous and invested with the splendid heritage which such a verdict carries with it (Gal. 3, Rom. 3-4). Everywhere justification is opposed to condemnation, and this must be regarded as decisive with respect to its forensic meaning. That the idea is connected with that of judgment might lead one to suppose that it must be regarded as having a primarily eschatological reference. But this would be a mistake. From the first, the question relates to the believer's present standing before God. The believer is justified even now, has peace with God now; and Paul can distinguish between this all-determining fact and salvation in the day of wrath. " Much more then, being now justified by His blood, shall we be saved from the wrath of God through Him. For if, while we were enemies, we were reconciled to God through the death of His Son, much more, being reconciled, shall we be saved by His life "—saved by Him, *i.e.* as the living Lord (Rom. 5$^{9f.}$, 1 Thess. 5^9).

Of the justifying verdict the grand feature is that it is given not in accordance with the facts, but in the teeth of the facts, God crediting the believer with a righteousness he is far from possessing. Paul does not shrink from the assertion that He justifies the ungodly; and in this paradox he sees the wonder and glory of the transaction (Rom. 4^5). In so acting, God is moved by pure grace. It is His gracious and sovereign will to justify the believer, and the believer receives justification from His hands as an unmerited gift (Rom. 3–5). That the Almighty can thus disregard the principle of recompense embodied in the Law, acquitting those whom the Law condemns, has its ground in the redemptive work of Christ. Christ having brought the Law's reign to an end, God is no longer bound by it, but is free to act in accordance with the dictates of His love.

Though justification is a free gift, it is not bestowed unconditionally. Only those obtain it who believe in Christ. Paul's demonstration of the title of faith to have such significance attached to it is developed in opposition to the legal views that were current not only in Judaism, but also in a section of the Church itself. His first care is to demolish his opponents' position, and this he finds a simple enough matter. If recompense, as he credits them with maintaining, is the sole principle to which God has respect in deciding a man's fate, if a man can be justified only when he has earned the verdict by a perfectly blame-less life, then must justification lie for ever beyond his reach. From the beginning of time until now there is no one who has not sinned and fallen short of the glory of God. " By the works of the Law," so Paul declares, summing up his criticism of legalism, " shall no flesh be justified in God's sight " (Rom. 3^{20}).

The positive side of his demonstration the Apostle finds to be a matter of much greater difficulty, and he essays various lines. He appeals to the fact that God has placed His seal upon faith by bestowing on the believer the gift of the Spirit and the power to work miracles (Gal. 3^5). He appeals to the witness of the Law and the Prophets: " Abraham believed God, and it was reckoned to him for righteousness " (Gal. 3$^{6ff.}$, Rom. 4). This Old Testament passage suggests to him the forensic idea of imputation, and he makes a passing attempt, which is not to be taken too seriously, to connect faith with justification in a forensic scheme: " To him that worketh not, but believeth on Him who justifieth the ungodly, his faith is reckoned for righteous-ness " (Rom. 4^5). But why should God accept faith as an equivalent for righteousness? In his glowing eulogy of the faith of Abraham, the Apostle is brought to the brink of the idea that it is because of its religious worth. It would then appear as a new and better work. The Apostle, however, has no real intention of regarding it in this light. In general, he opposes faith not merely to legal, but to all works (Rom. 4^{22}). We may remark in this con-nection that though the idea of vicarious merit was not unknown in Judaism, Paul nowhere speaks of God as imputing to the believer the righteousness of Christ. His only use of the imputation idea is the one just noted.

But the Apostle has a better reason for making justi-fication contingent on faith than any yet given. He shows that faith alone corresponds with the character of justification as an act of free and sovereign grace. Bearing this character, it cannot be earned by works of righteousness, but only believed in and humbly and thankfully accepted (Rom. 4⁵, Gal. 3¹⁸).

The central meaning of Paul's doctrine of justification by faith is sufficiently obvious. It is nothing else than the familiar truth that God forgives sin, and that forgiveness cannot be earned but only appropriated in faith. And the Apostle himself is not unaware of this fact. He can quote the Psalmist's words, " Blessed are they whose iniquities are forgiven," as a proof of the blessedness of the man to whom God reckoneth righteousness apart from works, and can speak of redemption as consisting in the forgiveness of sins (Rom. 4⁷, Col. 1¹⁴).

How then, it may be asked, did he come to employ phraseology so ill adapted to express the idea in his mind? for that the terms, justification, righteousness of God, obscure rather than illustrate the nature of forgiveness few now would deny. For one thing, they clothe with a form of legality an act which from a legal standpoint is unintelligible. And further, they involve an abuse of language which was bound to lead, and did as a matter of fact lead, to grave misunderstanding. To justify or pronounce blameless is one thing, to forgive sin quite another; and neither in the Old Testament nor in Jewish literature are the two phrases ever treated as synonymous (cf. Prov. 17¹⁵). In employing the first with the meaning of the second the Apostle was flying in the face of established usage; and we cannot wonder if Jewish opponents, hearing him declare that God justifies the ungodly, regarded the assertion as flat blasphemy, or, if they understood his real drift, as mere juggling with words.

The usual explanation given of the Apostle's use of legal terminology is a reference to his rabbinical past. He

brought with him into Christianity his old modes of
thought. But this, if he broke with established usage,
explains nothing. The real explanation is his endeavour
to set the Law and the Gospel over-against each other in
as antithetical a way as possible, and to confound his
Jewish opponents on their own ground. For a Jew the
great thing was to obtain by a scrupulous observance of
the Law the justifying sentence of God, to be adjudged
righteous. In contrasting the Gospel with Jewish legalism
Paul adopts the terminology of the latter, but reads into it
an entirely new meaning. That everything depends on a
man's righteousness, on his being justified, he concedes ;
and claims that the believer in Christ has reached this goal
and that none other can. The believer is clothed with
righteousness, only that righteousness proceeds not from
himself but from God ; he is justified, only not on the
ground of his own merits, but by an act of divine grace.
What the Jew was vainly seeking, the believer through his
faith holds as an assured possession.

In describing the believer's new standing before God,
Paul also makes use of the idea of adoption. Redeemed
from the Law, the believer is elevated from the status of
a slave to that of a son and becomes heir to the
inheritance of salvation (Gal. 4^{1-7}). Like justification,
adoption is a forensic idea, and indeed the two are hardly
distinguishable.

Of no small importance in its bearing on the character
of the Apostle's piety is the question whether he thinks of
justification or forgiveness as a thing continually repeated
throughout the course of the believer's life, or whether he
does not rather limit its significance to the initial act in
which his pre-baptismal sins are purged away and he
receives his Christian standing. Accustomed as we are to
the idea that we daily sin and daily need forgiveness, it is
difficult for us to believe that the Apostle could have

entertained any other.   But there are considerations that make us pause.

It cannot indeed be said that Paul shuts his eyes to the fact of sin in the life of the Christian.   In most of his Epistles we find him dealing with it by rebuke, warning and exhortation.   What we do miss, however, is a clear recognition of forgiveness as a daily need of the Christian life.   He bids the Church forgive and restore, and he himself forgives an offender—the offence had been committed against himself—in the face of Christ (ἐν προσώπῳ Χριστοῦ); but nowhere does he direct the penitent believer to seek forgiveness from God, or comfort him with the assurance that such is obtainable (Gal. 6^1, 2 Cor. 2^{10}). When he enforces the duty of Church members to forgive one another by an appeal to the fact that Christ forgave them, he is thinking, as the aorist shows, of the forgiveness they had obtained in baptism (Col. 3^{13}).   Nor is it otherwise when he declares that the goal of his desire is " to gain Christ, and be found in Him, not having a righteousness of mine own, even that which is of the Law, but that which is through faith in Christ, the righteousness which is of God by faith " (Phil. 3^9).   Certainly here as everywhere it is assumed that the standing given by the justifying verdict is something permanent.   But it is equally clear that what is in his mind is just this standing as opposed to the abandoned legal standing, and that he has no thought of connecting it with post-baptismal sins. However we may account for it, the fact can hardly be disputed that the petition, Forgive us our debts as we forgive our debtors, has no place in the Apostle's teaching. The sins from which the believer is justified are those committed before he became a Christian.   The message of forgiveness in Paul's gospel stands at the beginning, and has no reference to lapses in the Christian life.   For post-baptismal sins no provision is made.   The believer, if he would obtain salvation, must cleanse himself from all defilement of flesh and spirit, perfecting holiness in the *fear* of God (2 Cor. 7¹).

How are we to account for this so disconcerting feature of the Apostle's piety? That it is not due to any dullness of conscience need hardly be said. There are two things that go far to explain it.

The first is Paul's high conception of the radicalness of the renewing change wrought in the believer. How should one who had died to sin, who had been liberated from its bondage, and in whose soul the living Christ was present, how should he continue to sin? Sin in the believer is for Paul an anomaly, an enigma; and though he recognises it as a fact, he continues to regard it as something exceptional. His conception of the normal Christian life is that of a gradual development in knowledge and virtue; he hopes and expects that every believer will be established unblameable in holiness before Christ at His coming (1 Thess. 3¹³, Col. 1²⁸).

The second fact that throws light on the absence of the petition for forgiveness is that the sense of guilt does not play anything like the same part in the piety of Paul as it does in that, say, of Luther. In reconstructing his conversion and the experiences that led up to it, stress is often laid on his agonising and vain endeavours to obtain peace of conscience by scrupulous fulfilment of the Law. But all that is unsupported hypothesis. His own testimony is that he was, as touching the righteousness which is in the Law, found blameless (Phil. 3⁶). If we can take the seventh chapter of Romans as autobiographical, what weighed upon him in his pre-Christian days was less the sense of guilt than the sense of moral powerlessness; and what he found in Christ less forgiveness than liberation. " Who shall deliver me out of the body of this death? I thank God through Jesus Christ our Lord." It is true that justification occupies a prominent place in his thought; but it has to be borne in mind that the idea covers not only peace with God but the whole heritage of the Christian salvation (Phil. 3[8ff.]).

And if the sense of guilt and of pardon were not the dominant notes in Paul's conversion, they can hardly be said to be heard at all in his life as a Christian. Nowhere does he make any confession of wrong-doing or failure, nowhere betray any sense that he daily needs to be forgiven. Without a trace of self-righteousness and without making any claim to sinlessness, he yet nourishes a proud consciousness that he has run not as uncertainly, fought, not as one that beateth the air. What keeps him humble is not the sense of his own imperfections, but the all-dominating feeling that he is what he is solely through the grace of God (1 Cor. 15[10], 2 Cor. 12[7ff.]).

Paul's doctrine of justification by faith with its correlate the doctrine of redemption from the Law was a creation of his own, none of his doctrines more distinctly so. In it he brought to clear expression as against Jewish legalism one of the cardinal features of the new religion, and with it met the first great crisis in the history of the Church. Its enduring significance and vitality are sufficiently attested by the fact that fifteen centuries later Luther found in it a sword of sharpness with which to smite the formalism and legalism that had again fastened themselves on Christianity.

When we describe the doctrine as a creation of the Apostle we are thinking only of the form in which it is cast. With respect to the spirit embodied in it, its essential religious content, it was not new, but takes us back to Jesus and to the Hebrew prophets and psalmists. Jesus does not describe forgiveness as justification; but equally with Paul He exhibits it as the free gift of sovereign love; equally with Paul He rejects the whole conception of merit, and on the same religious grounds. The essential import of Paul's doctrine is all contained in the two parables of the Pharisee and the publican and the servant coming in from the field. No sooner has the servant fulfilled one task than another is imposed upon him (Luke 17⁷). Does his lord thank him because he did the things that were commanded? "Even so ye also, when ye shall have done all the things that are commanded you, say, we are but servants; we have done that which it was our duty to do." As against God a man can have no claim and can heap up no merit. In the parable of the Pharisee and the publican Jesus shows how the introduction of the merit idea poisons the springs of religious life, fostering self-righteousness and contempt for those unable to produce a like array of good works. The same parable may be cited as an illustration of Jesus' teaching with respect to the condition of forgiveness. Nothing is said about faith, and indeed the conception of faith as belief hardly anywhere emerges. If the publican rather than the Pharisee is justified, it is because he approaches God in a humble and contrite spirit. Jesus is content with the simple idea that God's gifts are for those who come to Him in the right temper and are prepared to use them worthily. That Paul hinges everything on faith is explained by the historical situation. Belief in Jesus' divine dignity had established itself as the condition of entrance into the community of the saved; and the Apostle was confronted by the task of vindicating the position which faith had assumed and showing what that position involved. In accomplishing this task he gives to faith an interpretation that makes it practically equivalent to the temper which Jesus illustrates in the figure of the publican. Does he not adduce as an argument for his doctrine that it renders all glorying void? At the same time his doctrine carried within it a peril which was all too soon to reveal itself. More and more the faith that justifies came to be understood as submission to the dogmas of the Church, and was turned into a new work, the chief recommendation of which was to the laity its easiness, and to the hierarchy its efficacy in safeguarding the ecclesiastical structure. We can understand how the writer of the Epistle of James, while conceding as a good churchman its rights to faith, should, as a man of moral earnestness, require that faith be supplemented by deeds of kindness and mercy.

CHAPTER III.

MORAL RENEWAL.

IF justification is for Paul not an ethical but a purely religious good, it does not stand alone, but is accompanied by a work of moral renewal. This work we have now to consider.

Uniformly it is presented under the form of a death and resurrection with Christ. United with Christ, the believer is involved in His two great archetypal experiences. "We are buried therefore with Him through baptism into death : that like as Christ was raised from the dead through the glory of the Father, so we also might walk in newness of life. For if we have become united with Him by the likeness of His death, we shall be also by the likeness of His resurrection ; knowing this, that our old man was crucified with Him, that the body of sin might be done away, that so we should no longer be in bondage to sin " (Rom. 6^1–8^{14}).

That in the experiences thus described the Apostle has in view, for one thing, a moral act of the believer, in which, under the constraint of Christ's love, he renounces the service of sin for the service of righteousness is unquestionable. "Know ye not," he says, "that to whom ye present yourselves as servants unto obedience, his servants ye are whom ye obey ; whether of sin unto death, or of obedience unto righteousness ? But thanks be to God, that, whereas ye were servants of sin, ye became obedient from the heart to that form of teaching whereunto ye were delivered; and being made free from sin, ye became servants of righteousness" (Rom. 6[16ff.], Gal. 5[24]).

But is this all that regeneration means for the Apostle, or the bottom meaning? Very far from it. His doctrine is through and through supernaturalistic. Behind the believer's act in renouncing sin and as the ground of its possibility, he assumes a mysterious process in which the metaphysical basis of the personality is the subject of a renewing change. Regeneration is not in the first place a moral act; it is an experience in which the will plays no active part.

In order to understand this experience we must recall the three formulas in which, as we have seen in a previous chapter, Paul sums up the work of Christ in delivering from the tyranny of sin seated in the flesh. Christ redeemed men from the right which sin as their legal master had to their obedience, from the sin-provoking Law and from the ultimate source of sin, the flesh. For all who are united with Christ the moral situation is changed in these three directions.

The believer is released from the legal claim which sin formerly had on his obedience. " For when ye were the servants of sin, ye were free in regard of righteousness. But now being made free from sin and become servants to God, ye have your fruit unto sanctification and the end eternal life."

Further, having died to the Law with Christ, paid its debt, the believer is no longer subject to its baleful action in provoking his fleshly lusts. " For when we were in the flesh, the sinful passions, which were through the Law, wrought in our members to bring forth fruit unto death. But now we have been discharged from the Law, having died to that wherein we were holden; so that we serve in newness of the spirit and not in oldness of the letter."

So far we cannot speak of any inner transformation,

but only of a change in the external situation. But when we take account of the third formula it is otherwise. According to this formula, sin in the flesh was in Christ's death struck by the judgment of God, and its power, if not annihilated, at least broken. The result for the believer is that united with Christ his flesh of sin is involved in the same destruction. And this is not all. Union with Christ carries also resurrection with Him. The believer's life is lifted into a region where a new force with far other working than that of the flesh comes into play. That the second moment in this process is conceived in wholly supernaturalistic fashion none will dispute. What Paul has in view is not any purifying or quickening of man's natural powers that shall set free or evoke his latent impulse toward the good. The activities of the new life are the product not of the believer's quickened mind ($\nu o \hat{\upsilon} \varsigma$), but of the working of the indwelling Spirit or again of the indwelling Christ. Love, joy, peace, meekness, temperance, knowledge, the gift of tongues and of prophecy—all the virtues and all the capacities of the redeemed life are traced to this supernatural and transcendent source (Gal. 5[22], 1 Cor. 12[4ff.]). "But ye are not in the flesh, but in the Spirit, if so be that the Spirit of God dwelleth in you. But if any man hath not the Spirit of Christ, he is none of His. And if Christ is in you, the body is dead owing to sin, but the spirit is alive as the result of righteousness" (Rom. 8[9ff.]). In this passage the Apostle speaks of the spirit or soul as coming to life as a result of the regenerative process. But in truth the soul plays as ineffective a part after conversion as before it. From being the bondservant of the flesh it becomes the seat of the Spirit—that, so far as the Apostle's theory of salvation is concerned, sums up its significance. When theory passes out of sight and he makes a practical appeal to the will, its efficiency is of course assumed.

What is true of the resurrection with Christ, that it is primarily an experience and one in which the factors are wholly supernatural, is not less true of the death with Him. Christ's experience with respect to the sin seated in His flesh, that it was condemned, executed, automatically reproduces itself in the believer. United with Christ, the believer, as regards his old man or sinful nature, is crucified with Him; he is dead to sin, the body of sin is done away so that he is no longer in bondage to sin (Rom. 6[6, 11], Gal. 2[20]). He is no more in the flesh but in the Spirit (Rom. 8[9]). He has been circumcised with a circumcision not made with hands, in the putting off of the body of flesh (Col. 2[11]). In a word, he is a new creature. What precisely happens Paul naturally finds difficulty in telling, but that he assumes that the sinful flesh receives a death-wound, that its tyranny is once and for all broken, can hardly be a matter of doubt. How closely he associates sin with the flesh and in how naively materialistic a way he can think of sin's destruction, appear from the incident of the scandalous offender (1 Cor. 5[1ff.]). The Apostle directs that such an one be delivered unto Satan for the destruction of the flesh, that the spirit may be saved in the day of the Lord Jesus. In the case of this man the death with Christ had somehow turned out to be ineffective; and the Apostle hopes that by a solemn dedication of him not merely to mystical but to actual death, his salvation may even yet be secured.

From the death and resurrection with Christ the believer comes forth a new creature. So radical is the change as described by the Apostle that one might infer that the very possibility of sin has been removed. But such an issue he certainly does not contemplate. What, however, he does teach is that the old compulsion to sin has passed and the way been opened for a sinless development. "But now being made free from sin, and become servants to God, ye have your fruit unto sanctification, and the end eternal life" (Rom. 6^{22}).

In Mystery religion regeneration was conceived as a divinising of our mortal nature. But such an idea cannot be attributed to Paul. The category with which he operates is not that of substance but that of power. Moral renewal follows not from any transmutation of human substance, but from the striking down of sin in the flesh. And similarly immortality is exhibited as the result of an act of God. "He which raised up the Lord Jesus shall raise up us also with Jesus, and shall present us with you" (2 Cor. 4^{14}). The nearest the Apostle comes to the idea of divinising is in the Pleroma passages in the Epistle to the Colossians (1$^{19ff.}$ 2^9). There Christ is presented as mediating to men the life-potencies of Deity. Into this characteristically Gnostic conception Paul would doubtless read a predominantly ethical meaning; in any case it forms no organic part of his theory, but is a mere occasional thought called out by the heresy he is combating.

We have said that regeneration, in Paul's conception of it, opens to the believer the possibility of a sinless development. His expectation is that in normal cases the Christian will advance day by day in the knowledge of Christ, practice keeping step with knowledge, until at last he apprehends that for which also he was apprehended and Christ is formed within him. That a Christian should deliberately sin appears to him not merely as an anomaly but as an enigma. "We who died to sin how shall we any longer live therein?" "Sin shall not have dominion over you, for ye are not under the Law but under grace." The contrast presented by the grey reality to this optimistic expectation cost the Apostle many a sad hour. That Christians could sin and sin badly was all too palpable a fact. The fact does not lead him to modify his view of regeneration, but it forces him to descend from the high

11

plane of the supernatural to the humbler region of the categorical imperative. Your flesh has been crucified with Christ, he again and again insists, therefore mortify its lusts; ye have received the Spirit, walk in it. By the stress of facts he is compelled to supplement his ethic of miracle with an ethic of will. The two stand side by side unrelated.

Behind the Apostle's account of regeneration we can see clearly enough his own individual experience. His conversion had signified for him nothing less than a death and a rebirth. But in giving a theoretical construction of his experience he passes by the purely ethical conception of repentance, which the prophets and Jesus had found sufficient, and operates with the categories of Hellenistic religion. Anthropological dualism, miraculous transformation, death and resurrection with a saviour-god—these conceptions came to him not from the Old Testament or from Judaism, but from the ecstatic, mystical piety of Philo and the Oriental cults.

CHAPTER IV.

Spiritual Gifts.

THE Christian life is for Paul a life in or under the power of the Spirit. Its every expression in feeling, knowledge, word and deed has the Spirit for its source. But with the Church in general the Apostle recognises certain manifestations of an extraordinary and exceptional character as bearing upon them in a peculiar way the Spirit's impress. These manifestations were generally known as gifts or pneumatic gifts (χαρίσματα τὰ πνευματικά). What value the Apostle attaches to them will be considered in a little; our first task must be to determine their nature.

In 1 Cor. 12–14 the whole subject comes up for exhaustive and highly instructive treatment. We are supplied with a list of the gifts. "To one," writes the Apostle, "is given through the Spirit the word of wisdom; and to another the word of knowledge, according to the same Spirit; to another faith, in the same Spirit; and to another gifts of healing, in the one Spirit; and to another working of miracles; and to another prophecy; and to another discerning of spirits; to another divers kinds of tongues; and to another the interpretation of tongues."

1. Of these various gifts the commonest and most typical, if we may judge from the prominence given to it, was that of tongues. As to the nature of this gift the description given leaves us in no doubt. It was not, as

the account in Acts would lead us to suppose, an ability to speak in a human language unknown to the speaker in his natural state. Paul compares it with foreign speech, which he could not have done had the two been identical, and declares, moreover, that without interpretation it was unintelligible not only to hearers of a particular tongue but to all hearers, and of no use for edification (1 Cor. 14[11. 2. 6]). The speaker was in a state of ecstasy; his utterances were involuntary, and unintelligible even to himself, unless he had the additional gift of interpretation. Carried away by a rush of religious feeling, he poured out a confused babel of sounds of which an ordinary listener could make nothing, and from which an unsympathetic listener would be apt to draw the conclusion that the man was either drunk or mad (1 Cor. 14[33], Acts 2[13]).

2. To translate such primitive language of the emotions into rational speech was the business of the interpreter of tongues. In the pneumatic's intonation he would probably find the clue which enabled him to judge whether the utterance was a song or a prayer, and whether it expressed penitence or aspiration, exultation or thanksgiving.

3. The gift of prophecy had this in common with glossolalia or tongues, that the speaker was carried away in an ecstasy, and was unable to restrain himself even if another held the ear of the meeting. It was distinguished from it by the fact that what was spoken was immediately understandable. With respect to their subject, the prophet's communications would relate mainly to the future (Acts 11[28] 21[11]). Paul plays the part of prophet when he assures the Thessalonian Christians that those who are alive at the Parousia shall in no wise precede them that are fallen asleep. What he says, however, of the effect produced by the prophet's words on unbelievers, that these feel themselves reproved and have the secrets of their hearts made manifest, would seem to indicate that the

prophet did not occupy himself exclusively with prediction
(1 Cor. 14^{24}).

4. With the gift of prophecy Paul couples that of dis-
crimination of spirits. Such a gift was highly necessary if
the community was not to be at the mercy of every ranter.
Lying, devil-inspired prophets were abroad as well as God-
inspired, and in outward respects the two classes were
much alike. The discriminator would need some store of
sobriety and a feeling for the genius of Christianity.

5. The ability to work miracles, while connected with
the Spirit, is connected also with extraordinary strength of
faith; and it is in all probability this extraordinary faith
the Apostle has in view when he speaks of it as a gift.
Among the miracles wrought, the cure of disease and
exorcism seem to have occupied the chief place. What we
have to think of is faith-healing.

6. But of all special endowments traced to the Spirit,
that of wisdom and knowledge—the difference between the
two can hardly have been considerable—was by far the
most significant. Knowledge, gnosis, played an immense
and not always a salutary part in the early history of
Christianity. A time speedily came when there was a real
danger that all that was distinctive in the Christian gospel
should be submerged in a flood of theosophical speculation.
Already in the Pauline Epistles we can trace the beginning
of the Gnostic movement. And, as we shall see, the
Apostle himself was in some sense a Gnostic. He was the
first to formulate a Christian gnosis. It is of the utmost
importance, therefore, that we understand what he means
by this gift and what value he attaches to it.

In Paul's judgment the gnosis which is a gift of the
Spirit is something altogether different from the wisdom
of the world, in other words, from pagan philosophy. The
latter he holds in the utmost contempt as a pretentious
futility which God has made foolish and will bring to

nought (1 Cor. 1–3). By all their philosophising, he asserts, the world's wise men have not succeeded in reaching any real knowledge of God. The true knowledge does not come through the exercise of man's native powers, but is supernatural in its origin. It is revealed to a man inwardly by the Spirit of God. "For the Spirit searcheth all things, yea, the deep things of God. For who among men knoweth the things of a man, save the spirit of the man which is in him? Even so the things of God none knoweth, save the Spirit of God. But we received not the spirit of the world, but the Spirit which is of God; that we might know the things that are freely given to us by God." Not only is such pneumatic knowledge inaccessible to the natural man; when it is presented to him he is unable to understand it. "The natural man receiveth not the things of the Spirit of God: for they are foolishness unto him; and he cannot know them, because they are spiritually judged."

From the fact that spiritual gnosis is classed among the special gifts we may safely infer that it was generally thought of as associated with the ecstatic state. It came to a man as an ecstatic vision. One must, however, in this connection interpret ecstasy in the wide sense, as signifying a state of exalted feeling. Paul had his strictly ecstatic visions in which, as it seemed to him, he ascended to the third heaven and heard words he might not utter; but he nowhere traces his doctrines to such a source.

What is the content of Christian gnosis? Since it is described as knowledge of "the things that are freely given to us by God," we must regard it as coextensive with Christian truth (1 Cor. 2^{12}). The Apostle claims to have received his whole gospel as a revelation from Christ (Gal. 1^{11}). At the same time he draws a distinction between the elementary truths which form the food proper for babes and the higher wisdom which only the fully initiated can understand (1 Cor. 2–3^{2}). His first preaching to the Corinthians was not with excellency of speech or of wisdom, but had the simple message of the Cross for its theme. In all probability it is the higher wisdom he has mainly in view when he speaks of gnosis as an exceptional gift. Such gnosis has for its subject the divine mysteries, even " the wisdom that hath been hidden, which God fore-ordained before the worlds unto our glory " (1 Cor. 2[7]). The wisdom referred to in this passage clearly relates to Christ's rank as the Lord of glory ; for the Apostle proceeds to say that had the demonic world-rulers possessed it they would not have compassed their own ruin by putting Christ to death. We may take it therefore that the higher gnosis consists in part at least in what we should describe as speculative christology. And this view of it is confirmed when we consider the manner of the Apostle's dealing with a Christian gnosis which he condemns as false. In the Epistle to the Colossians we read of believers who had been led into speculations regarding the functions of angelic powers in mediating to men the divine Fulness (2[8. 18]). Against this false gnosis—false as not holding fast the Head—Paul sets the true. In Christ alone the Fulness dwells and He alone can reconcile the world to God. Than the first two chapters of Colossians no better example of the Pauline gnosis can be given.

One must not, however, limit the term to speculative christology. It covers equally the wisdom of the Cross, that wisdom that seemed to the Greeks mere foolishness (1 Cor. 1[22], Col. 1[20]). It covers eschatology (1 Cor. 2[9]). Nor must we identify it too exclusively with doctrine. The man who understands that meat that has been offered in sacrifice to an idol cannot harm him, has gnosis (1 Cor. 8[1]). From the connection in which the word is frequently found we may legitimately infer that it shades into the meaning of practical moral insight. The Apostle prays that his readers may be filled with the gnosis of God's will in all spiritual wisdom and understanding, to walk worthily of the Lord (Col. 1⁹). When so wide a reach is given to the term it will at once be understood that between the gnosis to which all believers have access and that which is the privilege of the specially endowed no sharp line of demarcation can be drawn.

In these gifts—tongues, prophecy, gnosis—the early Church saw something wonderful and also something new. And the secret of their appearance was not unknown. From His throne in heaven Jesus had poured out on His people the gift of the Spirit (Acts 2³³). Men were living in the last days, in some sense in the messianic age, and the words spoken by the prophet Joel had received their fulfilment: "And it shall be in the last days, saith God, I will pour forth of my Spirit upon all flesh; and your sons and your daughters shall prophesy, and your young men shall see visions, and your old men shall dream dreams" (Acts 2¹⁷). If these wonderful phenomena had been unknown in the days of Jesus' earthly life, it was because the Spirit had not yet been given (John 7³⁹). The converse of this last statement would represent still better the primitive point of view: the Spirit had not yet been given since these wonderful phenomena had not yet appeared. This account of the pneumatic gifts is also the account of Paul. For him too they are a new thing in history, the sign-manual of the Spirit's working and of the messianic age.

It will be evident that this explanation does not belong to the domain of science and does not supersede the necessity for an investigation of historical causes. In undertaking such an investigation we shall limit ourselves to the ecstatic gifts and the gift of gnosis. The gifts of healing and exorcism are of less historical importance, and besides they have their analogies in Jesus' earthly ministry.

We have said that the Church regarded ecstatic gifts, at

least in the universality of their manifestation, as something new. Such gifts were in fact no native product of Hebrew or Jewish piety. Though the Hebrew prophets in describing their experiences make use of the terminology of primitive ecstatic prophecy, they were far indeed from being ecstatics. And the same may be asserted of the apocalyptic writers. They too describe the trance and vision; but not to speak of the fact that they locate these experiences not in the present but in the past, their descriptions to an even greater extent than those of the prophets betray the character of literary artifice (4 Esd. 14[38ff.], Bar. 20[5. 6]). Even if we grant that these descriptions may be based on direct knowledge and that there is other evidence for the existence of an ecstatic piety in certain Rabbinical circles,[1] all that can be made out is a rare and sporadic appearance of the phenomena in question, and that for the most part under the influence of Hellenistic religion. Of tongues, trances, visions in connection with the ministry of the Baptist or of Jesus we hear nothing. The question that has been raised, Was Jesus an ecstatic? must be answered with an emphatic no. From the side of Judaism the outburst of ecstatic phenomena in the primitive Church is not to be explained.

Something doubtless must be put down to the enthusiastic character of early Christian piety. Believers were on the strain, eagerly looking for the coming of God's Son from heaven. There was an enthusiasm of faith and hope such as Judaism had never known. In all times of religious convulsion and revival ecstatic manifestations have sprung up as if from the soil; they were familiar enough at the Reformation; how natural that they should have emerged in the greatest religious revival the world has seen!

Such an explanation, however, cannot be accepted as complete. It is impossible to ignore the fact that something analogous to the ecstatic gifts was in existence outside the

[1] Kennedy, *St. Paul and the Mystery Religions*, p. 46.

Church.   In Greece the excited shoutings of the Dionysos'
ecstatic had long been a familiar spectacle.[1]   And of the
Mystery cults ecstasy in its various manifestations formed a
constant feature.   The god descends upon the mystic, fills
him with his spirit, makes him a prophet and gives him
revelations.   It is difficult to resist the conclusion that the
appearance of ecstasy in the Church was not unconnected
with its existence outside.   Not without significance is the
fact that it was precisely in the Church at Corinth, where
contact with Oriental religion was of the closest, that
glossolalia and prophecy showed the most luxuriant growth.
And we have the Apostle himself for a witness that it was
no easy task to distinguish between a glossolalia and
prophecy that were Spirit-inspired and such as were devil-
inspired (1 Cor. 12[2, 3] 14[29]).   It is natural to suppose that
the latter were simply the Oriental articles in their un-
regenerate form.

The hypothesis of foreign influence would indeed be
rendered precarious had we to accept the account of Acts,
which carries back the gift of tongues to the very first days
of the Christian Church.   But that account shows many
legendary traits ; and we must suppose that the writer has
antedated a phenomenon the origin of which he was not in
a position to fix.

Not less foreign to the genius of Hebrew and Jewish
religion than the phenomena of ecstasy was the thing called
gnosis.   In Philo indeed gnosis appears in full-blown form,
and there is evidence that also in certain Rabbinical circles
the conception had been appropriated.[2]   But when we find
a Jewish gnostic piety, as when we find a Jewish ecstatic
piety, we are safe to infer influence from the side of Oriental
religion.   Indigenous to the soil of Hebraism or Judaism
gnosis certainly was not.   The prophets, it is true, frequently
speak of the knowledge of God and attach to it vital

[1] Rohde, *Psyche*, II. 4 ff., 69.   [2] Kennedy, *op. cit.* p. 49.

importance. " I will betroth thee unto me in faithfulness, and thou shalt truly know the Lord" (Hos. 2^{20}). " The spirit of the Lord shall rest upon him, the spirit of wisdom and understanding, the spirit of counsel and might, the spirit of knowledge and of the fear of the Lord " (Isa. 11^2). It would be untrue to say that between the knowledge the prophets have in view and that which Paul describes as gnosis there is nothing in common. Both are rooted in an ethical conception of God and of His relation to the world. At the same time there is this radical difference, that the theosophical and mystical element which gives to the latter its distinctive character is in the former entirely absent. Nowhere do the prophets and psalmists, or even the Wisdom writers, enter the domain of theosophical speculation, or contemplate a knowledge of God that shades into a mystical fellowship with Him. And the same can be said of Jesus. The knowledge of God which Jesus teaches is not speculative but ethical; that He is the Almighty Judge and also the merciful Saviour, that He is kind to the unthankful and to the evil, and that there is joy in His presence over one sinner that repenteth. For anything analogous to the Pauline gnosis we shall search the Synoptic sayings in vain. From the Old Testament, or from native Jewish thought, or from the teaching of Jesus, that gnosis is not to be explained.

The Pauline gnosis, if we leave out of account the ethical spirit that suffuses it, has its affinities not with the knowledge of God taught by the prophets and by Jesus, but with the gnosis of Hellenistic religion. Of this last we have already given some brief account, and all we need do here is to institute a comparison between it and the gnosis of the Apostle.

In respect of form the two are closely akin. For both the claim is made that they are supernatural · in their origin, and radically different in kind from human wisdom.

Inaccessible to the natural man, they come as an inner revelation, and are a gift of God, mediated through God's Spirit. Needless to say, much more is meant by this than the familiar truth that religious knowledge is morally conditioned. Again, in both cases gnosis is associated with the ecstatic state. Finally a distinction is in both cases drawn between the elementary knowledge of the neophyte and the higher knowledge which is the privilege of the fully initiated.

With respect to content also we can trace at least a general resemblance. In Oriental religion and in Paul what gnosis supplies is a philosophy of the present world and of the process of redemption : it will explain how so wretched a world of mortality and sin came to exist and how man may find deliverance from it. In both this philosophy is rooted in pessimism and dualism, and operates with categories that are half philosophical and half mythological. Common to both is the conception of an intermediate being or beings—logos, nous, aeons—the agent in creation and redemption.

These points of community are too numerous and too vital to be accounted for on any other hypothesis than that of dependence. The conception of gnosis passed into Christianity not from the Old Testament and not from Judaism, but from Oriental religion. It must be regarded as part of Christianity's Hellenistic heritage.

This is far from meaning that the gnosis of Paul stands on the same level with that of the Hermetic writings or even of Philo. The mere fact that within a few centuries the latter died a natural death, while the former, modified it is true in many directions, has dominated the religious thought of well-nigh two millenniums, is evidence enough of the wide gulf that separates them.

The Pauline gnosis lifts itself out of that of paganism for one thing by its sobriety. It is marked by no such extravagance of mythology and speculation as meets us in its pagan congeners. Never is speculation carried a step further than serves to bring out the character of the Christ-redemption; never is it other than the handmaid of a real religious interest. And further, we can say that the gnosis of Paul is separated from that of paganism by the immeasurably greater worth of its contents. If in both we find the same dualistic opposition of the natural and the spiritual, the same pessimism and the same conception of a mediating being, in the former case all this becomes the medium and instrument of a faith which in its ethical depth and purity not only stands high above any that Hellenism can show, but has never been transcended. If we may not identify Paul's gnosis with the gospel which Jesus brought to our race, we can say that it embodies that gospel. The treasure is there, if in earthen vessels.

To estimate the Apostle's gnosis from this standpoint is tacitly to affirm that its greatness does not lie in its speculative subtlety or in its originality. A philosophical genius like Plato or Plotinus Paul was not. What is imperishable in his gnosis has another source than speculation; it springs from a religious experience of altogether extraordinary range and depth. Of Hellenistic gnosis too it can be said that it was not without its root in experience. But here the experience had in it comparatively little that was either religiously or ethically profound. In the main it was one of the transitoriness and worthlessness of man's earthly existence and of an ecstatic and ascetic liberation from the fetters of sense. If these elements are not altogether foreign to the piety of the Apostle they are far from constituting its pith and marrow. Into his experience there entered something infinitely greater—a feeling for the guilt and tyranny of sin, a discovery of the sin-forgiving grace of God, an inward revolution that made the doing of God's will the law and impulse of his being. Paul's gnosis is the instrument of such an experience and receives from it what is highest in its content. And the Apostle's experience conducts us back to a second great reality in which his gnosis is anchored—the Person of Jesus Christ. In the Hermetic writings νοῦς or Mind plays substantially the same part as the risen Christ in the gnosis of Paul. But compared with the latter what a pale and empty abstraction it is! Paul's Christ is no abstraction, but the embodiment of what is most central in the supreme revelation of His character and will which God has given to our race. The Gnostics of a later day claimed Paul as their Apostle; and their claim was so far justified, in that he was the first to formulate a Christian gnosis. But further than this, no. From the gnosis of the Christian Gnostics as from that of the pagan, the gnosis of Paul, alike by its sobriety, by the worth of its thoughts, by its hold on reality and by the character of the piety that comes to expression in it, stands wide as the poles asunder.

If the pneumatic gifts entered Christianity from the outside, we can add that they received such Christian baptism as they were capable of. Naturally a gift like that of tongues emerged from the process less altered in character than did the gift of prophecy or of gnosis. Only in the last case can we speak of a radical transformation.

But the genius of Paul's religion appears not less in the position and value he assigns to the spiritual gifts than in the new spirit with which he informs them. With respect even to the more specifically ecstatic gifts of tongues and prophecy, his judgment is far from being depreciatory. As emphatically as the Corinthians themselves he regards them as of supernatural origin, and he declares that they are to be coveted (1 Cor. 14[5]). He himself had his moments of ecstatic rapture (2 Cor. 12[1ff.]). He was a prophet, and he spoke with tongues more than all his readers (1 Cor. 14[18]). But notwithstanding this high valuation of ecstatic gifts, what the Apostle does with them is to place their exercise under strict control and make it relative to the edification of the man himself or of the community. Not more than two or at most three ecstatics are to be permitted to speak at one meeting, and then only in turn. The speaker with tongues is not to demonstrate at all in the public assembly unless some one is present who can interpret. At all costs order is to be maintained; for, as the Apostle grandly remarks, God is not a God of confusion but of peace. To the objection that the ecstatic, being under the power of the Spirit, may find it impossible to restrain himself, he replies with the sober principle that the spirits of the prophets are subject to the prophets. That ecstatic manifestations are thus subjected to control means that their end is sought outside themselves. Not only does Paul guard against the dangers of a Corybantic Christianity; in a decisive way he makes the ecstatic the handmaid of the moral.

In the Apostle's treatment of the gift of gnosis the same principles are in evidence. Among all the gifts he ranks it highest. A standing prayer for his converts is that they may abound in it yet more and more (Phil. 1^9, Rom. 15^{14}, 1 Cor. 1^5, Col. $1^{9f.}$). It has to be said, however, that when he speaks of gnosis as a gift to be coveted by the ordinary Christian, what he has in view is mainly a practical knowledge of God's will (Col. 1^{10}). Whatever importance he attaches to what we should call the more speculative gnosis, nowhere does he regard it as the condition or the means of salvation. Even in Colossians, where this gnosis occupies a place of exceeding prominence, it is not it, but faith and love that appear as the distinctive marks of a Christian ($1^{4,\ 11}$). The Hellenistic idea of salvation through knowledge we do not find in Paul. Moreover, he is not ignorant of the perils that accompany the gift. "Knowledge," he declares, "puffs up, but love edifies." Along with the other pneumatic gifts gnosis must consent to be the handmaid of ethical religion (1 Cor. 8[1ff.]).

This so momentous principle receives its grandest and most decisive expression in the Apostle's never-to-be-forgotten eulogy of love. Among the Christians at Corinth the pneumatic gifts, and particularly those more distinctively ecstatic, were earnestly coveted and diligently exercised. Evidently they were regarded as the chief if not the only evidence of the Spirit's presence and activity. In answer to certain questions that had been sent to him Paul deals in a comprehensive way with the whole subject. What judgments he passes we have seen. He will have the Corinthian believers desire earnestly the greater gifts, prophecy and gnosis rather than tongues. But he knows of something that is of infinitely higher worth than them all. " If I speak with the tongues of men and of angels, but have not love, I am become sounding brass or a clanging cymbal. And if I have the gift of prophecy, and know all mysteries and all knowledge; and if I have all faith, so as to remove mountains, but have not love, I am nothing. Love never faileth : but whether there be prophecies, they shall be done away ; whether there be tongues, they shall cease ; whether there be knowledge, it shall be done away. For now we see in a mirror darkly ; but then, face to face ; now I know in part ; but then shall I know even as also I have been known. But now abideth faith, hope, love, these three ; and the greatest of these is love." Than this Paul has written nothing greater, nothing that places upon his piety a more decisive stamp. Consider what it means. The greatest thing in the Christian life is not any ecstatic rapture or vision, and not the ability to read the future or to penetrate the mysteries of God ; it is the everyday virtue of love—the love that cherishes the good and forgets self in the service of others. Love with its sister qualities

—joy, peace, long-suffering, kindness, goodness, faithfulness, meekness, temperance—constitute the best evidence of the Spirit's presence, the noblest fruits of the Spirit's working (Gal. 5^{22}). Paul is a mystic: he counts it one of his greatest privileges that he has enjoyed the mystic's ecstatic vision of God. But when he has to take his stand, he breaks with mysticism at the decisive point and gives in his allegiance to that ethical conception of religion that came to him from the Old Testament prophets and from Jesus. Paul values and cultivates gnosis, but in the last resort his piety is not gnostic. Much as he appropriates from Hellenism, his Hebrew heritage of ethical religion proves itself strong enough to give to the Hellenistic its own colour and to reduce it to a position of subordination.

CHAPTER V.

ETHICS.

WHEN we speak of ethics in connection with Paul we must dissociate our minds almost completely from any such study of morality as was pursued in the Greek schools. Questions regarding the chief good, the freedom of the will, the classification of the virtues, the relation of virtue to knowledge, lie outside his horizon. Only at two points does he approach the confines of ethical theory—in his derivation of sin and righteousness from the opposed principles of the flesh and the Spirit, and in his conception of conscience as a faculty that at once reveals to man the moral law and acquits or condemns according as he obeys or disobeys its mandates (Rom. 2$^{14ff.}$). And with respect to conscience it has to be said, that only in the case of pagans does it appear as the source of moral knowledge. For Jews this source lies in the written Law, and for believers in the indwelling Spirit (Rom. 2$^{12.\ 17f.}$). When the conscience of believers is referred to, what is in view is hardly more than a sense of right and wrong (Rom. 9^1 13^5, 1 Cor. 4^4 8$^{7.\ 10}$, 2 Cor. 1^{12} 4^2). It is no part of the Apostle's design to establish morality on a human basis that is the same for Jew and Gentile, believer and un-believer. Everywhere the insight and the virtues of believers appear as the product not of their exalted and purified natural faculties, but of the Spirit's working. If a certain *justitia civilis* is conceded to the unconverted man, there is no thought of placing it on the same level with the Spirit-inspired righteousness of the Christian. In his ethic as in his dogmatic Paul occupies the ground of a thoroughgoing supernaturalism. Between the natural man and the redeemed the breach is absolute.

In studying Paul's ethic what we have to consider, therefore, is not so much questions of theory as the outstanding features of his conception of the moral life. These features can be gathered up under two or three heads.

1. In the first place, it can be said that morality always appears as inseparably connected with religion. That the two should exist apart is a thing never contemplated (Rom. 1^{21-25}). The completeness of the fusion comes out in various ways.

It appears in this, that always the ethical norm is conceived as the law of God or of Christ, the will of God or of Christ (Rom. 12^2 7^{22}, 1 Cor. 9^{21}, Gal. 6^2). While occasionally making use of the Stoic conception of a law of nature, the Apostle has no thought of grounding morality with the Stoics in the nature of man or in the order of the universe (Rom. 1^{26}, 1 Cor. 11^{14}). Its one ground is the personal will of God. When he speaks of the pagan's natural moral perceptions, it is as an equivalent for the written Mosaic law. And as it is with the ethical norm, so is it also with the ethical ideal. It is described in terms of religion. The goal of the believer is Christlikeness, the formation of Christ within him (Rom. 8^{29}, Gal. 4^{19}).

The fusion of morality and religion comes out also in the kind of motives to which the Apostle makes his appeal. It would be untrue to say that he never appeals to motives that are simply ethical. Himself a man of the most delicate moral sensibility, he knows how to present goodness in its beauty and obligation, and vice in its deformity and shamefulness. "Finally, brethren, whatsoever things are true, whatsoever things are honourable, whatsoever things are just, whatsoever things are pure, whatsoever things are lovely, whatsoever things are of good report; if there be any virtue and if there be any praise, think on these things" (Phil. 4⁸). Nevertheless, in the vast majority of cases the springs of action which Paul touches are ethico-religious in character rather than purely ethical. He knows "the terror of the Lord" and can appeal to the motive of fear (2 Cor. 5⁹). He can also hold up before men the rewards of fidelity. "Whatsoever ye do, work heartily, as unto the Lord and not unto men; knowing that from the Lord ye shall receive the recompense of the inheritance" (Col. 3²³ᶠ·). Very frequently he seeks to inspire believers with a sense of their high vocation in Christ and their obligation to rise to the height of it. "Walk worthily of God who calleth you into His own kingdom and glory" (1 Thess. 2¹²). "Flee fornication. Know ye not that your body is a temple of the Holy Ghost which is in you, which ye have from God." Everywhere we find appeals based on the example of Christ and on His love and His sacrifice for our salvation. "Have this mind in you which was also in Christ Jesus." "Ye are not your own; for ye were bought with a price: glorify God therefore in your body." "The love of Christ constraineth us; because we thus judge, that one died for all, therefore all died; and He died for all that they which live should no longer live unto themselves, but unto Him who for their sakes died and rose again."

2. One or two important aspects of Paul's conception of Christian morality are covered by the great word, "liberty." What he means by this word is in the first place emancipation from bondage to Jewish ceremonialism. "With freedom did Christ set us free; stand fast therefore and be not entangled again in a yoke of bondage. For in Christ Jesus neither circumcision availeth any-

thing nor uncircumcision ; but faith working through love "
(Gal. 5$^{1-6}$).

Long before the days of the Apostle, the Hebrew
prophets had attained to a clear understanding of the
distinction between the moral and the ritual, and had
made it the burden of their teaching that what God requires
of men is not ritual but righteousness. But outside a
narrow circle, Jewish religion failed to maintain itself on
this level. Whatever uses the combination of the traditional
ceremonial with prophetic ideas which lies before us in
Deuteronomy and the Levitical books may have served,
one evil result was that the distinction won by the prophets
was in large measure obscured. The ritual came to be
regarded as equally binding on the conscience with the
moral, or, indeed, as possessing a superior obligation. One
of the main charges brought against the Pharisees by
Jesus was that they tithed mint and anise and cummin,
and left undone the weightier matters of the Law, judgment and mercy and faith.

In common with Jesus and the prophets, Paul makes a
clean sweep of ritual and establishes the moral in its
purity as the one reasonable and acceptable service of God.
Food proscriptions, feast days and Sabbath days are no
more than a shadow of things to come (Gal. 5^6, Col. 2^{16}).
" The kingdom of God is not eating and drinking, but
righteousness and peace and joy in the Holy Ghost "
(Rom. 14^{17}).

And the Apostle proceeds further on the same lines
when he presents Christian obedience as something
radically different from the punctilious regard for the
letter of the commandment that was the soul of Pharisaic
piety. It is a service in newness of spirit and not in
oldness of written law (Rom. 7^6). Apprehending the
commandment in its inner, spiritual meaning, the believer
meets it with a spiritual obedience. And such obedience

is not extorted by threats, but is a thing of spontaneity and freedom. The very idea of law tends to disappear. Inwardly enlightened by the Spirit, possessing the mind of Christ, the believer has no need of formulated commandments. Only on one or two occasions does the Apostle appeal to such. In general, what the law of Christ means for him is some broad principle like love or the bearing of one another's burdens (Rom. 13^8, Gal. 6$^{1f.}$). From such principles every particular commandment proceeds. " For this, thou shalt not commit adultery, thou shalt not kill, thou shalt not steal, thou shalt not covet, and if there be any other commandment, it is summed up in this word, thou shalt love thy neighbour as thyself. Love worketh no ill to his neighbour ; love therefore is the fulfilment of the Law." In dealing with the practical problems brought up before him for solution it is by such broad principles the Apostle is guided (Rom. 14, 1 Cor. 8$^{10ff.}$ 10$^{23ff.}$).

Under the idea of liberty Paul includes also elevation above ascetic scruples. There were those in the Church who had an ascetic repugnance to the use of flesh and wine (Rom. 14, Col. 2$^{16-23}$). Though the Apostle deals tenderly with them, he makes it clear that he himself is no ascetic. " I know and am persuaded in the Lord Jesus, that nothing is unclean of itself" (Rom. 14^{14}). " All things are lawful for me, but not all things are expedient. All things are lawful for me, but I will not be brought under the power of any. Meats for the belly, and the belly for meats ; but God shall bring to nought both it and them " (1 Cor. 6$^{12ff.}$). As we shall see, his depreciation of marriage is to be explained from other than ascetic motives.

There is still another feature of the moral life which Paul brings under the idea of liberty. It is that of the autonomy of the individual conscience. No man has the right to make his conscience a law to another. " Why is my liberty," he asks, " judged by another conscience "

(1 Cor. 10²⁹). " Let not him that eateth set at nought him
that eateth not; and let not him that eateth not judge
him that eateth : for God hath received him. Who art
thou that judgest the servant of another ? To his own
Lord he standeth or falleth " (Rom. 14³ᶠ·). Since conscience is the supreme guide a man must be careful not to
do violence to it. Always he must act with the clear
conviction that what he is doing is right. Even if he ,is
mistaken in his judgment, it is a less evil than that he
should out of deference to another man's perceptions override his own. " He that doubteth," the Apostle declares
in discussing the question of the legitimacy of eating flesh
and drinking wine, " is condemned if he eat, because he
eateth not of faith ; and whatsoever is not of faith is sin "
(Rom. 14²³).

Can we speak of freedom of thought as included in the
idea of Christian liberty ? In one sense no, since what we
mean by the phrase hardly comes up before Paul for judgment. But this we can say, that as regards himself he
refuses to acknowledge any external authority however
august (Gal. 1¹¹ᶠᶠ·), and that where the foundation in Christ
is not menaced he is ready to concede to others a similar
freedom (1 Cor. 3¹⁰ᶠᶠ·). Not once does he appeal to Jesus'
words as authoritative in matters of doctrine. It is true
that in glaring contradiction with his principle that the Law
has been abolished, he continues to treat the Old Testament as verbally inspired and the final court of appeal
(Rom. 1¹⁷ 3¹⁰ 4⁷· ¹⁷ 9¹³, 1 Cor. 9⁹). From the fact that
the word seed in God's promise to Abraham is not in the
plural but in the singular he can draw an important dogmatic inference (Gal. 3¹⁶). But notwithstanding this insist-
ence on the letter of Scripture he is as far as possible from
being fettered by it. Armed with the allegorical method
of exegesis, a method that was taken over by Judaism
from the Stoics, he can always find in Scripture a verbal

confirmation of his own doctrine. A good example is his treatment of the commandment, Thou shalt not muzzle the ox when he treadeth out the corn. "Is it for oxen," he asks, "that God careth, or sayeth He it altogether for our sake? Yea, for our sake it was written: because he that plougheth ought to plough in hope, and he that thresheth, to thresh in hope of partaking" (1 Cor. 9[9ff.]). With unlimited confidence Paul throws himself on inner illumination. "He that is spiritual judgeth all things, and he himself is judged of no man" (1 Cor. 2[15]). The day of the authoritative doctrinal formulas had yet to come.

The liberty of the Christian man is ranked by Paul with the most precious of his possessions. And yet he is not insensible to the dangers in the direction of licence and self-assertion that accompany its exercise. Nowhere does he touch a higher moral level than in his earnest admonitions that liberty must be controlled by conscience and by consideration for others. "For ye, brethren, were called for freedom," he writes to the Galatians, "only use not your freedom for an occasion to the flesh, but through love be servants one to another." Rather than wound the conscience of a brother and cause him to stumble, the Apostle will renounce the exercise of his liberty (1 Cor. 8[13]). The Christian man, if free from all men, is at the same time the servant of all (1 Cor. 9[19]).

Closely akin to the idea of liberty is that of inner independence with respect to earthly goods and circumstances. In the consciousness that his treasure lies elsewhere, the Apostle maintains and will have others maintain a certain detachment from all that belongs to the perishing world. While the world is his to use it, he will not be brought under its power (1 Cor. 6[12] 7[30]). He has learned the secret both to be filled and to be hungry, both to abound and to be in want, and in whatever state he finds himself, therein to be self-sufficing (Phil. 4[11ff.]).

In this ideal of independence and self-sufficiency (αὐτάρκεια) some have seen the influence of the Stoics.[1] And it is possible that in using the word αὐτάρκης as well as in formulating the general conception of liberty, the Stoic ideal of the wise man who has his world within himself and can maintain under all circumstances an imperturbabls serenity, was in the background of the Apostle's mind. Between the two ideals, however, there is no more than a superficial resemblance. Much that Paul includes under the idea of liberty has nothing to correspond with it in Stoicism. And his independence of earthly goods and circumstances is something very different from the Stoic apathy, and has another root than the Stoic belief in reason as the one constitutive principle of human nature. It is the product of a deep religious faith: " I can do all things in Him that strengtheneth me " (Phil. 4[13]).

3. Though Paul's ethic is in certain directions deeply affected by his belief in the nearness of the end and the consequent transference of his interest from earth to heaven, it is emphatically a social ethic and singularly free from anything like self-centred individualism and other-worldliness.

Where his apocalyptic outlook has left the deepest marks is naturally in his valuation of the institutions and goods of the existing age or order. With respect to the State, it would be untrue to say that his attitude toward it is one of indifference (Rom. 13). As performing the altogether necessary task of maintaining order, the civil magistrate is a minister of God for good. In punishing the evil-doer he is doing God's work ; and the power he wields has God for its source and sanction. Believers and men in general are under a moral obligation to render him submission and honour and to pay the taxes he imposes.

---

[1] J. Weiss, *Die christliche Freiheit nach der Verkündigung des Apostels Paulus*, pp. 24 ff.

All things considered, that is a notable pronouncement; and it must have had an incalculable influence in determining the attitude of the Church to the State in the days of stress that were to follow. It means for one thing that Paul has emancipated himself from Jewish particularism and Jewish hatred of the Roman Imperium. It means also that his thinking is not in every point dominated by the two-age doctrine. According to that doctrine the " powers that be " might be ordained by God, but certainly not " for good." The Apostle's favourable judgment was probably in part due to his own experience of the Imperium's beneficent action. On more than one occasion it had interfered to protect him from his Jewish persecutors. But we must also regard his favourable judgment as an evidence of his open eye for facts. He saw the absolute necessity for the controlling hand of Rome if the world was not to lapse into chaos (2 Thess. 2[7]). Such appreciation of the work of the civil power must not, however, be taken as equivalent to an affirmation of the State. Sir William Ramsay's view that Paul contemplated a moral reform of the Roman Empire has absolutely nothing to support it.[1] The Empire, though not without its use, belongs to the order of things that is passing away. Not in it has the believer his citizenship, but in heaven and in the Church (Phil. 3[20]). Of imperial and civic duties, apart from those of submission and tax-paying, the Apostle has nothing to say.

That the reform of the State does not enter into Paul's calculation, nor anything that can be called a social pro-gramme, is evident from his treatment of the question of slavery. Slavery was an institution with respect to which the pagan conscience was not altogether easy. Provision was made in Roman law for a slave purchasing his freedom ; and among philanthropically minded masters the practice of manumitting their slaves, particularly in their wills, was

---

[1] *The Cities of St. Paul*, p. 75.

not uncommon.[1] And desire for freedom was widespread.
That it should be intensified in slaves who had been
brought under the power of Christian truth was inevitable.
Had they not learned that God was no respecter of persons,
that for them as for their masters Christ had died? This
aspiration the Apostle considers, but does not encourage
(1 Cor. 7$^{20-24}$, Col. 3^{11}). The external conditions of his
life, like everything that belongs to the present order, should
be for the believer a matter of indifference. If he was
called as a slave, let him be content to remain a slave; if
he was called as a free man, let him remain a free man.
Enough for the Christian slave that he knows himself
inwardly emancipated, the freedman of Christ, and the
citizen of a kingdom in which earthly distinctions of race
and rank and sex have lost their meaning. But if Paul
does not contemplate a social revolution, he is concerned
that men should bring into existing relations the spirit of
Christ. The master must be just and considerate, he must
treat the believing slave as a brother in Christ; the slave,
on his side, must be obedient and conscientious in his work.

While condemning covetousness as a species of idolatry,
Paul does not impose on believers any vow of poverty.
They are to work with their own hands that they may
maintain an honourable independence and be in a position
to help their poorer brethren (1 Thess. 4$^{11ff.}$, 2 Thess. 3^{10},
Gal. 6^6). There is to be no withdrawal from the ordinary
avocations of life. At the same time they must never
forget that the fashion of this world passeth away and that
it behoves them to sit loose to all its goods (1 Cor. 7^{30}).

What of the institution of the family? Since the end
is at hand the natural necessity for marriage disappears, and
the tie can come into consideration only with respect to its
bearing on the religious interests of the parties involved.
Judging it from this standpoint, the most the Apostle can

[1] Dill, *Roman Society from Nero to M. Aurelius*, p. 117.

bring himself to concede to it is toleration. Unmarried himself, he counsels those who have not already contracted the tie to follow his example (1 Cor. 7). It is good for a man not to touch a woman. This negative attitude towards marriage is not rooted in any ascetic scruple, but in the consideration that marriage forges a new link with the world and distracts from a whole-hearted service of Christ. " He that is unmarried is careful for the things of the Lord, how he may please the Lord; but he that is married is careful for the things of the world, how he may please his wife."

But while Paul regards celibacy as the ideal, he recognises that it is not in every case practicable and disclaims the intention of imposing it as a law. Those who have not the necessary self-control are better married. Marriage is allowed as a concession to human weakness : " It is better to marry than to burn."

Though the Apostle nowhere attempts to establish marriage on a moral basis or betrays any feeling for the value of the home as a school where the affections are evoked and character built up, his strong moral interest asserts itself in the ideal of home life he inculcates. The wife is to be in subjection to her husband, as is fitting in the Lord, and the husband on his part is to love his wife and treat her kindly (Col. 3[18f.]). Children must obey their parents, and the father must not exercise the *patria potestas* in too despotic a fashion. It may be remarked here that notwithstanding his assertion that in Christ male and female are one, Paul does not in practice concede to the woman an equal place with the man. Both in the family and in the Church she is relegated to a position of subordination, and that on the ground of her natural inferiority. While the man is the image and glory of God, the woman is the image and glory of the man ; and as Christ is the head of the man so the man is the head of the woman (1 Cor. 11[3ff.]).

In this matter the Apostle abides by what was the antique view, both Jewish and pagan.

In a society in which divorce was easy and frequent, it meant a raising of the ideal when the Apostle, going back to a commandment of Jesus, proclaimed the indissolubleness of the marriage bond (1 Cor. $7^{10ff.}$). Even in the case of a mixed marriage he throws the responsibility of annulling it on the pagan partner. Only it must be said that in forbidding the believing wife to leave her unbelieving husband, so long as he is content to remain with her, he has in view less the sanctity of the tie than the possibility that through his wife's influence the husband may be won for the Christian faith.

For the vice of sexual impurity, so rampant in paganism, Paul shows an abhorrence that was in part at least an inheritance from his Jewish upbringing. Always he classes it with the deadliest of sins. Characteristic of his standpoint is the ground on which he bases his condemnation. He condemns fornication not as inflicting a wrong upon the woman or as destroying the relation of mutual respect and honour that ought to subsist between the sexes, but as a sin against a man's own body (1 Cor. 6^{13-20}, 1 Thess. 4^{3-7}, Rom. 12^1). The body no less than the spirit is for Christ; it is a member of Christ and destined for immortality. To make it a member of a harlot is to desecrate it. A religious rather than an ethical standpoint, and yet one that presupposes a lofty ethical ideal. We must glorify God with our body as with every faculty we possess.

We have explained Paul's predominantly negative attitude towards earthly institutions and relationships as the result of his apocalyptic outlook. These institutions and relationships belong to the world that is hastening to destruction. Outside Judaism a movement in many respects similar had long been in progress. The Hellenistic age witnessed the passing of the antique corporate conception of life and the rise of individualism. Among the factors responsible for this development were the collapse and ultimate submergence in the Roman Empire of the old free cities and nationalities, and the disintegrating action of philosophic thought on the time-honoured authorities that had held the self-assertion of the individual in check.[1] It was no longer possible for the individual to merge his life in that of the State. Loosed from the State and with his intellect emancipated, he thought of himself as a member of the cosmos; and his ethical ideal, as formulated in Stoicism and Epicureanism, was one of almost complete liberation from external claims and ties. The " wise man " looked within for the content of his life, and nourished the sense of his independence and self-sufficiency as a rational being. Naturally it was only among the cultured classes that such an ideal found acceptance. Among the mass the new sense of freedom and individuality sought satisfaction not in philosophy but in religion. And since the old State religions had nothing in this direction to offer, what appeal they possessed being solely to man as a citizen, the mass turned to the Oriental cults that were sweeping in successive waves over the Empire. The Cults appealed to man as an individual and offered him an individual good—liberation from the chains of the material, deliverance from the dark astral powers and the hope of a blessed and immortal existence beyond death.

In a mordant passage Sir James Frazer contrasts this new conception of life with that of the palmy days of Greek and Roman civic virtue. " Greek and Roman society," he writes, " was built on the conception of the subordination of the individual to the community, of the citizen to the State ; it set the safety of the commonwealth, as the supreme aim of conduct, above the safety of the individual whether in this world or in a world to come. Trained from infancy in

---

[1] Wendland, *Die hellenistisch-römische Kultur*, 2nd ed. pp. 45 ff.

this unselfish ideal, the citizens devoted their lives to the public service and were ready to lay them down for the common good; or if they shrank from the supreme sacrifice, it never occurred to them that they acted otherwise than basely in preferring their personal existence to the interests of their country. All this was changed by the spread of Oriental religions which inculcated the commune of the soul with God and its eternal salvation as the only objects worth living for, objects in comparison with which the prosperity and even the existence of the State sank into insignificance. The inevitable result of this selfish and immoral doctrine was to withdraw the devotee more and more from the public service, to concentrate his thoughts on his own spiritual emotions, and to breed in him a contempt for the present life which he regarded merely as a probation for a better and an eternal. The saint and the recluse, disdainful of earth and rapt in ecstatic contemplation of heaven, became in popular opinion the highest ideal of humanity, displacing the old ideal of the patriot and hero who, forgetful of self, lives and is ready to die for the good of his country. The earthly city seemed poor and contemptible to men whose eyes beheld the city of God coming in the clouds of heaven. Thus the centre of gravity, so to say, was shifted from the present to a future life, and however much the other world may have gained, there can be little doubt that this one lost heavily by the change. . . . The revival of Roman law, of the Aristotelian philosophy, of ancient art and literature at the close of the Middle Ages, marked the return of Europe to native ideals of life and conduct, to saner, manlier views of the world. The tide of Oriental invasion had turned at last. It is ebbing still." [1]

That in these strictures, directed mainly against Christianity, there is the proverbial grain of truth will hardly be

[1] *Adonis, Attis, Osiris,* p. 252.

disputed. The decay of the sense of civic duty involved in the individualism of the Hellenistic age is not to be denied. But there are two things Sir James Frazer fails to take account of. He does not see that the old tribal conception of morality had become impossible, that the human mind had advanced beyond it. And limiting his attention to the negative aspect of the new movement, he allows nothing for its positive ethical contribution. If philosophy was indifferent to the interests of the State it introduced the conception of the unity of the race and essayed the task of establishing morality on a human basis. And if the Cults cannot be credited with leading a moral advance, they did not a little to foster the human sympathies out of which morality springs. Indifferent with regard to the State, and concerned about the future life rather than about the present, they were yet far from being antisocial. Everywhere there sprang up, in place of the old civic and national communities fallen into decay, new communities in which distinctions of race and rank and nationality were obliterated, and rich and poor, the slave and the free man, Oriental and Occidental, could meet as brethren on the platform of a common religious interest. That the Cults offered to men a refuge from isolation, some kind of human fellowship, was one of the secrets of the attraction they exercised.

But it is when we take account of Christianity that the exaggeration and one-sidedness of Frazer's view becomes most apparent. Granted that in Paul's teaching the present is overshadowed by the future, and earthly institutions in large measure lose their significance, it is still true that his ethic is emphatically a social ethic and as free from self-centred individualism and other-worldliness as well could be. We have only to think of the position he assigns to love. The greatest thing in the world, greater than faith and hope, the root of all virtue, is the love that

suffereth long and is kind, that envieth not, is not puffed
up, seeketh not its own, rejoiceth not in unrighteousness
but rejoiceth with the truth, beareth all things, believeth all
things, hopeth all things, endureth all things. And everywhere the Apostle's teaching moves on this level. The
follower of Christ, if he walk worthy of his vocation, does
not seek his own but makes himself the servant of all.
For the sake of others he renounces his rights and restricts
his liberty. He is content to be poor that he may make
others rich. He does nothing through faction or vain-
glory, but follows the things that make for peace. He
shows forbearance, and when injured he is ready to forgive.
He blesses those who persecute him, returning good for
evil. He is kind and sympathetic, rejoicing with those
that rejoice and weeping with those that weep. Though
sitting loose to the world's relationships and goods, he is
an obedient and peaceable citizen, a loyal and affectionate
husband, a considerate and just master, a conscientious
servant, a diligent man of business.

That is not the ideal of the ascetic, nor of the man
whose chief thought is to secure for himself a blessed immortality. It is rooted in a social conception of life ; from
its relation to other lives the individual life derives its
content.

One may feel surprise that the social conception of life
should have maintained itself with such force and purity,
combined as it was with an outlook which emptied all
existing social institutions and relationships of permanent
meaning and value. The same problem meets us in Jesus,
who with His Apostle shared the apocalyptic outlook.
Judging Jesus' ethic from what this outlook would require
it to be rather than from what it actually is, men have
described it as an "interim ethic." The description,
however, has but little appropriateness. Jesus' ethic,
like that of Paul, is through and through social. One

13

or two considerations may throw some light on the problem.

Notwithstanding the fact that in the teaching both of Jesus and His Apostle the state, the city and the family retire into the background, and such interests as commerce, art, science, literature receive no recognition whatever, human beings are far from being thought of as isolated units whose sole or chief business is to make sure of their place in the future world. They are members of a kingdom —the Kingdom of heaven. And while this kingdom is regarded as lying beyond the clouds, there is no attempt at an imaginative construction of it, or at an adjustment of morality to new and ideal conditions. Its righteousness is the righteousness that obtains here on earth. What really happens is that there is a concentration of interest on those relationships that are universally human, and that the ethico-religious ideal becomes the one object of pursuit. That men are brothers, the children of the Father in heaven, this appears as the one all-determining social fact. On this fact every social duty is based—that men live together in peace, that no one injure another or use him for his own selfish ends, that they treat one another with generosity and kindness and find their greatness in being the servants of all. If the State disappears as the object of devotion and sacrifice another and a larger object comes into view, the realisation of the divine purpose with our race the bringing in of the Kingdom. In the service of this cause it is required that a man, in the vivid language of Jesus, be ready to hate father and mother, yea and his own life also.

To look upon all this as a decline from the civic virtue of Greece and Rome is to rank patriotism as the supreme duty and a tribal morality above a human. And in the long-run, one dare assert, the particular relationships did not suffer from their temporary eclipse; rather were they set in a larger horizon and guarded by a holier sanction. We may complain of the indifference of early Christianity to the goods of civilisation; and certainly we cannot share it. But it has to be remembered that every great movement has had the same one-sidedness. Paul could not have accomplished what he did if religion had been for him only one interest among others, if it had not been everything to him. To send a man into the world with a single consuming passion in his soul is God's way of enriching the heritage of the race. And God Himself adjusts the balance. What is true of individual men is true also of movements. Moreover, this also has to be borne in mind, that if the moral and religious interest is not the sole interest in our human life, it claims the place of supremacy. It is the organising principle in life; and only when other interests submit to its control do they reach their fullest development and contribute their richest blessing.

The ethic of Jesus and not less that of Paul is thus grounded in the conception of a kingdom of God which is also a kingdom of humanity. In the case of the Apostle there is another fact to be taken into account. A new society has formed itself within the old, and in this new society believers have their place and work. They are members of the Church, and the Church unites them in a social whole, imposes upon them reciprocal duties and enlists them in a common cause. "And whether one member suffereth, all the members suffer with it; or one member is honoured, all the members rejoice with it." One dare assert that the Church bound men together by closer and deeper ties—ties of faith and hope and love—and elicited a purer devotion, a nobler service, a more uncalculating sacrifice than any State, ancient or modern, has ever done.

That the shield has another side is true. The concentration of interest in the Church involved a certain limitation in the conception of the social ideal and of social duty. It is the Church and not humanity that appears as the body of Christ; the Church and not humanity that the Christian is under obligation to serve. The world outside is for Paul a profane thing, within which no breath of the Divine Spirit stirs, under the dominion of sin and hastening to destruction. In it the follower of Christ has neither part nor lot; he has been crucified to the world and the world to him (Gal. 6¹⁴, Phil. 3²⁰). It is not merely on the evil in the world that he turns his back, but on the world itself (2 Cor. 6¹⁴⁻¹⁸). The adjective holy, which Paul applies alike to the Church and to the believer, carries with it the idea of separation from the profane world no less than that of dedication to God (Rom. 11¹⁶, 1 Cor. 3¹⁶· ¹⁷ 7¹⁴· ³⁴, Col. 3¹²). A narrowing of the social ideal is undeniable; and equally undeniable is a narrowing of the field of duty. To assert that Paul recognises no positive duties towards those outside the Church unless to bring them inside, would indeed be a gross exaggeration. Believers are to render unto no man evil for evil, but to bless those that persecute them; they are to show love and goodness not only towards one another, but towards all (1 Thess. 3¹² 5¹⁵). They are to walk in wisdom toward them that are without (Col. 4⁵). The Apostle is far from teaching a sectarian morality. And yet what he understands by love, if not indeed exclusively, is still in the main love of the brethren (Rom. 12¹⁰). In the vast majority of cases it is to the brethren that the services of love are to be rendered. The larger idea of human brotherhood is to some extent overshadowed by the narrower if more intense idea of Christian brotherhood. But here too we can trace a providential order. The big human sympathies had to be nourished in the Church before they were strong enough to reach out to those who had no claim on them but that of a common humanity.

That the ethic of Paul is in all essential respects that of Jesus hardly needs to be demonstrated. The fact stares us in the face. In both we find the same complete fusion of morality and religion, the same grip of the distinction between the moral and the ceremonial, the same inwardness, the same respect for the autonomy of the individual conscience. In both, morality appears as something radically social and is summed up in the commandment of love. It is the same vices that are singled out by Jesus and by His Apostle for condemnation—pride, the presumption that sits in judgment upon others, self-righteousness, anger, revenge, lasciviousness, worldliness. It is the same virtues that are exalted—humility, kindness, pitifulness, gentleness, peaceableness, liberality, forgiveness, self-renunciation, self-sacrifice. If Jesus forbids us to resist evil, Paul tells us to overcome evil with good. The list of parallels could easily be extended. There is but one way of accounting for this so striking agreement. The Apostle stood under the influence of the Master.

CHAPTER VI.

The Church and its Sacraments.

THE CHURCH.—What created the Christian community and held it together was the belief that the crucified and risen Jesus had been exalted by God to the messianic throne and would speedily reappear to judge the world and bring in the Kingdom. This belief did not at once lead those who shared it to separate themselves from Judaism—they continued to frequent the Temple and the synagogue—but from the outset it must have made them conscious that they were a people apart. They and they alone were believers—one of the earliest names by which they called themselves—and waited for the coming of Christ from heaven. They were a company of brethren —another early name—bound together by their common faith and hope. To them alone salvation in the approaching catastrophe was assured.

Though it is little likely that the primitive community made its own place and significance a subject of reflection, the march of events must have compelled it to define in some way its relation to the Jewish faith and people. From the attitude of James and those who thought with him to the Gentile mission, we may safely infer that it held fast not merely to its spiritual, but as well to its racial continuity with Israel. The demand that Gentile converts should be circumcised and observe the Law was in effect an assertion than the messianic salvation was

primarily for the Jews, and that Gentile converts to participate in it must incorporate themselves with the people of
promise. Since it speedily became clear that the mass of
the Jews was not to be won for Christ, the idea of the
Christian community as the faithful remnant in which the
destinies of the nation resided must early have come to
the front. There would in all probability be no occasion
or impulse to proceed beyond these simple and obvious
thoughts.

Nor do we find much more in Paul. While he has a
great deal to say about particular churches, the idea of the
Church as a whole but rarely emerges on his pages. Only
in the Epistle to the Ephesians is this idea the centre of
religious interest, and its extreme prominence there is one
of the main reasons for doubting the Epistle's genuineness. Nowhere in the Epistles of undoubted authenticity
is it made the subject of dogmatic determination. The
peculiarly Pauline conception of the Church as the body
of Christ is not, as we shall see, presented as an answer to
the question as to its place and significance in the world.

For Paul as for the primitive community, the fundamental fact about the Church is that it is the fellowship
of the saved (1 Thess. 5⁹). And his more developed conception of salvation enables him to give to this thought a
new sharpness. It is assumed that all who have connected
themselves with the Church have died and risen with Christ,
that in all Christ or the Spirit dwells as the animating
principle of their being (Rom. 6³ff.). That all do not live a
life becoming the Gospel does not for Paul alter this basal
fact. Believers are saints, holy, not as ethically faultless,
but as the temple of the Spirit and the property of God.
If God has begun a good work in them, He must needs
carry it to completion (Phil. 1⁶). Ultimate rejection of the
unworthy indeed remains as an abstract possibility, but
even in the case of the scandalous offender of 1 Cor. 5

the Apostle clings to the belief that his spirit may be saved in the day of the Lord Jesus. Outside the Church there is no salvation, nothing but the evil world that hastens to its doom (Gal. 1⁴).

This is not to be taken as meaning that Paul holds the later view of the Church as guaranteeing salvation to its members through its ministry and sacraments. Salvation comes through faith in Christ; only he can assume that true believers and Church members are equivalent terms. The Church is not the institution of salvation, but the sum of the saved.

Not less than the Jewish Christians, Paul is concerned to maintain the continuity of the Church with God's ancient people. "We are the circumcision who worship by the Spirit of God and glory in Christ Jesus and have no confidence in the flesh" (Phil. 3³). The Old Testament is taken possession of as an exclusively Christian book. "For our sake it was written," and Christ is the yea and the amen to all its promises (1 Cor. 9¹⁰, 2 Cor. 1¹⁹). It is not, however, to racial but to spiritual continuity that the Apostle attaches importance. When he makes use of the remnant idea he connects it not with the Church, but with the slender company of elect Jews (Rom. 11⁴ᶠᶠ·). In Christ there is neither Jew nor Greek, circumcision nor uncircumcision. Notwithstanding the fact that in a burst of patriotic feeling he speaks of the Gentiles as having been grafted like a wild olive into the ancient stem, Jewish descent has become a matter of complete indifference (Phil. 3⁴ᶠᶠ·). "He is not a Jew who is one outwardly, neither is that circumcision which is outward in the flesh; but he is a Jew who is one inwardly, and circumcision is that of the heart, in the Spirit, not in the letter" (Rom. 2²⁸ᶠ·). What makes a child of Abraham is not fleshly descent, but the possession of Abraham's faith (Gal. 3⁷).

As the true Israel, the children of promise, the Church is the chosen or elect community (Rom. 8^{33} $9^{23f.}$, Col. 3^{12}). It is made up of those whom God has separated from the doomed world to be vessels of His mercy. The idea is of frequent occurrence in the Old Testament and in Jewish Apocalyptic, and it was from these sources the Apostle derived it.

So far the Church has been defined only in terms of its members: it is the company of believers, of the saved, of those who having Abraham's faith are the true Israel, the elect, the heirs of the promises. Does Paul also think of it as an institution and attempt to determine its character as such?

To his hand there lay the idea of the Kingdom. How natural that he should declare the Church to be the Kingdom in its incipient stage, the Kingdom militant, soon to become triumphant! Was it not marked off from the profane world, the kingdom of darkness, by the presence of Christ, the presence of the Spirit within it? Two or three passages can be quoted as seeming to point to some such conception. Of the Kingdom it is said that it is not in word but in power, and that it does not consist in eating and drinking, but in righteousness, peace and joy in the Holy Ghost (1 Cor. 4^{20}, Rom. 14^{17}). This might seem to bring it into the present. But it does not really do so. That Paul can speak of the great realities of the Kingdom as even now with us does not really in his case, any more than in that of Jesus, carry the implication that the new order has opened. Two Colossian passages may be thought to carry us further (Col. 1^{13} 4^{11}). But in the first of these, in which believers are described as having been delivered out of the kingdom of darkness and translated into that of the Son of God's love, the Apostle is speaking proleptically; and in the second, which refers to certain disciples as " my fellow-

workers unto the Kingdom of God," it is the ultimate
end of their activity that is in view.   Paul has no thought
of bridging the gulf between now and then.   Believers
are those who shall inherit the Kingdom, but they do
not in any sense constitute it.

But if Paul does not think of the Church as the
Kingdom, there is another conception under which he
brings it in its organic character and one peculiar to
himself.   The Church is the body of Christ.   What he
means by this figure we learn from 1 Cor. 12$^{12-27}$, where
it is developed in detail.   Though made up of many
members, the Church is yet essentially one, an organism,
as we should express it (1 Cor. 10^{17}).   Individual believers
are not isolated, independent atoms; they are so closely
linked with one another that if one suffers all the others
suffer with him.   Each has his place and function in the
whole, and on the right performance by each of his special
task the welfare of the whole depends.   Into the one
body each has been baptized in the one Spirit.   But
while all this shows us the appropriateness of the figure
of a body, it does not show us why the Church should
be described as the body of Christ.   Nor is the Apostle
at pains to make this point clear.   He assumes that it
will be at once understood.   Christ is the Head "from
whom all the body, being supplied and knit together
through the joints and bands, increaseth with the increase
of God" (Col. 2^{19} 1^{18}).   The Church is His as it is God's;
He suffered for it, and its well-being is His constant care
(Rom. 16^{16}, Col. 1^{24}).

In the Epistle to the Ephesians the idea of the Church
as the body of Christ is reproduced, but in a distinctly
mystical form.   The Church is the body of Christ, not
as having Him for its Head, but as containing His Fulness
—"the Fulness of Him that filleth all in all" (1^{23}).   Still
further, the oneness of Christ and His Church is described

as a great mystery (5^{32}). Usually it is assumed that in the other Epistles also the relation is regarded as a mystical one. But without any sufficient reason. In Colossians Christ mediates the Divine Fulness not to the Church but to the individual, and the great mystery is His indwelling in the individual (2^{10} 1^{27}). There is nothing to show that in the Epistles of unquestionable genuineness Paul carries over the idea of a mystical union from the individual believer to the Church as an institution. In these the Church has not yet become an object of speculative interest.

Baptism.—Paul assumes that it was through baptism that every believer, himself included, entered the Christian community (Rom. 6^3, 1 Cor. 12^{13}). From his comparison of the rite to a burial and a resurrection we may infer that it was by immersion. Can we add anything more with respect to its form? It is described as baptism in or into—the prepositions ἐν, εἰς, ἐπί are interchangeable and carry no difference of meaning—the name of Jesus (1 Cor. 1^{12} 6^{11}, Rom. 6^3). From this description and from other indications we may regard it as in the highest degree probable that in the baptismal act the name of Jesus was pronounced or invoked both by the convert and by the dispenser of the rite. The Book of Acts speaks of Saul as having been baptized " calling upon the name "; and it is probably the same invocation the Apostle has in view when he declares that whosoever shall call upon the name shall be saved (Acts 22^{16}, Rom. 10^{13}). And in the Epistle of James believers are warned against the rich who " blaspheme the honourable name called over you " (τὸ καλὸν ὄνομα τὸ ἐπικληθὲν ἐφ᾿ ὑμᾶς) (2^7). It is natural to suppose that the calling of the name here referred to is that of the dispenser of baptism. And it is the same invocation which is in Paul's mind when he describes believers as having been washed, sanctified, justified in the name of the Lord Jesus Christ and in the Spirit of our God (1 Cor. 6^{11}). It may be remarked that the trinitarian formula, which appears first in Matt. 28^{19}, did not come into use till toward the end of the first century (Acts 2^{28} 8^{14} 10^{48}).

How are we to interpret this invocation of the Name? By Heitmüller [1] and others it is interpreted in the light of certain superstitious notions, survivals from a primitive stage of religious culture, regarding the connection of a person's name with his personality and the power which a knowledge of his name gives one over him. His name is part of a god's being, and one has only to pronounce it to have his power at one's disposal. The invocation of Jesus' name in baptism was meant to act as a spell. It drew down upon the convert Jesus' Spirit and power and had thus a consecrating virtue. It also placed the convert under Jesus' protection and stamped him, in a way analogous to the pagan practice of tattooing the god's name on the body of the devotee, as Jesus' property. In support of this hypothesis examples are adduced of a superstitious use of Jahveh's name in the Old Testament, and of a similar use of the name of Jesus in subapostolic times and even in the first generation (Num. 6^{27}, Matt. 7^{22}, Mark 9^{38}, Luke 9^{49} 10^{27}, Jas. 5^{14}, Acts $3^{6.\ 16}$ $4^{7.\ 10.\ 30}$). Devils were cast out and cures wrought by the mere utterance of the Name. Satan was supposed to tremble and withdraw when he heard it.

That a superstitious use of Jesus' name, particularly in exorcism, gradually found its way into the Church must be conceded. But there is nothing to show that such was current in the first generation. Certain it is that to the utterance of the Name in baptism Paul attaches no importance whatever. He can describe baptism without

---

[1] *Im Namen Jesu. Taufe und Abendmahl im Urchristentum*, p. 12.

introducing the Name, as a baptism into Christ, or more specifically into His death (Gal. 3²⁷, Rom. 6³).

In the absence of sufficient data one cannot speak with any certainty, but the probabilities are that the utterance of the Name meant on the part of the convert a confession of faith in Jesus as Messiah and Lord, and on the part of the dispenser of the rite, either a condensed prayer or a declaration that henceforth the convert belonged to Jesus. It is natural to suppose that the confession of Jesus with the mouth, of which Paul speaks in Rom. 10⁹ as ensuring salvation, is that of the decisive hour of baptism. And when he tells the Corinthian Christians that he had avoided baptizing them himself, lest any should say that they were baptized into his own name, pledged to be his followers, he assumes that baptism into the name of Jesus signifies a designation of the convert as belonging to Jesus (1 Cor. 1¹³ᶠᶠ·). Since it was just such a confession of faith in Christ and dedication to Christ that distinguished Christian from other baptisms, and in particular from that of John, we can easily understand how they should have been included in the descriptive title.

Confession of Jesus and dedication to His service must therefore be regarded as entering into the meaning which baptism possessed for Paul and for the Church in general. But these two ideas are far from exhausting the significance of the rite ; they are indeed only preliminary to others of a more essential character. Baptism in Paul's references to it appears under three distinct aspects, as a rite of entrance into the Church, a rite of cleansing and a rite of regeneration. Whether he views it as possessing an *ex opere operato* virtue or only as symbolic will appear in course.

1. Only once does the Apostle present Baptism in the light of a rite of initiation. Speaking of believers as

members of the body of Christ, he says, " For in one Spirit were we all baptized into one body, whether Jews or Greeks, whether bond or free; and were all made to drink of one Spirit " (1 Cor. 12^{13}). What constitutes the believer a member of the Church is the possession of the Spirit, and it is at his baptism the Spirit is imparted.

We are here face to face with a question of cardinal importance and one which will come up in other forms. Does Paul think of the Spirit as sacramentally mediated by baptism, or does he only regard its communication as synchronising with the baptismal act? At the present time the tendency among scholars is to adopt the former alternative.

In attempting to answer the question we begin with the fact that in the vast majority of cases in which Paul speaks of the giving of the Spirit there is no reference to any material medium. In definite terms he makes its communication contingent on faith. " Received ye the Spirit," he asks, " by the works of the Law or by the hearing of faith ? " (Gal. 3^2). Often he describes it as sent by God into the heart or as given by God (Rom. 8^{11}, 2 Cor. 1^{22} 3^5 5^5, Gal. 3^5 4^6, Phil. 1^{19}). All these passages tell strongly against the sacramental view. And what can be adduced in favour of it? Only two passages, and these very far indeed from being explicit. The first we have already quoted : " For in one Spirit were we all baptized into one body." Here the giving of the Spirit is indeed associated with baptism, but it is not asserted and not necessarily implied that the former is mediated by the latter. One can understand how the Apostle should have brought the two together without any thought of establishing a causal connection. Baptism must as a rule have followed close on conversion. In baptism the convert made a public confession of faith and was received into the fellowship of the Church. Often it would

be accompanied by new and thrilling experiences. How
natural that the Apostle should run conversion and baptism
together and single out the latter as marking the decisive
moment! Does the second passage carry us further? In
1 Cor. 6¹¹ Paul refers to certain in the Church who had
formerly lived an evil life, and continues, " But ye were
washed, ye were sanctified, ye were justified in the name
of the Lord Jesus and in the Spirit of our God." The
washing being taken as referring to baptism, we have the
statement that the effective instrument in it is the Spirit.
But no more here than in the first passage is it asserted or
implied that the operation of the Spirit is bound to the
ritual act. That the Apostle speaks of renewal as washing
rather gives the impression that the rite is no more than
the symbol of a spiritual change spiritually wrought. In
view of the fact that in general he speaks of the Spirit as
given directly by God and explicitly establishes faith as the
condition of its reception, nothing short of an unambiguous
statement would justify us in attributing to him the idea
that it is communicated through a material agency. But
such is nowhere to be found.

And there is another consideration which is not without
a bearing on the question. According to the primitive
view, the Spirit was not a universal but a special gift, the
possession of which carried with it extraordinary powers.
Its communication could not therefore have been connected
with a universal rite like baptism. And the Book of Acts
does not so connect it, but speaks of the Spirit as descend-
ing of its own motion, or after the preaching of the Word
and before baptism, or again as given by the laying on of
hands. While it is true that Paul was not bound by the
primitive view, the burden of proof lies on those who assert
that he broke with it.

We have been able to find in Paul only one passage in
which baptism appears as the rite of reception into the

Church. But this aspect of its significance must have been much more prominent in early days and indeed in Paul's own day than such an isolated reference would indicate. Every religious community had its sacrament of initiation. Through a lustral washing the heathen proselyte was received into Judaism, and by the same rite John sealed those who gathered round him as belonging to the company that waited for the coming of the Kingdom. Even so in Christian baptism the believer was sealed as a member of the Christian community. But while this can be asserted, it must be added that baptism would not have been adopted as the rite of initiation had it not possessed some intrinsic meaning that fitted it to occupy such a position. What this meaning was we have now to consider.

2. From immemorial times baptism had held a place as a rite of cleansing. In the primitive stage of religious development the defilement or infection which the lustral bath was supposed to wash away was that resulting from contact with a person or object which, as charged with a noxious magic force or an evil spirit, was regarded as tabu— dangerous. The water was thought of as absorbing the infection, or as drawing out the evil spirit; or, again, cleansing from visible impurity was regarded as carrying with it by sympathetic magic cleansing from invisible. In the lustrations of the Levitical code the idea of tabu has been superseded by that of ceremonial uncleanness; and what was originally avoided as charged with a dangerous force—a dead body, a menstruous woman, swine's flesh— is now avoided because contact with it would render a man unfit to appear before God and to mingle with his fellow-worshippers. And in cases of defilement the efficacy of the lustral bath is no longer based on the magic virtue of the water, but on the fact that it is a divinely appointed means of purification. Neither in the Old Testament nor

in Jewish writings is there any evidence that purificatory washings were thought of as removing moral stains. But in the great prophets, for whom as rites they have ceased to possess any validity, they appear as symbols of such a cleansing (Isa. 1^{16}, Ezek. 36^{25}, Zech. 13^{1}, Ps. 51^{7}). And it was probably in attachment with the prophets that John the Baptist gave to the rite itself, so far as we know for the first time, a moral significance. His baptism was a baptism of repentance unto the remission of sins. Since what he emphasises is not the efficacy of the rite but the obligation to bring forth fruits worthy of repentance, and since, further, he contrasts it with an efficacious Spirit-baptism of the future, there can hardly be a doubt that he views it as no more than an outward seal of the inner reformation. And if we regard the Christian baptism, as we are justified in doing, as modelled on that of John, it would have originally the same meaning. It would be a symbol of repentance and forgiveness. Such, as a matter of fact, is the significance attached to it in the Book of Acts, though there the idea of an *ex opere operato* virtue has begun to assert itself (2^{38} 2 2^{16}).

In Paul the conception of baptism as a rite of cleansing is no more prominent than the conception of it as a rite of initiation. All we have are two somewhat slight allusions : " Ye were washed, ye were sanctified, ye were justified "; " You being dead through your trespasses and the uncircumcision of your flesh, did He quicken together with Him, having forgiven us all our trespasses, having blotted out the bond written in ordinances that was against us " (1 Cor. 6^{11}, Col. 2$^{13f.}$). In the last passage the word " blotted out " is probably a play on lustral washing. The reason for this almost complete disappearance of the idea of cleansing will be noted presently. In this connection no one would contend that the Apostle thinks of a magical efficacy as attaching to baptism. When he discusses

14

justification or forgiveness the rite does not once come into account.

3. For the Apostle every other aspect of baptism is practically swallowed up in this, that it is a rite of regeneration. "We who died to sin," he writes in Rom. 6, "how shall we live any longer therein? Or are ye ignorant that all we who were baptized into Christ Jesus were baptized into His death? We were buried therefore with Him through baptism into death, that like as Christ was raised from the dead through the glory of the Father, so we also might walk in newness of life." The same complex of ideas recurs in Gal. 3^{27} and also in Col. $2^{11\text{ff.}}$. From the passage itself we can see that Paul was not singular in giving this interpretation to baptism. He assumes that the Roman Christians share it with him. As has already been shown, its origin is to be sought in Oriental religion. The idea of a death and a resurrection with Christ, borrowed from that source, impressed itself not only on Christian piety, but on the conception of the Christian sacraments.

The only question to be discussed is whether Paul regards baptism as merely symbolical of the two great Christian experiences or as the effective agent in their production. We have strong reasons for believing that there were those in the Church for whom the idea of a magical virtue attaching to the rite was far from foreign. In Rom. 6, Paul argues on the assumption that the ethical significance of baptism had been left out of account. But if the Roman Christians did not interpret it ethically they must have looked upon it with the Cults as effecting a divinising of our mortal nature. Again, in 1 Cor. 10^{1-5}, the Apostle has to issue a warning that participation in the sacraments does not by any means carry with it the certainty of salvation. Though the Israelites were all baptized unto Moses in the cloud and in the sea and partook of sacred meat and drink, most of them perished miserably in the wilderness. Finally, the practice of a vicarious baptism for the dead to which Paul refers could have sprung up only under the influence of superstitious notions as to the efficacy of the rite (1 Cor. 15[29]). We have to reckon with the fact that already in Paul's time sacramental ideas were current in the Church. But it does not follow that the Apostle shared them. The evidence points distinctly in the opposite direction.

Nowhere do we find a hint that the lustral water is charged with supernatural virtue, or that it is the medium of the Spirit. What we get is a superficial analogy between the disappearance of the convert in the water, followed by his re-emergence and the process of death and resurrection. Moreover, this analogy is by no means essential to the Apostle's thought. He can speak of baptism as a putting on of Christ, and again as a circumcision not made with hands—note the negation of the material—in the putting off of the body of flesh (Gal. 3[27], Col. 2[11]). In view of this lack of definiteness it is difficult to resist the conclusion that baptism is no more than a graphic symbol of what for Paul is the vital thing, union with Christ in His death and resurrection.

And there are other considerations that point in the same direction. Wherever Paul touches on efficient causes, he has recourse not to the rite, but to the power of God, or to the working of faith, or again to the working of the mystical union. "Our old man," he says, "was crucified with Christ, that the body of sin might be done away; for he that hath died is justified from sin" (Rom. 6[6]). It is the actual death—that death which is an essential moment in the mystical union—that sets the sinner free. And in Colossians the resurrection with Christ that succeeds on the death with Him is traced to faith in the working of God. Similarly the statement in Galatians that those who

were baptized into Christ did put on Christ is preceded by
the statement that all are sons of God through faith.   In
general, one can say, salvation is made to hang not on
participation in any sacrament, but on the Word of God
received in faith.   " The word works in you that believe ";
" In Jesus Christ I begat you through the Gospel " ; " By
faith ye have access into this grace wherein we stand."
By faith Paul knows Jesus and the power of His resurrection and the fellowship of His sufferings, becoming conformed unto His death (Phil. 3¹⁰).   In this last passage the
idea of death and resurrection with Christ is presented
without any reference to baptism.

It is true that Paul does not condemn the superstitious
practice of a baptism for the dead, but on the contrary
argues on the assumption that it is legitimate.   But is the
idea of an *argumentum ad hominem* unthinkable?   In any
case the practice is out of keeping with the whole structure
of his thought.   All we can infer from the use to which
he puts it is that he has not fully grasped the distinction
between symbol and efficient cause, or its far-reaching
importance.

Whether, as Bousset[1] maintains, the conception of
death and resurrection with Christ entered Christianity as
an interpretation of baptism, is a question not easy to
decide.   Certainly if Paul derived it from the cultus he
not only radically transformed its meaning, but almost completely detached it from its original ground.   The mystical
union is in his thought essentially independent of any
ritual act.   Not the sacraments but the word is the power
of God unto salvation.   " Christ," the Apostle can declare,
" sent me not to baptize, but to preach the Gospel."

The Supper.—In the eleventh chapter of the First
Epistle to the Corinthians we find a description of the

[1] *Kyrios Christos*, pp. xv, 171.

Supper as it was actually celebrated in the Church at
Corinth. The description is of peculiar interest as afford-
ing us, apart from a meagre reference in Acts 2[46], our
earliest glimpse of the institution that was to play so
notable a rôle. What we see is a common meal to which
the Christians in the neighbourhood have gathered. The
meal, in other respects an ordinary one, bears a religious
character. The table is " the table of the Lord," and the
Lord Himself is believed to be present. Through eating
and drinking the celebrants seek to enter into some sort of
union with Him (1 Cor. 10[14ff.]). In their conception of it,
the Supper is a mystic means of union with the exalted
Christ. If they thought of it as also a means of cementing
their fellowship with one another, their conduct was in
strange contradiction with their theory. The brotherhood
was broken up into cliques, partly it would seem on lines
of social status ; and each clique brought its own provisions
and itself consumed what it brought. While the richer
members feasted to the point of excess, the poorer sat
apart, hungry and neglected spectators. And this was not
all. Without waiting for a full assembly each clique
started its meal on the moment of its arrival. There was
no tarrying for each other. The picture, it must be confessed, is far from a pleasing one.

As thus observed, the Christian Supper was hardly
distinguishable from the religious meals that were a feature
of the paganism of the time.[1] Pagans too described their
festal table as " the table of the Lord." " Chairemon," we
read in a papyrus of the second century, " invites you to
sup at the table of the Lord Serapis, in the Serapeion,
to-morrow, the 15th, at the 9th hour." And the religious
good sought in these common meals was, as in the
Corinthian Supper, union with the deity. How precisely
the food and drink were thought of as mediating the

[1] Hepding, *Attis, seine Mythen und sein Kult.*, pp. 177 ff.

union is a question not easy to answer. Of the crude idea of an eating of the god, which obtained in the ancient Thracian Dionysos' rites, there is in the Hellenistic cults of the Imperial time no clear trace. The conception would, however, be realistic enough. It was a widespread belief that evil spirits could find their way into the human body and into the soul through the medium of food dedicated to them.[1] If a demon could avail itself of such an avenue, why not a divinity? It is also possible that there was no explicit theory, but that the consecrated meat and drink was regarded as endowed with mystic powers that were somehow effective in bringing the worshipper into contact with the god.

Paul himself is quite aware of the resemblance between these heathen meals and the Christian Supper, and sets the two in a sort of parallelism ($10^{18ff.}$). And what is more, there were believers in Corinth who thought it no sin to frequent both tables. Such conduct is intelligible only if we suppose that they regarded the religious good offered as in both cases substantially the same, immortality, namely, through union with the god. In that day it was no uncommon thing for men to seek an augmentation of grace through participation in the rites of more than one cult. Whoever was responsible for it, the Supper as celebrated at Corinth was in all substantial respects identical with the sacred meals at which Serapis or Attis was the presiding divinity.

If we have taken the Supper as observed in Corinth as our starting-point, it is not because we would find there, with Heitmüller, Weiss and Lake, the best index to the Apostle's fundamental ideas. Very much the contrary. We start from the Corinthian observance for the reason that every single thing that Paul says about the Supper is said in connection with that observance. Outside the tenth

---

[1] *Clementine Homilies*, ix. 9. Dieterich, *Eine Mithrasliturgie*, pp. 99 ff.

and eleventh chapters of First Corinthians there is not the remotest reference to the rite, not in the Second Epistle, not in Romans or Galatians or Philippians or Colossians. To appreciate what Paul says about the Supper we must keep before us the fact that he is speaking with his eye on the observance of the Corinthian Church.

That he should condemn the so painfully obtrusive moral abuses is a matter of course. In effect he demands, in order to their suppression, that the Supper be dissociated from the idea of a meal, and treated as a purely religious rite. " Have ye not houses to eat and drink in, or despise ye the Church of God? If any man hunger let him eat at home." The Supper is on the point of being differentiated and separated from the love-feast. But this is not all, or the main thing.

When the Apostle roundly declares that it is not possible under the existing conditions to celebrate a real Supper, he has something more in his mind than the moral abuses (11^{20}). For he immediately proceeds to set over-against the Corinthian practice the rite as Jesus Himself had instituted it, and as he, the Apostle, had delivered it to the Church. And in the account which he gives of the first Supper there is nothing that bears on the abuses reprobated, but everything turns on the ideas embodied in it. Can we resist the conclusion that Paul missed in the Supper as observed in the Corinthian Church what for him was its essential import, and that in the well-known passage beginning, " For I have received of the Lord that which also I delivered unto you," he has the deliberate design of bringing before his readers what that essential import is? In this passage, if anywhere, we must seek his doctrine of the Supper. What he says of the rite in the tenth chapter must not indeed be ignored, but it must not be taken as the starting-point of our interpretation.

In his account of the first Supper, Paul would seem

to attach himself, not to tradition, but to an inner revelation from the risen Lord: " I received of the Lord that which also I delivered unto you." Here, doubtless, as in Gal. I[11], he asserts his independence of all merely human authority. But no more than in Galatians can this assertion be taken as implying a complete indifference to tradition. From tradition he took over at least the historical data ; and the comparison of his narrative with those of the Synoptists will show that even with respect to dogmatic interpretation his freedom has its limits.

But before comparing the Synoptic accounts of the Last Supper with that of Paul, it may be well to compare them with each other. Our ulterior task may turn out to be thereby simplified.

The first result of such a comparison is the elimination of Matthew as an independent source. Its narrative is based on that of Mark ; and its two material divergencies —the transformation of Mark's " They all drank of it " into a command, " Drink ye all of it," and the clause, " Unto the remission of sins " added to the cup-words— are both of the nature of explanatory amplifications.

The Lukan narrative presents a much more difficult problem. To begin with, the text is not free from uncertainty. In the manuscript D, which represents a text that was widely current in the West, the narrative ends with the words, " And He took bread, and when He had given thanks, He brake it and gave to them, saying, This is My body " (22[14-19a]). Scholars of eminence have adopted the view not only that this short text is the authentic one, but that it embodies the earliest of all the extant traditions about the Supper. The narrative, it is affirmed, is complete as it stands ; there are the cup and the bread, with their accompanying words ; and the continuation in other MSS. (22[19b-20]), which is in almost verbal agreement with I Cor. II[24b-25], can be best understood as the work of some harmonising scribe.

To the present writer this hypothesis seems built on the sand. The evidence for the authenticity of the longer text on which our English versions are based is overwhelmingly strong. It is true that this text seems to reduplicate the cup. But verses 15–19 can quite well be taken not as an account of the rite proper, but as an introduction to it. Mark as well as Luke has the saying about not drinking again of the fruit of the vine until the coming of the Kingdom, though he places it not at the beginning but at the end. We may suppose that Luke, finding in some source unknown to us the saying, "With desire I have desired to eat this Passover with you before I suffer," conjoined it with the saying given by Mark, prefixing both to his account of the rite proper as an introduction. If this part be introductory, the objection that the long text involves a reduplication of the cup disappears. It is impossible to believe that Luke, or whoever the writer was, intended the farewell cup to be taken, as the short text would involve, as the model of and warrant for the sacramental. Accepting therefore verses 19, 20 as the Lukan account of the rite, a comparison of these verses with 1 Cor. 11[24, 25] will show that Luke is dependent, if not on 1 Cor. 11, then on the usage of Pauline Churches. The third Gospel must, therefore, along with the first be set aside as an independent source. We are thus left with only two primary sources, that of Mark and that of Paul.

Comparing the narratives of Paul and Mark, we find that the most considerable divergence occurs in the words accompanying the distribution of the bread. According to Paul, Jesus, when He had given thanks and broken the loaf, said, "This is My body, which is for you: this do in remembrance of Me." In Mark, Jesus' words are briefer, no more than, " Take, eat, this is My body." Which of the two represents the more primitive and correct tradition ? In general, it is a safe rule to prefer the shorter to the longer form, since a saying is more likely to be expanded than abbreviated. And this rule may be so far applied in the present case. Christ's command to repeat the act in memory of Himself, if not added by the Apostle, was taken by him from a source less primary than that which Mark had at his disposal. There are strong reasons for believing that Jesus did not contemplate the founding of a rite that should survive His death. So far we seem to be on firm ground. When, however, the brevity rule is applied to excise as a later addition the Pauline words, " Which is for you," doubts rise in our mind. So enigmatical a saying as " This is My body " Jesus certainly did not utter. Whatever words He spoke we may be sure that their meaning lay on the surface, and that it would be intelligible to every one. And certainly in the mind of Mark himself, as we can see from the cup-words he attributes to Jesus, the saying, " This is My body," carried a sacrificial reference. Jesus' body was offered as a sacrifice for many—that unquestionably is the meaning he read into it. How in some circles of the Church the saying should have been preserved in a truncated form is not difficult to understand, when we remember that in all probability it was not used in the liturgical way it is to-day, and that its meaning was always regarded as self-evident.

Passing to the cup-words we find that Paul gives them in a form slightly different from that in which they appear in Mark. What we have in Mark is, " This is My blood of the covenant, which is shed for many "; and in Paul, " This cup is the new covenant in My blood." Here it is easy to decide which is the more primitive form. It is that of the Evangelist. The Apostle freely alters the

saying in order to bring it into line with his more developed
and explicit theology. For him Christianity is a *new*
covenant established by Christ's death, as opposed to the
old covenant of the Law (2 Cor. 3[6ff.]). That he retains in
this connection the covenant idea is a proof of his attachment to the common tradition; for had he been freely
inventing he certainly would not have presented Christ's
blood in the light of covenant blood. Such a conception
is hardly in the line of his theology.

From this investigation of sources two results stand
out as assured. With respect to the form and meaning
of the first Supper and the circumstances of its institution,
the two primary sources—Paul and Mark—are in substantial agreement. Both represent Jesus as holding on
the night of His betrayal a parting meal with His disciples,
—whether it was also the Passover meal need not here be
decided. In both, Jesus appears as taking a loaf, uttering
a thanksgiving prayer, and breaking the loaf with at least
the words, " This is My body." In both He proceeds to
take a cup and to describe it as signifying His blood shed
in connection with the Covenant. That is the first
assured result. And the second is, that in both the
Supper is exhibited as a celebration of Christ's sacrificial
death.

Is this tradition in the substance of it authentic? In
face of the fact that Paul must have been familiar with the
rite from the time of his conversion, some two or three
years after the crucifixion, the modern suggestion that the
story of the last Supper is nothing more than an etiologi-
cal myth seems utterly unwarranted. Nor do we see any
reason to doubt that the thoughts to which Jesus gave
verbal and symbolic utterance on that last tragic evening
of His earthly life were substantially such as the traditions
have handed down to us. Among many scholars of the
present day there is a violent reaction against the old

discredited notion that Jesus regarded His mission in the world as being simply to die. Every reference of Jesus to His death as having saving significance is dismissed as "Church theology," and, to escape such a reference in the Supper, resort is had to all sorts of far-fetched interpretations of its symbolism. The fundamental idea is sought in the common meal and the fellowship or brotherhood which, according to ancient notions, the common meal established. Jesus would bind His disciples with Himself and with each other in a fellowship that would outlast death. And He offered them His own body, His own personality, as the bond which should unite them. But all that must be brushed aside as mere irrelevancy, without a particle of support in the oldest sources. The point of the symbolism does not lie in the eating and drinking; in Jesus' accompanying words it is not this that is emphasised. It lies in the breaking of the bread and in the resemblance between wine and blood. In all the narratives Jesus is represented as breaking the bread—an unintelligible prominence if the act were nothing more than the necessary preliminary to its distribution; and in the primitive community the Supper was described pregnantly as "the breaking of bread" (Acts 2$^{42.\ 46}$ 20^7). And does not the Old Testament speak of wine as "the blood of the grapes" (Gen. 49^{11}, Deut. 32^{14})? If such be the point of the symbolism, the idea which Jesus sought to convey through it could have been none other than that of His death as a sacrifice.

Why should not Jesus in that meal with His disciples, held under the shadow of the approaching tragedy, have endeavoured to prepare them for the staggering blow, and to root in their minds the assurance that what might seem the ruin of their hopes was in reality the divinely ordained means of their fulfilment? Why should He not have sought to communicate to them this faith, which He

Himself unquestionably possessed, and of which, as we
know, they stood in bitter need? And is it incredible
that Jesus should have thought and spoken of His death
as a sacrifice, of His blood as the blood of the eternal
covenant that assured salvation to the people of God?
In just this idea the great prophet of the Restoration found
the support of his sorely tried faith as he contemplated
the mysterious fate of his people, doomed to unparalleled
sufferings in the service of the Highest. One can say that
for Jesus, in that crisis of the Kingdom's fortunes, it was
the one inevitable idea. From this standpoint, and from
this alone, can the symbolism of the broken bread and
the cup of red wine, with Jesus' accompanying words, be
understood. Had Jesus pushed the symbolism further,
had He intended His disciples to draw a meaning out of
their eating and drinking, He would only have obscured
His central thought.

In our attempt to show what Paul had to start from,
and to demonstrate his substantial fidelity to the common
tradition, we have had to break the thread of our exposition of his doctrine, and we must stop to pick it up
again. Setting out from the Supper, as observed in the
Corinthian Church and Paul's strictures on it, we noted
that his own interpretation of the rite, given in 1 Cor. 11$^{23-26}$,
is to be understood as deliberately set over-against that
defective and perverted observance, and as embodying all
that he feels to be vital.

What is it then that the Apostle in this passage brings
into the foreground. Is it that the Supper is a means
towards mystical union with Christ—such union as the
Corinthians sought in it? Of that there is not one
solitary word. Even the conception of the rite as binding
believers into a fellowship with one another never emerges.
Nor is there any indication that in eating the bread and
drinking the cup believers partake of Christ's spiritual

body or receive into themselves the potencies inherent in His being. While participation in the elements is treated as part of the rite, no particular significance is attached to it. Indeed, from the words attributed to Jesus, "This do, *as oft as ye drink it*, in remembrance of Me," one might legitimately infer that the drinking is no more than an *occasion* for the celebration of the Lord's death. Whenever believers eat a meal, the broken bread and the cup of wine are to call up before them the great sacrifice on Calvary. Had Paul thought, as Heitmüller and Weiss think he did, of a kind of transubstantiation of the elements, and of a literal eating and drinking of Christ's flesh and blood (Weiss refuses to go further than the idea of fellowship with the transformed elements), he would hardly have changed the traditional words, "This cup is My blood of the covenant" into "This cup is the new covenant in My blood."

Two passages in particular are appealed to in support of the view that Paul teaches the doctrine of a real presence. The first is that which relates to unworthy partaking. "Wherefore whosoever shall eat the bread or drink the cup of the Lord unworthily, shall be guilty of the body and blood of the Lord. . . . For he that eateth and drinketh, eateth and drinketh judgment unto himself, if he discern not the body. For this cause many among you are weak and sickly, and not a few sleep." The unworthy partaking, it is urged, of which the Corinthians were guilty, consisted in this, that they did not recognise the true character of the sacred objects on the table, but treated them as if they had been ordinary bread and wine. And the divinity-charged elements reacted against the profane users by smiting them with sickness and death.[1] Now it may be conceded that if the doctrine of a real presence were capable of being demonstrated from other

---

[1] Heitmüller, *Taufe und Abendmahl im Urchristentum*, pp. 66 ff.

passages, it might perhaps be legitimately read into this. But it cannot be thus demonstrated. And, as we shall see, the words about not discerning the Lord's body are capable of another interpretation more in harmony with the context and with the general character of the Apostle's thought. As regards the judgment upon unworthy partakers, this is exhibited in the succeeding verses as effected not by the divinity-charged elements, but by the chastening hand of God. Not any more conclusive is the second passage to which appeal is made. In the beginning of the tenth chapter Paul writes: " I would not, brethren, have you ignorant, how that our fathers . . . did all eat the same spiritual meat, and did all drink the same spiritual drink: for they drank of a spiritual rock that followed them, and the rock was Christ." That the Supper is in the Apostle's mind is clear; and we may legitimately infer that he could think of the Supper, as well as of the desert manna and water, as spiritual food and drink. But it by no means follows that he conceives the nourishment as provided in a physical way, or that the word spiritual must be translated as simply supernatural. It is Christ Himself, not His flesh and blood, that is pointed to as the food and drink of the soul. The rock was Christ.

We have spoken of what Paul does not teach in that passage in which he deliberately sets himself to unfold the true purport of the Supper. He does not teach that the Supper is the medium through which the soul's mystical union with the exalted Christ or the fellowship of believers with one another is sustained. He does not teach any doctrine of " the real presence," does not say that in partaking of the sacramental bread and wine the believer receives into himself elements charged with supernatural and divine potencies. What then does he teach? The Supper is for him a memorial of Christ's sacrificial

death.   "This do in remembrance of Me.   For as often as
ye eat this bread and drink the cup, ye proclaim the
Lord's death till He come."   In these sentences the meaning of the rite is summed up.   The last is of particular
importance as an index to the Apostle's thought, since it
formed no part of the tradition, but was added by himself.
A memorial of Christ's sacrificial death, a means of proclaiming it—that and that alone is what the Supper
signifies for Paul.   And if we are right in supposing that
he finds the Corinthian observance not merely disfigured
by moral abuses but also defective in the matter of knowledge, may we not say that what he misses in it is
precisely the vital thing—a recognition of Christ's
sacrificial death (cf. 1 Cor. 2$^{1f.}$).   With all their striving
after mystic knowledge and mystic union, the Corinthian
Christians failed to "discern" in the Supper the Lord's
broken body and shed blood.   They were guilty of the
body and blood of the Lord in the sense that they ignored
and flouted the significance of these divine realities.

In asserting that the idea of union with the exalted
Christ forms no essential part of Paul's interpretation of the
Supper, we have left out of account the tenth chapter.
There the idea is unmistakably present.   Let me cite the
passage in which it appears.   "Wherefore, my beloved,
flee from idolatry. . . . The cup of blessing which we
bless, is it not a fellowship with the blood of Christ
(οὐχὶ κοινωνία ἐστὶν τοῦ αἵματος τοῦ Χριστοῦ)?   The
loaf which we break, is it not a fellowship with the
body of Christ?   Seeing that we, who are many, are one
loaf, one body: for we all partake of the one loaf.   Behold
Israel after the flesh: have not they which eat the
sacrifices fellowship with the altar?   What say I then?
That a thing sacrificed to idols is anything, or that an idol
is anything?   But I say that the things which the Gentiles
sacrifice, they sacrifice to devils and not to God, and I

would not that ye should have fellowship with devils (οὐ
θέλω δὲ ὑμᾶς κοινωνοὺς τῶν δαιμονίων γίνεσθαι). Ye cannot
drink the cup of the Lord and the cup of devils : ye cannot
partake of the table of the Lord and the table of devils."

In this paragraph the chief exegetical problem is the
meaning that is to be given to the word κοινωνία. Is the
fellowship with Christ or with the demons,—the two are
placed in parallelism,—which is the result of partaking at
the sacred table, to be understood as nothing more than a
table-companionship, the divinity being thought of as the
host ; or has the Apostle in his mind a real union, the
divinity entering into the soul of the communicant ?
Both interpretations are possible, but the latter is to be
preferred as more in keeping with the Apostle's general
train of thought. If it be objected that he could not have
thought of the Jewish sacrificer as united with the altar
but only as entering into a close relation with it, the answer
is that he shrank from presenting the sacrifice as a medium
of union with God. Undoubtedly Paul in this passage
speaks of union with Christ as effected by participation in
the Supper, and, as ever, of union with Him in the likeness of His death. That he speaks, not of fellowship with
Christ in His death, but of fellowship with Christ's body
and blood, is explained by the necessity for accommodating
himself to the symbolism of the rite.

Must we then conclude that Paul offers two parallel
and complementary interpretations of the Supper, that it
is a celebration of Christ's sacrificial death, and a means
towards union with Him ? There is more than one consideration to make us pause.

We take this first, that the conception of union with
Christ as mediated through an external rite is wholly
foreign to the general character and trend of the Apostle's
thought. That baptism is connected with the mystical
union only in symbolic fashion we have already seen, and

15

that the real ground of the latter lies nowhere else than in faith.   Further, the fact is surely of weight that often as Paul refers to the mystical union, in no other passage than the one we have been dealing with does he bring it into relation with the Supper.   The truth is, that the Supper did not lend itself in the way baptism did to body forth the mystical union as Paul conceived it.   While it might express the idea of union with Christ in His death, it could not express the complementary idea of union with Him in His resurrection.   And even in the Corinthian passage there are indications that he is consciously digging in a field of thought that is not his own.   Speaking of fellowship with the sacramental body of Christ, with a play on the word body (the loaf, which is a symbol of the body offered on Calvary ; the body of Christ, which is the Church), he transforms the idea into that of fellowship with one another in the Church (v. 17).   An incidental thought this last, and hardly entering as a vital element into his conception of the Supper.

The truth we believe to be this, that in the argument of 1 Cor. 10$^{14-22}$, which has for its object to show the inconsistency of participation in heathen religious meals with a profession of Christianity, the Apostle is working less with his own categories than with those of his readers.   What we have is a parallel to his argument from the practice of baptizing for the dead.   He could the more easily take the Corinthians' standpoint, since the idea of union with Christ was one with which in itself he could find no fault.

At the present time the tendency is to read into Paul the crudest sacramentarianism.   The sacraments are declared to be for him the Christian " Mysteries," through which the Christian salvation is mediated.   How little foundation there is for such a view of his teaching we have tried to show.   It is a significant fact that while he frequently speaks of the Gospel as a mystery, he nowhere uses the term where we should most expect to find it—in connection with the sacraments. In the circle of his ideas these occupy but a subordinate place. He does not bind the working of God to material agencies. Of the sacraments he might have said what he said of circumcision, that neither their observance nor their non-observance avails anything, but faith working through love.

CHAPTER VII.

THE CONSUMMATION.

To an extent which it is difficult for us to realise to-day the religion of the first Christian generation was dominated by the thought of the approaching end. Any hour the clouds might part and the Son of God appear with His angels. In Jewish Apocalyptic circles, from which the expectation was taken over, the various events which would mark the passing of the old and the coming of the new and eternal order had long been a subject of interest and speculation, and a more or less uniform and consistent programme had secured general acceptance. To this programme no less than to the expectation itself the Church served itself heir.

Down to the close of his life Paul cherished the belief that the Lord was at hand, though the precise hour of His coming he did not pretend to know (Phil. 4^5, 1 Thess. 5^2). And he has numerous references to the various events that make up the great drama of the last days. When, however, we essay the task of fitting these references into a consistent scheme we are confronted by difficulties, some of which are perhaps insurmountable. Nowhere does he himself supply us with such a scheme. Something approaching it we do indeed find in the two passages, 1 Thess. 4$^{16-17}$, 1 Cor. 15$^{20-28}$; but in both not only are events of cardinal importance omitted, but no place seems to be left for them. To these difficulties we shall return

later. In the meantime we submit the following programme
as perhaps open to fewest objections: the Messianic birth-
pangs; the Parousia and the Messianic war; the resurrection of believers who have died and the transformation of
those remaining alive; the millennial reign and the final
destruction of the demonic powers; the general resurrection
and the Judgment; the destruction of the wicked and the
coming of the eternal Kingdom.[1]

1. *The Messianic Birth-pangs.*—While the day of the
Lord will come as a thief in the night, events of a startling
character will herald its approach—the messianic birth-pangs,
as Jewish Apocalyptic describes them. The Apostle speaks
of a great "apostasy," a "mystery of lawlessness," a con-
spicuous "working of error." "The man of sin will be
revealed, the son of perdition, he that opposeth and exalteth
himself against all that is called God or that is worshipped;
so that he sitteth in the temple of God, setting himself
forth as God" (2 Thess. 2[3ff.]). Under the leadership of
this Antichrist iniquity will muster its forces for one last
desperate onset.

Whence did Paul derive this mysterious figure? In
part, at least, the description is taken from a passage in
the Book of Daniel, which tells of a tyrant (Antiochus
Epiphanes) who in the last days will exalt and magnify
himself above every god, speak marvellous things against
the God of gods and corrupt by his flatteries such as do
wickedly against the covenant. Some traits may also be
borrowed from the Emperor Caligula who, to the horror
of the Jews, attempted to set up a statue of himself in
the Temple at Jerusalem. Already in the later Jewish
Apocalypses the Daniel tyrant had been developed into the
figure of an Anti-messiah. For Jewish writers the Anti-
messiah was naturally a heathen potentate; but for Paul

[1] Knopf, *Zukunftshoffnungen des Urchristentums.*

he is unmistakably Jewish.   The apostasy from God which he leads is a Jewish apostasy ; and in the bitter hostility of the Jews to the Christian faith the Apostle sees the " mystery of lawlessness" already at work.   Meanwhile the "revelation" of Antichrist and the full flood of apostasy are held back by the strong hand of Rome.   But in a brief space this restraining power will be taken out of the way, and then !

2. *The Parousia and the Messianic War.*—In describing the Parousia Paul is sparing in the use of circumstance, and what he gives is traditional.   The Lord Jesus, surrounded by His retinue of angels, will descend with a shout, with the voice of the archangel and with the trump of God (1 Thess. 4[16], 2 Thess. 1[7, 8]).   The shout and the trumpet blast are a summons to the dead.   But from other passages we learn that the raising of the dead is not Christ's first task, that sterner work must precede it. Unbelievers will be destroyed from the face of the earth. "When they are saying, Peace and safety, then sudden destruction cometh upon them, as travail upon a woman with child ; and they shall in no wise escape " (1 Thess. 5[3]). And in Second Thessalonians we read that the Lord at His coming will slay the lawless one with the breath of His mouth (2[8]).   What we have in these two passages is the equivalent of the messianic war of Jewish Apocalyptic.   In the older apocalyptic writings this war appears as a real flesh-and-blood struggle.   Under the leadership of God or of the Messiah, the remnant of faithful Jews will put their heathen oppressors to the sword.   But as eschatological conceptions became more transcendent the war was stripped of its human character.   The host of the faithful disappear from the field, and the Messiah, unaided and in supernatural fashion, accomplishes the work of destruction.[1]   So is it in Paul.   Antichrist and his followers offer no real resistance:

[1] Windisch, *Der messianische Krieg u. das Urchristentum.*

they are brought to nought by the mere manifestation of Christ's coming. We may add that the war has also been purged of the last remnant of political motive.

3. *The Resurrection of Believers.*—With the disappearance of the wicked from the earth the way is cleared for the resurrection of believers who have died before the Parousia and the transformation of those remaining alive, that all may share in the millennial reign.

Of a resurrection of the wicked Paul nowhere speaks; though declaring as he does that they must appear before God's judgment bar, he must have presupposed it (Rom. 2^{6-16}). For his silence several reasons may be adduced. If, as we assume, he holds a millennial reign, he could not suppose the wicked raised at its opening along with believers, but only as in the Book of Revelation (20^{11}), immediately in front of the great assize. This, however, does not carry us far. More relevant is the fact that in the Apostle's mind resurrection is always associated with life and glory. It is in Christ that men shall be made alive (1 Cor. 15^{22}). To attain to the resurrection is to experience the power of Christ and to grasp the great prize (Phil. 3^{11}). In the utterances of Jesus we meet with a similar association. Jesus speaks of the good as recompensed at the resurrection of the just, and describes them as children of the resurrection. And in Jewish writings the idea of a resurrection limited to the just stands side by side with that of a resurrection of the just and unjust. It cannot be said, however, that all this amounts to a complete explanation of Paul's silence with respect to a resurrection of the unjust. His silence is part of a wider problem, that of the obscurity in which he leaves their fate.

What we have to consider, therefore, at the present point is the resurrection of believers. And the term believers has to be taken in the restricted sense of believers in Christ.   Of the saints of the old dispensation we hear nothing.

Resurrection for Paul means two things : the recall of the soul from Hades, and its reclothing with a body.   And this is the only form in which he knows the hope of immortality.   When the resurrection is denied, he treats it as tantamount to the denial of a future life (1 Cor. 15$^{12-19}$).

Sometimes this identification of the two conceptions is represented as springing from a desire on the Apostle's part to carry not merely man's soul, but his entire personality into the future world.   But no such motive is discoverable. The truth is, that he occupies here traditional Jewish ground.   The belief in immortality entered Jewish religion with Apocalyptic and under the form of a belief in a resurrection (Isa. 24-27, Dan. 12^2).   In Hellenistic religion the conception of immortality was different, the body as the soul's unworthy prison-house being consigned to eternal destruction.   Escaping the body, the soul rises as an immaterial spirit to God.   This conception is also found in certain circles of Jewish thought that had come under Hellenistic influence.   Philo, the Book of the Wisdom of Solomon, Fourth Maccabees, Slavonic Enoch know nothing of a resurrection of the body.   That Paul is not altogether unaffected by the Hellenistic view we shall see in a little.

What of the soul's state during the period between death and the resurrection ?   Where does the note of the last trump find it ?   Paul does not directly tell us ; but from certain references we can conclude that he shares the current Jewish belief—a belief that had come down from immemorial times—in a place of the dead, Hades, or, as the Hebrews named it, Sheol.   In Hades the soul was supposed to lead a bodiless, shadowy existence not worth the name of life.   The First Epistle of Peter informs us that to this spectral land the crucified Christ descended, to preach the Gospel to certain disobedient spirits of the

diluvian age (3$^{19ff.}$). If we could accept Ephesians as
authentic we should have from Paul a reference to the
same descent (4^9). In any case it can hardly be anything
else than the place of the dead he has in his mind when he
expresses a shrinking from death as from an unclothing
and making naked of the soul (2 Cor. 5$^{2-4}$). With regard
to the nature of the intermediate state the Apostle does not
speculate. His description of deceased believers as asleep
cannot be treated as a doctrinal statement. That he
thought of their death as involving a certain separation
from Christ we may perhaps infer from the kind of comfort
he gives to the Christians of Thessalonica, who were in fear
lest their dead should not participate with those alive in
Christ's millennial reign, but should have to remain in
Hades until the general resurrection. The dead in Christ,
he tells them, shall be raised to accompany Christ at His
coming (1 Thess. 4$^{13-17}$). Had he been able to say, they
are with Christ even now, he would surely have given them
that for their consolation.

With what bodies shall the saints arise? According to
the traditional Jewish view the old earthly body, gathered
from the dust by a miracle of power, will be restored to
them. But this crude notion Paul refuses to accept.
"Flesh and blood cannot inherit the kingdom of God,
neither doth corruption inherit incorruption" (1 Cor. 15$^{35ff.}$).
The new body will be spiritual in character and, unlike the
old, above the reach of decay. It will be composed of the
same radiance-substance as that of Christ's glorious body
(Phil. 3^{21}), and be adapted to the new mode of existence.
With respect to its precise relation to the discarded earthly
body the Apostle has nothing more definite to give us than
a reference to the relation of the springing corn to the seed
cast into the earth. When speculation moves in such
tenuous regions too many questions must not be asked.
The attempt sometimes made to show that the resurrection

body is regarded as in process of formation within the believer during his earthly life may at once be dismissed as without the slightest support.

Analogies to Paul's conception of a glorified body meet us alike in Jewish and in Hellenistic thought. According to the Apocalypse of Baruch, the earth will yield up the dead as she received them ; but after the Judgment the bodies of the wicked will suffer an evil change in appearance, while the bodies of the just will be so transformed as to shine with beauty and glory (50–51). And in the Hermetic writings the transfigured body of the regenerated, which has come from the birth of true being, will, unlike the old, be indissoluble and immortal.[1] While these parallels reveal a general tendency, they do not necessarily imply the Apostle's dependence on outside sources.

4. *The Millennial Reign and the final destruction of the demonic powers.*—In the Book of Revelation we read of a binding of Satan and a reign of Christ on earth with His martyred saints that lasts a thousand years (20^{4-15}). This, the seer tells us, is the first resurrection. The rest of the dead lived not until the thousand years should be finished. At the end of the millennial reign Satan will be loosed out of his prison, and will come forth to deceive the nations which are in the four corners of the earth and to lead them against the beloved city and the saints. But the issue for these demonic and human powers will be swift destruction. On their destruction will follow the second or general resurrection and the Judgment. The last scene shows us the final ruin that overtakes the workers of iniquity and the untroubled and endless bliss of God's people. Death and Hades, together with those whose names are not found written in the Book of Life, are cast into the lake of fire. The new Jerusalem descends out of heaven, made ready as a bride adorned for her husband.

---

[1] Reitzenstein, *Poimandres*, pp. 344 f.

Such is the eschatological programme of the Book of Revelation. While this book was not written until some thirty years after Paul's death, it embodies conceptions that had long been current in the Christian community, and we are amply justified in making use of it to light up obscure tracks in the Apostle's scheme. The millennial reign and the closely connected universal judgment form one such track. This reign he nowhere mentions by name, nowhere indeed makes any quite unambiguous reference to it. But that it forms part of his programme a study of 1 Cor. 15$^{22-26}$, in the light of the passage from the Book of Revelation, will make in the highest degree probable.

It lies in the plan of God, the Apostle declares, that Christ shall reign until He hath put all His enemies under His feet. During His reign, or, as it would rather seem, at the close of it, He will bring to nought the demonic hosts that have so long and cruelly lorded it over mankind,—all rule, and all authority and power,—the last foe to fall being the fell power of death. This reign Paul describes as the Kingdom, and tells us that when the work of subjugation is complete Christ will surrender His delegated authority to God. The parallelism with the millennial reign of the Book of Revelation is close enough to justify us in identifying the two. And it is a confirmation of this view that it provides a stage for that reign of the saints with Christ and their judgment of angels of which the Apostle elsewhere speaks (Rom. 5^{17}, 1 Cor. 4^8 6^3).

5. *The general Resurrection and the Judgment.*—Regarding the position of these two events in the drama of the End, Paul leaves us completely in the dark; and in placing them after the millennial reign we assume that he follows the traditional apocalyptic scheme.

For the pious Jew the Judgment was the outstanding religious fact. He thought of God above all as the sovereign Judge before whose awful eye we go in death.

To this conception the moral earnestness that remained a feature of the best Judaism was largely due. And for Jesus too the Judgment was a great solemn fact with which every man must reckon. It is hardly less so for Paul. Paul knows the terror of the Lord (2 Cor. 5¹¹). Believer and unbeliever alike must appear at the bar (Rom. 2³⁻¹⁶ 14¹⁰, 1 Cor. 3¹³ 4⁵). "We must all be made manifest before the judgment seat of Christ; that each one may receive the things done in the body, according to what he hath done, whether it be good or bad" (2 Cor. 5¹⁰).

In the verse quoted it is Christ who occupies the throne of judgment, and this must be taken as the Apostle's dogmatic view (Rom. 2¹⁶, 1 Cor. 4⁵). But that he does not attach importance to the point is shown by the fact that he can also speak of the judge as God (Rom. 2⁶· ¹¹ 14¹⁰). The same vacillation meets us elsewhere in the New Testament[1] and also in the literature of Jewish Apocalyptic.[2] Everywhere the one vital thing is that the Judgment is divine and final. The idea that it is the position of Christ as Judge that gives to it its specifically Christian character has no support in the New Testament.

With the Judgment the drama of the last days reaches, or almost reaches, its close. The wheat has been winnowed from the chaff, a final separation made between the righteous and the wicked. One other scene the Apostle opens for an instant before our eyes.

6. *The destruction of the wicked and the coming of the eternal Kingdom.*—"Then cometh the end, when Christ shall deliver up the Kingdom to God, even the Father: when He shall have abolished all rule and all authority and power. And when all things have been subjected unto Him, then shall the Son also Himself be subjected to

[1] In Matt. 7²² 25³¹ the Judge is the Son of Man; in Matt. 10²⁸, Mark 10⁴⁰, Rev. 20¹¹, he is God.
[2] In En. 45¹⁻³ 51¹· ² 61⁸, the Messiah; in Dan. 7⁹· ¹⁰, 4 Esd. 7³³, God.

Him that did subject all things unto Him, that God may be all in all" (1 Cor. 15$^{24ff.}$). The work of redemption and judgment is complete. There is no more in the universe any power that lifts itself against God. We also hear of a redemption of the material creation from the bondage of corruption, but the speculation is not pursued (Rom. 8^{20}). Not earth but heaven is the scene of the Kingdom. There the ransomed saints, transformed into the image of their Redeemer, are gathered. Their bliss the Apostle does not attempt to paint.

What of the lost? The Book of Revelation gives us two pictures, one of the redeemed in Paradise, the other of devils and condemned souls in the lake of fire. Of the second picture there is not in the Pauline Epistles a single trace. The wicked simply disappear from the scene, the nature and term of their punishment being left shrouded in obscurity. By bringing together a number of scattered indications one may, however, arrive at a fairly certain notion as to what the Apostle thinks regarding their fate.

That he contemplates a universal restoration is an idea that may at once be put aside. Support has been sought for it in certain statements of a general character: "As in Adam all die, so also in Christ shall all be made alive": " God hath shut up all unto disobedience that He might have mercy upon all" (1 Cor. 15^{22}, Rom. 11^{32}, Col. 1^{19}, Eph. 1^{10}). But such statements cannot be pressed in their letter against the many passages that proclaim in unambiguous terms the final ruin of the ungodly (Rom. 2$^{5.~12}$, Phil. 3^{18}, 2 Thess. 1^{9}). They are but examples of the Apostle's sweeping and antithetical way of putting things. Quite decisive against the idea of restoration is the fact that nowhere do we find a single syllable that suggests a future probation.

One point only is open for argument, whether the Apostle has in his mind annihilation or an eternity of suffering. With regard to this point the words used to describe the fate of the lost are not in themselves decisive. Prominent among these words is death ($\theta\acute{a}\nu a\tau o\varsigma$); death is sin's specific penalty, its wages (Rom. 5^{12} $6^{21.\ 23}$ 8^6). Death may carry the meaning of annihilation, but not necessarily so, since the dead, according to current ideas, continued to maintain in the under world a certain phantasmal existence in separation from God. All we can read into the word is the loss of everything that gives to life its value and makes it worth living. Not different in any essential respect is the connotation of another equally prominent term—destruction ($\dot{a}\pi\acute{\omega}\lambda\epsilon\iota a$). What it means is that the wicked are swept from the place of the living and the presence of God—brought to utter ruin (2 Thess. 1^9).

But if a study of these terms leaves the question of annihilation or endless suffering an open one, the general tenor of the Apostle's thought points conclusively to the former. The universe he contemplates as the goal of redemption is one reconciled to God in all its parts. Of angels in chains or men in a lake of fire we hear nothing. If the demonic powers are not reconciled, they are abolished. God has become all in all. The vision which the Apostle leaves with us is that of a world which is without a devil and without a hell, without a shadow on its brightness or a discord in its harmony.

Already we have had occasion to draw attention to certain perplexing silences, and it is necessary to give to these somewhat fuller consideration. The Apostle's failure to supply an ordered programme of the various eschatological events to which he refers is not the main difficulty. The main difficulty is that in the programmes which he gives us events of cardinal importance are omitted and, as it would seem, no place left for them. From the account of the End in 1 Thess. 4^{13-17} no one would infer that the gathering to Christ of risen and living believers is to be followed by the millennial reign, the general resurrection and the Judgment before the grand consummation of being ever with the Lord has been reached. And in one or two passages not only these events, but the Parousia and the Resurrection as well, drop out, the whole apocalyptic drama thus falling away. In 2 Cor. 5^{1-8} and Phil. 1^{23} the Apostle looks on death as opening an immediate entrance into the heavenly world. Immediately at death the soul of the believer will be clothed upon with its habitation which is from heaven and be at home with the Lord. To depart is not to pass into the intermediate state, there to wait for the Parousia, the Resurrection and the Judgment; it is " to be with Christ."

On the strength of the last two passages eminent scholars like Holtzmann, Teichmann, Pfleiderer, Clemen, Schmiedel, Sokolowski, etc., suppose a change of view on the Apostle's part, under the influence of Hellenistic conceptions. But the hypothesis has little to support it. Even in the earliest of the Epistles (1 Thess. $4^{15ff.}$), as we have seen, cardinal events are passed over and no room left for them. And if in Phil. 1^{23} Paul speaks of death as conducting into the presence of Christ, he can in the same Epistle bid his readers expect the Parousia (4^5). Similarly 2 Cor. 5^{1-8} is followed by a reference to the Judgment (5^{10}). That the Apostle ever consciously and deliberately broke with the apocalyptic tradition in any of its main parts must be pronounced in the highest degree improbable.

Much more can be said for the hypothesis that in the two passages in question Paul is simply overleaping intervening events in order to hasten, in the ardour of his longing, to the goal of union with Christ. Jesus also, though retaining the apocalyptic scheme, can speak of Lazarus as carried immediately after death to Abraham's bosom. But this in all probability is not the full explanation.

More than once in the course of these lectures we have drawn attention to the effect of the Apostle's conception of a completed redemption in dislocating the traditional apocalyptic scheme. The real struggle of Christ with the powers of darkness is transferred from the future into the past. Christ's triumph being already an accomplished fact, the struggle of the future inevitably loses in the Apostle's mind something of its significance. And the same thing is true of an event so outstanding as the Judgment. In Jewish Apocalyptic the Judgment has its main significance as an instrument for effecting a separation between the righteous and the wicked. But for Paul this separation has already been virtually effected. The wicked are already condemned by the fact of their unbelief; the righteous already justified by the fact of their faith. " There is now no condemnation to them that are in Christ Jesus." It is true that Paul does not think of the believer's present state of salvation as absolute, and that he bids him remember the judgment bar; but against this we have to set that element of assurance which is one of the cardinal features of his piety. " Who shall lay anything to the charge of God's elect? It is God that justifieth. Who is he that shall condemn? It is Christ Jesus that died." Paul does not break with Apocalyptic, but the unconscious movement of his thought is away from it. The Fourth Gospel travels farther on the same road.

CHAPTER VIII.

PHILOSOPHY OF HISTORY.

HISTORY means for Paul but one thing, the story of re-demption. The complexity which the conception possesses for the modern man for him does not exist. In the Cross of Christ he finds the grand centre to which everything is related. All that happens before has for its single purpose to prepare the way for the Cross; all that happens after is but the working out of the redemption there achieved. And until the moment of Christ's death the drama transacts itself within the circle of the Hebrew nation. On the teeming multitudes outside the Apostle casts scarcely a glance.

His scheme of history, as we have already shown, is built on the apocalyptic idea of the two ages—the existing age, demon-ridden, given up to sin and under the bondage of mortality, and the coming age of righteousness, im-mortality and glory. While in some sense the Cross appears as the point of transition from the one to the other, effecting as it did the liberation of the race from the powers of evil and bringing new supernatural forces into play, formally the Apostle abides by the traditional view that the transition comes only with the events of the last days.

It is part of Paul's gnosis to explain how the world came to be in so miserable a condition. In Hellenistic gnosis also the same problem was in the foreground. There the solution was found in a creation myth.   A god, whose proper home is the ideal world, descends into the lower region of matter with the purpose of reducing its chaos into order.   But in the act of creation he himself is involved in the meshes of the material and held a helpless prisoner, though without losing the ability to raise himself out of the depths of death to the divine world.   So comes it to be that in man there is a higher spiritual element and also a lower material element, and that the former is in bondage to the latter.[1]   Paul, in dealing with the problem, attaches himself to a far more sober and ethical story—that of the Fall given in Genesis, though, as we shall see, he puts upon it his own interpretation.

We begin with the passage Rom. 5[12-21]. "Therefore, as through one man sin entered into the world, and death through sin ; and so death passed unto all men, for that all sinned.   Sin was indeed in the world before the giving of the Law, but in the absence of the Law sin is not imputed. Nevertheless death reigned from Adam until Moses, even over them who had not sinned after the likeness of Adam's transgression, who is a figure of Him that was to come." That here the twin miseries of sin and death are traced to our first parent's notorious act of disobedience is clear. What is not so clear is the precise character of the connection established.   The idea of a merely legal implication of the race in the sin of its representative may at once be set aside.   Paul plainly declares that the doom of death that fell upon the race was the direct result of its own sin— "for that all sinned"; and the object of the parenthesis (vv. 13, 14) is to point out that his familiar doctrine of sin as the product of lust and the Law is not to be taken as meaning that there was no sin in the world until the time of Moses.   Those between Adam and Moses could not indeed sin in the full sense of the word, since they lacked

---

[1] Bousset, *Kyrios Christos*, pp. 166 ff.

the specific prohibition imposed on the former and the formulated code of the latter. None the less, they were sinful in the sense of being fleshly, and this unconscious sinfulness was in itself sufficient to bring down upon them the doom of death. Our difficulty is not, however, yet at an end.

Does Paul teach or assume an integrity of Adam's nature anterior to his transgression and a corruption of it as the consequence of that transgression, the corrupt nature being handed down to his posterity by natural generation? No such doctrine is to be found in Judaism. Judaism was familiar with the idea of a radical evil impulse in human nature; but in this impulse Fourth Esdras sees not the fruit but the root of Adam's disobedience (3[31f.]). And one must hesitate to ascribe the doctrine to Paul. In 1 Cor. 15[47] the first man is described as "of the earth earthy"; his being, that is to say, was from the beginning fleshly, and consequently sinful. For the Apostle Adam is simply the representative of natural humanity as Christ is of redeemed humanity; and his transgression is not so much the cause of the sinfulness of the race as the first and typical act in which that sinfulness exhibits itself. Everything happened according to the divine plan. The natural had to precede the spiritual (1 Cor. 15[46ff.]). God shut up all unto disobedience that He might have mercy upon all (Rom. 11[32]).

Dark as are the colours in which the existing age is painted, that age cannot be described as, in the Apostle's view, God-abandoned. Even before the advent of Christ God was active in it, though only as lawgiver and judge, preparing the way for the great redemption that was to come. To the giving of the Law through Moses a degree of significance is ascribed very strange to a modern reader, but not unintelligible when one remembers what the Law was to a pious Jew. That event is regarded as marking

an epoch in the history of the race.   Not only did it bring
men for the first time to a knowledge of their sinful state,
it also created sin in the full meaning of that term.   Before
the giving of the Law men were indeed sinful in the sense
that their every impulse was evil ; but having no divine norm
by which to judge these ·impulses—Paul takes no account
of the law written in the heart—their sinfulness was unconscious, and therefore irresponsible and not reckoned by
God as guilt (Rom. 5^{15}).   "What shall we say then?   Is
the Law sin?   God forbid.   Howbeit, I had not known
sin except through the Law ; for I had not known coveting
except the Law had said, Thou shalt not covet : but sin,
finding occasion, wrought in me through the commandment
all manner of coveting : for apart from the Law sin is
dead.   And I was alive apart from the Law once : but
when the commandment came, sin revived and I died"
(Rom. $7^{7ff.}$ 5^{15}, Gal. $3^{19.\ 22}$).   This theory, which is the
product of profound psychological observation, has obvious
points of connection with modern evolutionary accounts of
the genesis of sin.   The Apostle does not, however, always
bear it in mind ; for he can speak of Abraham, who lived
long before the days of Moses, as not only possessed of a
full moral consciousness, but as attaining unto the righteousness which is of God by faith (Rom. $4^{1ff.}$).

In thus lifting men from the level of unconscious to
that of conscious and deliberate transgressors, in bringing
them to a knowledge of their sin and of their utter inability
to free themselves from its bondage, the Law fulfilled its
God-appointed end.   Not until men had learned what sin
is, and had drunk the cup of humiliation to the dregs, were
they in a position to receive the great salvation.

One may legitimately find in Paul's account of the
preparation for the Gospel some faint adumbration of the
idea of historical development.   Only the development he
recognises is not of the immanent kind, but is imposed

from without, by the external act of God. How little it was able to help him to mediate the transition from the old revelation of law to the new revelation of grace we have already seen. He could think the supersession of the first by the second as taking place in no other way than by a divine act of abrogation. The idea of an immanent development would have simplified his task, but it was not at his disposal.

Sometimes one meets with the assertion that among Paul's ideas we have to number that of the solidarity of the race. But the truth is that of solidarity in the modern sense of a causal interconnection of all human beings in society and of one generation with another, the Apostle knows nothing at all. If natural humanity is represented as forming a moral unity with its progenitor, it is not because it is attached to him by invisible threads of influence, but because it has in him either its legal representative or the prototype of its metaphysical constitution (Rom. 5$^{12ff.}$, 1 Cor. 15$^{47. 48}$). And as little can we speak of a solidarity of Christ with believers or of believers with Christ. Here again it is the idea of legal representation that the Apostle has before him. The death of one on behalf of all can be described as the death of all, for the reason that the act of the Head is valid for the members and equivalent to their own act (2 Cor. 5^{14}). And believers are one with Christ, not in virtue of ties of sympathy and moral influence— though these doubtless are assumed—but in virtue of a mystical union. The nearest the Apostle comes to the idea of solidarity is when he describes the reciprocal relations of believers in the Church. "And whether one member suffereth, all the members suffer with it; or one member is honoured, all the members rejoice with it" (1 Cor. 12^{26}). But in Paul's philosophy of history and of salvation this conception of interdependence plays no part.

For the Apostle, history is a drama in which God and

Christ are the only real actors. Human beings are but the
clay in the potter's hand, the subjects of divine plans and
operations. Everything that happens happens according
to the divine foreknowledge and appointment. It was in
the plan of God that man should sin and sink ever deeper
into the abyss; in His plan also that when he was shut up
in his disobedience and helplessness his redemption should
be achieved. And man's salvation is from beginning to
end the work of God, or, what is the same thing, of Christ.
It is God, through Christ, who strikes down the hostile
powers that hold the soul in bondage; and every motion
of the redeemed soul towards truth and goodness has the
supernatural agency of the Spirit behind it. Nay, that
very faith by which a man brings himself within the sweep
of the divine salvation is itself spoken of as God-wrought
(1 Cor. 2⁴, Rom. 12³, Eph. 2⁸). Paul knows nothing of
synergism. He can set forth the whole process of salvation without once introducing the human will as a co-
operating factor. "Whom He foreknew, He also fore-
ordained to be conformed to the image of His Son; and
whom he foreordained, them He also called: and whom
He called, them He also justified: and whom He justified,
them He also glorified" (Rom. 8²⁹). The sovereignty and
sole-causality of God is, one may say, the corner-stone not
only of the Apostle's philosophy of history, but of his
whole theology.

This idea of the divine sovereignty comes to clearest and
strongest expression in the Apostle's doctrine of Election.
The doctrine has its roots in the Old Testament. Frequently in the Old Testament Israel is spoken of as God's
elect or chosen people. And it is emphatically affirmed
that her election was an act of pure grace on God's part,
that she could urge no right or claim to God's favour.
"The Lord did not set His heart upon you or choose you
because ye were more in number than any people: for ye

were the fewest of all people: but because the Lord loveth
you, and because He would keep the oath which He sware
unto your fathers, hath the Lord brought you out with a
mighty hand, and redeemed you out of the house of
bondage. Speak not thou in thine heart, after that the
Lord thy God hath cast them out from before you, saying,
For my righteousness the Lord hath brought me in to
possess this land " (Deut. 7^8 9^4). Now in the Apostle's
view it is Christian believers who are the true Israel and
the real objects of the divine election. Frequently he
describes such as the elect or chosen of God. And he
has occasion to vindicate the freedom of God in choosing
them from among the Gentiles rather than from among
the Jews. The growing predominance of the Gentile
element in the Church and the growing certainty that
Israel as a whole was not to be won for the Gospel,
carried with it the corollary that Israel from a chosen
people had become a rejected people. To Jews outside
the Church, and doubtless to many of Jewish extraction
inside, such an idea could not be other than an offence.
Paul boldly accepts the facts as divinely ordered, and
beats down every cavil lifted against them (Rom. 9–11).
It belongs to the sovereign right of God to select as the
objects of His favour whom He will. His election is an
act of pure grace, undetermined and uninfluenced by any
considerations with respect to the worthiness or the willing-
ness of those elected. "It is not of him that willeth, nor
of him that runneth, but of God that hath mercy." Even
in the choice of ancient Israel the sovereignty of God and
that His election is not of works, but by grace, was manifested. For Rebecca having conceived and children being
not yet born, "neither having done anything good or bad,
that the purpose of God according to election might stand,
not of works, but of Him that calleth, it was said unto her,
The elder shall serve the younger. Even as it is written,

Jacob I loved, but Esau I hated." The Jews, therefore, and this is the point at which the Apostle is driving, have no valid ground of objection to the fact that the election has passed from them to the Gentiles.

Paul does not shrink from working out this doctrine of election to its logical completion in a doctrine of reproba-tion. Esau was rejected before he had done either good or bad ; and " the Scripture saith unto Pharaoh, For this very purpose did I raise thee up, that I might show in thee my power, and that my name might be published abroad in all the earth. So then He hath mercy on whom He will, and whom He will He hardeneth."

That such a conception of God's sovereignty seems to menace His justice and the foundations of His moral government Paul is well aware. " Thou wilt say then unto me, Why doth He still find fault ? For who withstandeth His will ? " But he beats down the objection by denying the right of the creature to question the doings of his Creator. " Nay but, O man, who art thou that repliest against God ? Shall the thing formed say to Him that formed it, Why didst thou make me thus ? " What a word is that to those who throw themselves in futile rebellion against the order of the universe ! The Apostle does not, however, leave the matter there. He will vindi-cate the ways of God by establishing God's own glory as the one supreme end of all His action. " Hath not the potter a right over the clay, from the same lump to make one part a vessel unto honour, and another unto dishonour ? What if God, willing to show His wrath, and to make His power known, endured with much long-suffering vessels of wrath fitted unto destruction : and that He might make known the riches of His glory upon vessels of mercy, which He afore-time prepared unto glory ? "

It is not to be denied that in these passages the sover-eignty of God is maintained at the expense of His moral attributes. A God whose supreme end is the display of the power of His wrath and of His mercy, and who uses human beings as the mere means of that display, is not the God of Jesus, nor a God who can command the homage of our conscience or our heart. But one must not isolate these passages. Side by side with them we find others, which show that the Apostle has been carried by his logic and his polemic farther than his conscience dares follow. Israel's rejection is traced also to her own unbelief, and that rejection explained as a means towards a fuller realisation of the purpose of grace. " For as ye (the Gentiles) in time past were disobedient to God, but now have obtained mercy by their (the Jews') disobedience ; even so have these also now been disobedient, that by the mercy shown to you they also may now obtain mercy " (Rom. 11[30]). Paul has never, indeed, any thought of surrendering or modifying his doctrine of God's sovereignty in election and sole agency in the work of salvation ; but no more does he dream of ascribing to Him an arbitrary will, or of elevating His power above His moral attributes. His God is not a despot, but the God of grace whose supreme object is the world's salvation. " He hath shut up all unto disobedience, that He might have mercy upon all " (Rom. 11[22]).

So far as the main argument in Rom. 9–11 is concerned, one might plausibly contend that Paul thinks of the elect not individually, but collectively, that what he has in view is a choosing not of this and that individual, but of the Church as a whole. But from many passages and from the whole structure of his doctrine of salvation, it is abundantly clear that he teaches an individual election and an individual reprobation. In selecting proof-examples from the Old Testament—Esau, Jacob, Pharaoh—it is precisely on individuals that he fixes. And the individual reference in such passages as 1 Cor. 1[26f.]—Not many wise after the flesh, not many mighty, not many noble, are called ;

Rom. 9^{24}—Vessels of mercy, which He afore prepared unto glory, even us, whom He also called, not from the Jews only, but also from the Gentiles; Rom. 16^{13}—Salute Rufus the chosen in the Lord—is unmistakable. Those who love God are the called according to His purpose. Always the calling is represented as something effectual and irresistible : whom God calls, He also justifies (1 Thess. 5^{24}, 2 Thess. 2^{14}, Gal. 1^{15}, 1 Cor. 1$^{8f.\ 26}$, Rom. 1^6 8^{28}). Finally, the very purpose of that enumeration in Rom. 8^{29} of the links of the chain that binds believers to God, is to assure individuals that their final salvation is secure, as grounded in God's eternal counsel. It may be remarked that the doctrine of reprobation loses in Paul's hands much of its harshness, since he nowhere thinks of an endless torment of the wicked, but only of their destruction.

While Paul teaches the sole agency of God in the work of salvation and the irresistibleness of His decrees, this does not embarrass him in the practical work of warning and exhorting. In his practical appeals he presupposes human freedom and responsibility, and assumes that a fall from grace is possible (Rom. 2$^{4-10}$ 6$^{12.\ 13}$ 11^{20}, 1 Cor. 10$^{1-12}$, 2 Cor. 6^1, Gal. 5^4, Col. 1^{23}). Nowhere does he attempt a reconciliation of the two standpoints, or, indeed, betray any consciousness of a problem.

Paul's doctrine of election has, as we have seen, its roots in the Old Testament. It is not, however, to be regarded as something which he simply took over from tradition and subjected to further elaboration. Rather is it organic to his thought and, in some measure, to his religion. In it he finds support for two cardinal religious interests, the primacy of grace, namely, and the need for assurance. And it is involved in his whole conception of God as the sole agent in salvation. That the doctrine leaves out of account and reserves no place for moral initiative and moral responsibility, elements equally vital to the Christian life, will hardly be questioned. But this is only to say that it partakes of a weakness belonging to every scheme and every formula ever constructed by the human mind. Big as Paul's conception of a redemptive purpose of sovereign grace working itself out in history is, it is not big enough to cover the complexity of the facts.

CHAPTER IX.

PAUL AND JESUS.

HOW does the gospel of Paul stand related to that of Jesus? The far-reaching character of this question no one will dispute. From the point of view of the history of our Christian religion it is by far the most important that can be raised: in it the whole problem of the origin of historical Christianity is summed up. And its dogmatic importance is hardly less. The contrast which the Pauline gospel with its complex constructions presents to the simple gospel of Jesus raises the question as to the place and right of these constructions in our Christian religion, the place and right of speculative constructions in general. It is the historical problem that must first engage our attention.

At many points in the course of our discussion we have instituted a comparison between the teaching of the Apostle and that of the Master. And what we have found as the result of our study has been a combination of striking agreement with no less striking difference. In much Paul is substantially at one with Jesus; in much he is independent, following paths which Jesus never trod. It may be well to gather up these scattered conclusions, presenting both the points of agreement and the points of difference in as succinct form as possible. We begin with the latter.

1. In Paul we meet with a fully elaborated doctrine of redemption of which Jesus can scarcely be said to know

anything at all. The apocalyptic redemption of the last
days is, indeed, common to both; but what of that redemption from the Law and from sin in the flesh which for the
Apostle constitutes the meaning of the Cross and the basis
of his gospel? Nowhere does Jesus contemplate such a
deliverance as the result either of His life or of His death.
Never is the Law treated by Him as a uniform magnitude
which must stand or fall as a whole, and as possessing only
a temporary validity. With a sovereign freedom He rejects, deepens, enlarges, wherever it contradicts or falls
short of His own inward perception of the divine will; and
in the new form He gives it He assumes and indeed asserts
its abiding character. With its central principle of recompense He finds no fault; nor does He betray the slightest
consciousness that this principle limits in any way the
freedom of God's forgiving love. Of the Pauline doctrine
that God can justify or forgive only after the vicarious
payment of the penalty demanded by a violated Law there
is no trace. Forgiveness has no other ground than the
royal goodness that is kind to the unthankful and the evil.
Jesus proclaims the divine mercy as something that is
always in the heavens; and as God's representative He can
bestow forgiveness without a hint of a coming event, apart
from which the forgiveness would not be valid.

And of an objective redemption from the power of sin
Jesus knows as little as of a redemption from the Law.
So far from sharing Paul's pessimistic estimate of the
natural man, He appeals to him with a confidence that is
rooted in a splendid optimism. Repentance and the
attainment of the new righteousness are frankly staked on
man's ability to follow the higher when he finds it. This
does not mean that Jesus ignores the initiative of God in
salvation or His ever-present help. He speaks of the
shepherd going out to seek the lost sheep, and prays for
Peter that his faith fail not. But what we do not find is

the doctrine that the powers of evil must first be broken in objective fashion before man is in a position to fulfil the divine requirements.

To His death Jesus is far from attaching the same exclusive significance it receives in Paul. If toward the close of His career He speaks of a divine necessity that He should suffer and of giving His life as a ransom, He can also describe His mission as being to preach the gospel, to bring the Law to its fulfilment, to call sinners to repentance, to seek the lost. And in His words about His death He has no thought of formulating a doctrine of redemption, but only of giving expression—under the one form which Jewish thought provided—to His invincible trust that the tragedy which seemed to His disciples the end of all things, would in the Providence of God contribute to the ultimate victory of His cause.

2. Paul's doctrine of redemption carries with it a series of presuppositions and corollaries, and these also, as we should expect, have nothing to correspond with them in the teaching of Jesus. Where among Jesus' words do we find the suggestion, that hitherto Israel had known God only as lawgiver and judge, and that His own death would for the first time open a way for the experience of God's grace and give men the right to call God Father? Jesus has no doctrine of adoption. For Him every man is a child of God, though so long as he wanders in sin he is a lost child; and his task is to live as a child of God by trusting God and being generous and merciful as He is. Where again do we find in Jesus that absolute condemnation of our human nature so characteristic of the Apostle's theology? Jesus has no doctrine of human depravity. He takes men as He finds them, seeing the evil in them and condemning it, seeing also the good and welcoming it. If He will call none good in the absolute sense save One, He knows of such as are merciful, generous and strong in

faith, and that without any suggestion of their having been redeemed. The many travel the broad road; but all can repent and enter the strait gate. Still again, there is nothing in Jesus' teaching to correspond with the Pauline doctrine of the Spirit. Human goodness is traced not to the Spirit's supernatural operations, but to the human heart and will. Among other auxiliary redemption conceptions foreign to Jesus we may mention that of sin as having its seat in the flesh, the connection of sin with the Law, election and reprobation, the bondage and liberation of the material creation.

3. How vital to Paul's gospel is the element of Christology and how fully developed one does not need to say. His gospel, if the story of redemption, is also the story of the pre-existent Son of God, the mediator in the work of creation, who descended into our world, clothing Himself in human flesh, and, His task completed, was exalted to divine honour and power. And it is Paul's sense of standing in a vital relation with this exalted Christ that is the mainspring of his piety.

It would be wrong to say that in the teaching of Jesus there is nothing that can be called Christology. Jesus shared the messianic expectation of His people. And although the fact is denied by Wrede, Wellhausen and others, there can hardly be a doubt that He thought of Himself as the Messiah of promise.[1] How exactly He conceived of this figure is a question not easily answered. Sometimes He attaches to Old Testament passages in which the work of the Messiah is described as human and ethical in character. But as it became clear that the Kingdom was not to come as the result of His earthly ministry, His thoughts seem to have turned to the transcendent Messiah of Apocalyptic who at the close of the age would descend with the clouds of heaven. He speaks

---

[1] E. F. Scott, *The Kingdom and the Messiah*, pp. 146 ff.

of His reappearance after death in heavenly glory. This much of Christology we find in Jesus, but of the characteristic doctrines of Paul not a trace. Nowhere does He speak of His pre-existence, or of having created the world, or of a surrender of heavenly glory and an assumption of human flesh. The Pauline conception of a mediator between God and creation, God and man, is altogether foreign to Him. He leads men to the Father and teaches them to expect everything from the Father's mercy and goodness. Most important fact of all, Jesus founded no Christ-cult. Nowhere does He offer Himself as an object of worship, or indicate that He will become such when exalted to the messianic throne. If He calls men to Himself and requires of them a loyalty to which on occasion the most sacred natural ties must be sacrificed, it is because He knows Himself the representative and leader of God's cause in the decisive hour of the world's history. Of Jesus' gospel Christology forms no vital part. This is placed beyond question when we take into account the condition he attaches to salvation.

4. For Paul the one condition of salvation is faith, the faith that has for its object the Redeemer and His redemption. It is true that in the last resort what Paul understands by such faith is trust in the sin-forgiving grace of God. But it is also true that the grace of God has no meaning for him apart from the redemption drama. A series of speculative constructions—the incarnation, the abrogation of the Law, the destruction of sin in the flesh, the communication of the Spirit, the exaltation of Jesus to the dignity of Kyrios—is made the basis of religion.

That in the teaching of Jesus it is otherwise is a fact that can neither be denied nor explained away. Never does Jesus put forward His messianic dignity as the ground of His proclamation, or require a recognition of it as the condition of discipleship. In His interviews with individuals the messianic question never emerges. To the rich young man who asks how he may attain to life He replies, Keep the commandments; and when His reply is treated as insufficient, He imposes another commandment harder than any known to the Decalogue. "This do and thou shalt live"—that is no piece of irony, but a typical statement of Jesus' conception of the way of life. Not that He overlooks the importance of faith. Trust in God is the source of that elevation above worldly anxieties that makes untroubled obedience possible, the source also of spiritual power—"all things are possible to him that believeth." But what He means by faith is always such trust: never the acceptance of doctrinal constructions. If sometimes He relates faith to His own person, what He has in view is not a recognition of His dignity or of the significance of the death He is to die; it is trust in the mighty power of God that works through Him.

5. Foreign to Jesus is also the strain of mysticism that forms so distinctive an element in the piety of His Apostle. The piety of Jesus moves throughout in personal and ethical relations.

6. For those who find in Paul a pronounced sacramentarian strain this must appear as one of the most outstanding of the differences between him and the Master. But rejecting as we do such a view of his teaching we must dismiss it as non-existent. Jesus did not condemn ritual in itself; on the contrary, He observed such parts of the Law as seemed to Him capable of expressing or nourishing any real religious impulse. And if He cannot be regarded as having instituted the Christian sacraments, there is nothing in these as interpreted by Paul that is out of harmony with the spirit of His religion.

But if the differences between the teaching of Paul and that of Jesus are undeniable, not less so are the

17

agreements.   And indeed one can say that the latter are more radical and far-reaching than the former, and for the most part underlie the former.   Since, however, they relate not so much to the domain of doctrine as to that of spirit and motive, they are much less easy to formulate.

1. Only minor importance can be attached to the fact that the thought of both Master and Apostle is largely dominated by the apocalyptic outlook.   This element represents not what is original in one or the other, but only what is traditional.   It may be remarked in passing that while Paul is deeply tinged with the pessimism in which Apocalyptic was rooted, the native purity and force of Jesus' spirit preserve Him unaffected. To Jesus creation appeals not as sighing for liberation from the bondage of corruption, but as instinct with the Providence of a God who feeds the sparrows and clothes with beauty the lilies of the field.

2. Fundamental to every religion is its conception of God; and with respect to this we can say that Master and Apostle are substantially at one.   Of Jesus' conception the unapproachable greatness lies in its combination of the character of severity with that of tenderness.   God is the Lord of heaven and earth, the power behind the moral law, the sovereign and judge who is able to destroy both soul and body in hell, before whose eye we continually stand, and to whom we must answer for even the secret motions of our heart.   And He is also the Father of mercy and grace, kind to the unthankful and evil, who does not willingly consent to lose even one of His children and who in His wondrous love goes out to seek and save the lost.   His justice and His mercy go hand in hand; justice clothing mercy with moral earnestness, and mercy tempering justice so that it shall be something else than a devouring fire, and establishing for it as end a kingdom of the redeemed.

While it is true that in Paul's teaching these attributes are set over-against each other in a temporal scheme foreign to Jesus, they none the less burn with steady radiance and give to his religion its stamp and character. No less than Jesus, Paul brings men up before the righteous Judge who rewards every man according to his deeds. And what is it but the divine grace that is the foundation of all his trust and hope? In the revelation of grace he finds the essence of the new dispensation; and the consciousness of it vibrates in every utterance of his personal experience. When all dogmatic wrappings have been stripped off, the basal fact on which religion rests will be found to be for Paul what it is for Jesus—holy love the supreme might in the universe, at once the constitutive principle of the divine nature and the law of human conduct. If his doctrine of election leads the Apostle perilously near the point of setting the will and power of God above His moral attributes and of narrowing the love of God to a love for the elect, he himself is hardly conscious of the fact. The end to which he uniformly looks is an undimmed triumph of grace. " Where sin abounded, grace did abound more exceedingly; that as sin reigned in death, even so might grace reign through righteousness unto eternal life through Jesus Christ our Lord."

3. Further we can say that Paul reproduces the essential notes of Jesus' piety, that in faith and love and hope Master and Apostle are one. In contrast with Judaism we find in both the same complete subordination of the ceremonial and statutory to the ethical. If Jesus can declare that the great things of the Law are judgment, mercy and faith, Paul can add that the Kingdom of God is not meat and drink, but righteousness, peace and joy in the Holy Ghost. Both place the service of God in the service of man, teaching a perfectly ethicised religion.

And both equally break with Judaism in their repudiation of the merit doctrine. The substance of Paul's doctrine of justification by faith is all contained in the parables of the Pharisee and the publican and the servant returning from the field. What we have in both cases is a piety of absolute humility and trust in the presence of the judging and sin-pardoning God. Finally Paul's sense of inward freedom as against everything traditional, statutory and ascetic is surely not unconnected with the sovereign way in which Jesus, trusting the inner light, deals with the moralities and ordinances of the sacred past. If the essentials of Jesus' piety are all included in the Beatitudes, we can say that there is not a single one of these that has not its correspondent in the Pauline Epistles.

4. The striking similarity of the ethic of Paul to that of Jesus has already been sufficiently demonstrated, and all we need do here is again to draw attention to it.

5. Even with respect to those points in which the Apostle seems farthest removed from the Master the influence of the latter is unmistakable. It is a departure from Jesus when he establishes as the object of faith a construction of Christ's person and work. And yet it is far from his intention to exhibit faith as an act of intellectual submission, " an obedient affirmation of the preaching of redemption." At bottom what he has in view is trust in the grace of God that has come to men in Jesus Christ. For him as for Jesus such trust is the secret of peace and the wellspring of power.

Again, while it was not from Jesus that Paul derived the mystical strain in his piety, his mysticism is none the less penetrated through and through by Jesus' spirit. Death and resurrection with Christ mean for him a death to sin and a resurrection to righteousness and God; communion with the indwelling Christ, a communion with the eternal Power from whom every pure thought and noble impulse ultimately proceed.

It would be too much to say that under a new form Paul reproduces all that is vital in Jesus' life and teaching. Not to any single individual or to the Church as a whole has it been given to do that. But this we can affirm, that his gospel is not really another gospel. The God into whose presence he brings us is the God and Father of Jesus, and his faith and love and hope are the faith and love and hope of the Master. Of all the Apostles Paul understood the Master best and laboured most abundantly in His service.

How account for this mingling of agreement with difference? With respect to the former the matter will seem to many very little of a problem. Does Paul pretend to be anything else than an apostle of Jesus Christ? But, as we have seen, the question is not quite so simple. His disconcerting silence with regard to all in Jesus' historical life that lies outside the institution of the Supper and the Crucifixion, the paucity of unambiguous reproductions or even echoes of Jesus' words and his reiterated assertion that he received his gospel not through tradition but from inner revelation, constitute a problem the seriousness of which none conversant with the facts will be disposed to deny. Already the problem has been discussed, and all that it is necessary to do here is to gather up the results.

The agreement of the Apostle with the Master with respect to the fundamental matters of religion is too general and too close to be explained on any other hypothesis than that of dependence. Wrede's [1] assertion that Paul stands farther apart from Jesus than Jesus from the nobler forms of Jewish piety, and that the points of agreement are sufficiently accounted for by their common

[1] *Paulus*, p. 95.

Jewish heritage, must be dismissed as for the most part fantastic. In whatever way the Apostle reached his knowledge of the historical life and teaching, the facts compel us to assume that he possessed such knowledge. And his failure to make a larger use of the historical material though disconcerting is not inexplicable. It is due mainly to these two facts, that the object of his faith is not Jesus as He lived among men, pursuing His ministry of teaching and healing, but Jesus as exalted to the dignity of Kyrios, the present God to whom all power in heaven and on earth has been entrusted ; and that with respect to Jesus' earthly ministry, all significance is concentrated in the two great events, the death and the resurrection. Nor is the Apostle's emphatic assertion of independence inconsistent with the measure of dependence for which we have contended. His claim relates only to his construction of Christ's person and his interpretation of Christ's death and resurrection. With respect to the historical basis of his gospel, he definitely asserts that he had received—plainly from tradition—what he had delivered to the churches ; and if he mentions only the death, the burial and the resurrection, we need not suppose that he regards these saving facts as exhausting his debt (1 Cor. 15[3ff.]).

Far more difficult to solve is the problem of the differences. Where shall we look for the sources of those elements in the Apostle's gospel that distinguish it from that of the Master?

1. Something can be set down to the fact that the gospel of Paul is to a considerable extent what the gospel of Jesus is not at all, a product of reflection and speculation.

Jesus is no theologian, and in His teaching there is nothing that can be called doctrine in the usual meaning of the term. The simple conceptions under which He brings His mission—to call to repentance, to preach the gospel, to save the lost, to give His life as a ransom— are not in their character theological. Against the genuineness of the one distinctively theological saying, that of Matt. 11[27ff.], objections can be urged that to me at least seem decisive. Jesus does not make His work a subject of speculative elaboration and as little does He make His person. If He thinks of Himself as the promised Messiah, He makes no attempt to define the conception, unless indeed in a practical direction. The task He sets Himself is to act the part of a physician and saviour, not to instruct as to the secret of His person or the nature of the process through which salvation will be effected. In the production of His thoughts, system, theory, speculation play no part. From direct spiritual vision He derives the truths He proclaims, and these truths appeal to receptive hearts as self-evident.

To pass from Jesus to Paul is to find oneself in a different atmosphere. The element of direct insight, the prophetic element, is far indeed from being absent in the Apostle's teaching; it is present in amazing abundance. But how much there is that is not prophecy, but palpably theology! Everywhere reflection is at work, everywhere there is the attempt to explain. Paul is in part an apologist and constructive thinker. He will demonstrate the world-significance of Christ and His work, and establish the truth of the new religion as against the old. His Christology, his doctrines of the flesh and of the Law, of redemption and of justification, are one and all theological constructions. Without question one main source of the difference between the teaching of Paul and that of Jesus is the presence in the former of a speculative activity that is almost completely wanting in the latter. The Apostle essays to solve problems which the Master never raises or contemplates. His theology is a new phenomenon.

In conservative circles it has been the custom to trace back at least the germs of Paul's speculative conceptions to Jesus, and to find in this origin their ultimate authentication. The attempt must always end in failure. Paul himself never pretends to found on words spoken by the historical Jesus. Of his gospel he declares that he received it not from tradition, but by an inward revelation.

To say that the Pauline constructions constitute a new element in the Christian gospel is not to reject them as worthless. The theological task which the Apostle performed was one the Church was bound sooner or later to undertake. Sooner or later Christian men must have faced the questions, Who is this Jesus who has been to us what none other can be? What precisely is it that we owe to Him? If there was to be religious thought at all, a doctrine of Christ's person and work was inevitable. And only those afflicted with a blind hostility to theology will question the value of the gift Paul bestowed on the Church. To mention only one thing, it was the possession of the system of formulated doctrine bequeathed by the Apostle and his successors that preserved the Church from being engulfed in the maelstrom of Gnostic speculation.

2. Not infrequently the transformation of Jesus' simple gospel of sin, forgiveness and the Kingdom under Paul's hand is represented as due entirely to the new theological character stamped upon it. But this is certainly a mistaken view. The theology was a product of the transformation rather than its cause. What led the primitive community and led Paul to attribute to the exalted Messiah all the functions of Deity and to regard Him as a present God, was not primarily a process of reflection on the moral glory of the earthly Jesus or on the work He had done for man's salvation. The impression made by Jesus on the heart and conscience is indeed a presupposition of the new position assigned Him, but it is not by

itself sufficient to account for it. Appeal is often made to the resurrection as the decisive factor in the elevation of Jesus to the throne of Deity. But all that the resurrection did or could do was to create or re-establish belief in His Messiahship; and between this and belief in Him as the creator and ruler of the world there lies a gulf that is both wide and deep. Only when we take into account the Hellenistic atmosphere in which historical Christianity was developed can we understand how this gulf was bridged. To Gentile minds the messianic idea, if not unintelligible, was at least foreign, and without any of the sacred associations it possessed for a Jew. Inevitably, Gentile Christians gravitated towards a conception of the risen Christ rooted in their own modes of religious thought and feeling. Christ was thought of as a God to whom prayers could be addressed and from whom all help was to be ex-. pected. He could enter into the believer's soul and impart to it His own divine life. In a word, He was thought of as Kyrios. And as Kyrios He became the centre of a Cultus. This development lies behind all Paul's Christological determinations. It is not the outcome of these determinations, but the presupposition.

And what is true of Paul's Christology is true also of his doctrine of redemption. Certainly his doctrine embodies in rich measure a real experience of salvation through Christ. In all its branches it is rooted in fact. But while this is true, it is also true that the experience itself was in certain aspects of it determined in its form by Hellenistic modes of thought and feeling. It was from Hellenistic religion that the conception of a death and resurrection with Christ and of Christ's indwelling entered Christianity. Nay, that the Gospel was preached not as the message of the Kingdom, its righteousness and its benefits—the gospel of Jesus—but as the message of a completed redemption, was due to the fact that it was unconsciously shaped to meet the need and cry of the Hellenistic world.

As has been more than once pointed out, the transformation to which the Gospel was subjected affected its form rather than its substance. One change of ominous import has, however, to be noted. A series of speculative constructions of high complexity advanced into the centre of religion. Faith is directed not primarily to the Father of mercy and love, not to the God whom we know in Jesus, but to the story of the incarnate Son and His work of redemption. To some extent religion is made to hang on speculation. This too was the result of Hellenistic influence. The conception of a saving gnosis, which has for its content a philosophy of salvation, was carried from Hellenistic religion into Christianity. In Paul the evil effects of the change are hardly observable, but all too soon they were to disclose themselves. The consideration of this point conducts us from the domain of history into that of dogmatic.

Up to the present the Christianity professed by the various Christian Churches and embodied in their formularies has been, broadly speaking, Pauline. The great Pauline constructions have been treated as the basis of our religion, the far simpler religion of Jesus being either lost sight of or regarded as peculiar to Himself and inaccessible to human beings. The Reformation which signified in so much a breach with tradition was a return not to Jesus, but to Paul. But since the Rationalistic movement of the eighteenth century, the Pauline constructions have been steadily crumbling. More and more men have been asking whether the fate of our Christian religion is really bound up with these constructions, whether Christianity is not a much simpler thing than it appears in the pages of the Apostle and the creeds of the Church. The alternatives have been formulated, Jesus or Paul; and the cry raised, back from Paul to Jesus. Ultimately it is a question as to the meaning to be given to the term revelation. In what does the Christian revelation essentially consist, in an authoritative construction of Jesus' person and work, or in the historical personality as it discloses itself to us in word and deed? On this question our study of the genesis of the Pauline theology is not without an intimate bearing.

The Pauline constructions have, as we have seen, a history behind them. One and all they are built of conceptions taken over from the thought of the time. While some of these—the Messiah, the Spirit, vicarious suffering —can be traced back to the Old Testament, of the majority of them it must be said that their home was neither Hebraism nor Judaism, but Oriental religion. To this source we must assign such conceptions as that of Kyrios, a mediator of creation and redemption, death and resurrection with Christ, an indwelling God. But how does the fact that we are able to explain historically the genesis of the Pauline constructions affect our estimate of them?

By some it is used to depreciate the Apostle's originality, but with little justice. His theology is not to be explained as the result of a mere transference to Christ of conceptions already current in another connection. In truth Paul borrowed nothing that he did not transform, and his system as a whole is a work of the noblest creative genius.

Not less illegitimate is it to urge the origin of Paul's conceptions as a disproof of their validity. By this time we have surely learned that an idea is not to be measured or judged by the rude form in which it first emerged in human thought. We do not dispose of the Apostle's conception of the Spirit, for example, by tracking it to its source in primitive religion. Of every idea it can be said that it has a history that conducts us back to a stage of mentality that has long been transcended. And what though the majority of the Pauline conceptions sprang up on another soil than that of Hebraism or Judaism? Is it necessary to suppose that religious truth was the absolute monopoly of the chosen people, that the great pagan world had nothing to contribute to the religious heritage of the race? Few now would venture such an assertion. A conception like that of Christ as Kyrios is not to be regarded as tainted because of its origin. It may well be that it is more adequate as a description of what Jesus is to the soul than the messianic conception native to Judaism.

An historical treatment of the Pauline constructions does not prejudice the question of their validity. But one thing it does; it puts us in a position of freedom with regard to them. It is no longer possible to look upon them as truths supernaturally communicated, the proper attitude to which is one of unquestioning submission. It is no longer possible to treat them as the ultimate data of our faith. We can go behind them. We know their source and the facts which through them the Apostle sought to interpret. These facts—the historical figure of Jesus, His death on the cross, the liberation He brings to the souls that surrender themselves to Him, the new faith and hope and love He awakens—are before us to-day as they were before Paul; and we have the right, nay the obligation, to judge how far the Apostle's interpretations or explanations of them are adequate or tenable.

That it is possible for us to make the Pauline constructions our own in the precise form in which they were promulgated few probably to-day will venture to assert. Some of these, the doctrine of the flesh, for example, and of the Law's abrogation, and of death and resurrection with Christ, were never taken up by the Church, but silently dropped out of sight. And of those that found their way into the creeds not one but suffered substantial modification.   The traditional doctrines of the person of Christ, the incarnation, the atonement, while closely akin to those of Paul are far from being identical with them. And to-day the talk is not of modification but of recon- struction.   As a theological system Paulinism, notwith- standing its wealth of pregnant thoughts, belongs to a past that cannot be revived.   Its Jewish and Hellenistic cate- gories are not ours, cannot really be appropriated by us. When we try to describe what Jesus is for our faith it is not to the idea of the Messiah nor to that of the Logos nor even to that of Kyrios in its Hellenistic meaning that we have resort.   And in giving an account of Jesus' work we do not think of it as a disarming of demons, or as an abrogating of the Mosaic law, or as an objective de- struction of sin in the flesh.   The Pauline constructions are not without their historical justification, but they belong to a thought-world that lies behind us.

What in the Epistles of Paul is still vital and creative is not their theology, but their religion.   It is the faith and love and hope that in almost every page come to direct and glowing expression.   And the faith and love and hope are not really dependent on the theology.   For the revela- tion through contact with which they are born is not in the last resort any speculative construction, but divine reality, above all the great reality of the historical life of Jesus.[1]   In the domain of reality or fact it is that revela- tion lies.   What from age to age generates religion are the grand realities that meet us in our experience—the mighty universe over-against us with its wonders and splendours, the moral law within, a moral order in human affairs, a kingdom of God developing itself in history and calling

[1] Fairbairn, in his *Philosophy of the Christian Religion*, pp. 438 ff., contends for the former view of revelation ; Herrmann, in his *Communion with God*, for the latter.

us to its service with a high calling, a force of love and truth and self-sacrifice lifting itself up against all mean and selfish striving and authenticating itself as from the burning centre of things, the great personalities in which the spiritual facts and forces find embodiment.   Speculative constructions may in a more or less adequate way bring up divine reality before us, but they can never without loss be accepted as a substitute for it.   The first come and go ; the second abides.   It is among the great realities in-dicated that the Hebrew prophets and psalmists move. And what is true of them is true of Jesus.   He comes to us with no speculative constructions.   The God to whom He directs us is the God who manifests Himself in the Providence that orders the world and our human life, in the voice of conscience, in the love and generosity that dwell in human hearts, in the wondrous working that is bringing in the Kingdom.   His religion is the birth of immediate contact with divine fact.   Paul also has an open eye for reality ; but between the soul and reality he interposes a system.   Need we ask which of the two represents the permanent type of our Christian religion ?

INDEX

Printed by MORRISON & GIBB LIMITED, *Edinburgh*

The International Theological Library

'A Series which has won a distinct place in theological literature by precision of
workmanship and quite remarkable completeness of treatment.'—*Literary World.*

VOLUMES NOW PUBLISHED.

**AN INTRODUCTION TO THE LITERATURE OF THE OLD
TESTAMENT.**
Prof. S. R. Driver, D.D.   10s. 6d. net.

CHRISTIAN ETHICS.
Newman Smyth, D.D.   9s. net.

APOLOGETICS; OR, CHRISTIANITY DEFENSIVELY STATED.
Prof. A. B. Bruce, D.D.   9s. net.

HISTORY OF CHRISTIAN DOCTRINE.
Prof. G. P. Fisher, D.D., LL.D.   10s. 6d. net.

A HISTORY OF CHRISTIANITY IN THE APOSTOLIC AGE.
Prof. A. C. McGiffert, Ph.D., D.D.   10s. 6d. net.

CHRISTIAN INSTITUTIONS.
Prof. A. V. G. Allen, D.D.   10s. 6d. net.

THE CHRISTIAN PASTOR AND THE WORKING CHURCH.
Washington Gladden, D.D., LL.D.   9s. net.

CANON AND TEXT OF THE NEW TESTAMENT.
Prof. Caspar René Gregory, D.D., LL.D.   10s. 6d. net.

THE THEOLOGY OF THE NEW TESTAMENT.
Prof. G. B. Stevens, D.D.   10s. 6d. net.

THE ANCIENT CATHOLIC CHURCH (A.D. 98–451).
Principal R. Rainy, D.D.   10s. 6d. net.

THE GREEK AND EASTERN CHURCHES.
Principal W. F. Adeney, D.D.   10s. 6d. net.

OLD TESTAMENT HISTORY.
Prof. H. P. Smith, D.D.   10s. 6d. net.

THE THEOLOGY OF THE OLD TESTAMENT.
Prof. A. B. Davidson, D.D., LL.D.   10s. 6d. net.

THE CHRISTIAN DOCTRINE OF SALVATION.
Prof. G. B. Stevens, D.D.   10s. 6d. net.

HISTORY OF THE REFORMATION.
Principal T. M. Lindsay, D.D.
    Vol. I. The Reformation in Germany.   9s. net.
    Vol. II. In Lands beyond Germany.   9s. net.

THE CHRISTIAN DOCTRINE OF GOD.
Prof. W. N. Clarke, D.D.   9s. net.

**AN INTRODUCTION TO THE LITERATURE OF THE NEW
TESTAMENT.**
Prof. James Moffatt, D.D.   10s. 6d. net.

THE DOCTRINE OF THE PERSON OF JESUS CHRIST.
Prof. H. R. Mackintosh, D.Phil., D.D.   9s. net.

THE PHILOSOPHY OF RELIGION.
Principal George Galloway, D.Phil., D.D.   10s. 6d. net.

THE HISTORY OF RELIGIONS. Vol. I.
Prof. George F. Moore, D.D.   10s. 6d. net.

THEOLOGICAL SYMBOLICS.
Prof. C. A. Briggs, D.D.   9s. net.

THE LATIN CHURCH IN THE MIDDLE AGES.
André Lagarde.   10s. 6d. net.

A HISTORY OF CHRISTIAN MISSIONS.
Canon C. H. Robinson, D.D.   9s. net.

The International Critical Commentary

'Scarcely higher praise can be afforded to a volume than by the statement that it is well worthy of the "International Critical Commentary" Series.'—*Church Quarterly Review.*

VOLUMES NOW PUBLISHED.

GENESIS.
Principal JOHN SKINNER, D.D.   10s. 6d. net.
NUMBERS.
Prof. G. BUCHANAN GRAY, D.D.   10s. 6d. net.
DEUTERONOMY.
Prof. S. R. DRIVER, D.D.   Third Edition.   10s. 6d. net.
JUDGES.
Prof. G. F. MOORE, D.D.   Second Edition.   10s. 6d. net.
SAMUEL I. and II.
Prof. H. P. SMITH, D.D.   10s. 6d. net.
CHRONICLES I. and II.
Prof. E. L. CURTIS, D.D.   10s. 6d. net.
EZRA AND NEHEMIAH.
Prof. L. W. BATTEN, D.D.   9s. net.
ESTHER.
Prof. L. B. PATON, Ph.D.   9s. net.
PSALMS.
Prof. C. A. BRIGGS, D.D.   Two Vols.   9s. net each.
PROVERBS.
Prof. C. H. TOY, D.D.   10s. 6d. net.
ECCLESIASTES.
Prof. G. A. BARTON, Ph.D.   7s. 6d. net.
ISAIAH.
Vol. I (Ch. i.–xxvii.).   Prof. G. BUCHANAN GRAY, D.D., D.Lit. 10s. 6d. net.
AMOS AND HOSEA.
President W. R. HARPER, Ph.D.   10s. 6d. net.
MICAH, ZEPHANIAH, AND NAHUM, Prof. J. M. P. SMITH; **HABAKKUK,** Prof. W. H. WARD; and **OBADIAH AND JOEL,** Prof. J. A. BEWER.   One Vol.   10s. 6d. net.
HAGGAI, ZECHARIAH, Prof. H. G. MITCHELL; **MALACHI,** Prof. J. M. P. SMITH; and **JONAH,** Prof. J. A. BEWER.   10s. 6d. net.
ST. MATTHEW.
Principal W. C. ALLEN, M.A.   Third Edition.   10s. 6d. net.
ST. MARK.
Prof. E. P. GOULD, D.D.   9s. net.
ST. LUKE.
ALFRED PLUMMER, D.D.   Fourth Edition.   10s. 6d. net.
ROMANS.
Prof. W. SANDAY, D.D., and A. C. HEADLAM, D.D.   Fifth Ed.   10s. 6d. net.
I. CORINTHIANS.
The BISHOP OF EXETER and Dr. A. PLUMMER.   Second Ed.   10s. 6d. net.
II. CORINTHIANS.
ALFRED PLUMMER, D.D.   10s. 6d. net.
EPHESIANS AND COLOSSIANS.
Prof. T. K. ABBOTT, D.Lit.   9s. net.
PHILIPPIANS AND PHILEMON.
Prof. M. R. VINCENT, D.D.   7s. 6d. net.
THESSALONIANS.
Prof. J. E. FRAME, M.A.   9s. net.
ST. PETER AND ST. JUDE.
Prof. CHAS. BIGG, D.D.   Second Edition.   9s. net.
ST. JAMES
Prof. J. H. ROPES, D.D.   9s. net.
THE JOHANNINE EPISTLES.
A. E. BROOKE, D.D.   9s. net.

A GREAT ENCYCLOPÆDIA.

VOLUMES I.-VIII. ALREADY ISSUED.

Encyclopædia of Religion and Ethics

EDITED BY

Dr. JAMES HASTINGS.

THE purpose of this Encyclopædia is to give a complete account of Religion and Ethics so far as they are known. It contains articles on every separate religious belief and practice, and on every ethical or philosophical idea and custom. Persons and places that have contributed to the History of religion and morals are also described.

The Encyclopædia covers a distinct department of knowledge. It is the department which has always exercised the greatest influence over men's lives, and its interest at least, if not its influence, is probably greater at the present time than ever. Within the scope of 'Religion and Ethics' come all the questions that are most keenly debated in PSYCHOLOGY and in SOCIALISM, while the title will be used to embrace the whole of THEOLOGY and PHILOSOPHY. Ethics and Morality will be handled as thoroughly as Religion.

It is estimated that the work will be completed in Twelve Volumes of about 900 pages each, size 11½ by 9.

PRICE—

In Cloth Binding . . 28s. net per volume.
In Half-Morocco . . 34s. net per volume.
Volumes I.-VIII. may also be had in 12 Monthly Parts, price 2s. 6d. net each.

Volume IX. will be published :—

In Cloth Binding . . 30s. net.
In Half-Morocco . . 36s. net.

A full Prospectus may be had on application.

'The general result of our examination enables us to say that the editor has risen to the height of his great undertaking. The work deserves the fullest and best encouragement which the world of readers and investigators can give it.'—*Athenæum.*

'The scope of this encyclopædia is immense, and as for the quality of the articles, the list of the contributors proves that it is in general very high. . . . It will be one of the most reassuring and encouraging signs of the times if this great and magnificent enterprise receives adequate encouragement and recognition.'—*British Weekly.*

'No library could be better provided with what men have said and thought through the ages on Religion and Ethics and all they imply than by this one library in itself. . . . Some of the articles themselves summarise a whole literature.'—*Public Opinion.*